Special Judicial Mechanism for the Crime of Aggression Committed against Ukraine

Developments in International Law

VOLUME 83

The titles published in this series are listed at *brill.com/diil*

Special Judicial Mechanism for the Crime of Aggression Committed against Ukraine

Edited by

Pavel Šturma and Milan Lipovský

BRILL | NIJHOFF

LEIDEN | BOSTON

This work was supported by UNCE – Human Rights Research Centre (HUM/011) and the Cooperatio (2022).

Library of Congress Control Number: 2025949040

Typeface for the Latin, Greek, and Cyrillic scripts: "Brill". See and download: brill.com/brill-typeface.

ISSN 0924-5332
ISBN 978-90-04-74093-8 (hardback)
ISBN 978-90-04-74094-5 (e-book)
DOI 10.1163/9789004740945

This book is printed on acid-free paper and produced in a sustainable manner.

Contents

PART 3
The Crime of Aggression Definition and Immunities from Foreign Criminal Jurisdiction

PART 4
Trial Issues

Notes on Contributors

Simon De Smet
has served as a Legal Officer at the International Criminal Court since 2003. He has mainly worked in the Pre-Trial and Trial Divisions of the Court. Prior to joining the ICC, he served as a judicial fellow for Judges Thomas Buergenthal and Kooijmans at the International Court of Justice. He also teaches International Criminal Law at Cambridge University as an Affiliated Lecturer. His academic research focuses on evidence and methods of proof.

Patrycja Grzebyk
is a professor at the University of Warsaw, member of the Board of European Society of International Law, member of the International Law Association Committee on the Use of Force, member of the Council of Advisers of the Global Institute for the Prevention of Aggression, and President of the Network on Humanitarian Action. She graduated from the University of Warsaw (MA in Law, MA in International Relations, and Ph.D. in Political Science) and obtained her habilitation in law from the Institute of Legal Science of the Polish Academy of Science. Her field of research includes international humanitarian law, international criminal law, and law on use of force. She is an author of over 150 publications, including *Criminal Responsibility for the Crime of Aggression*, Routledge 2013; *Human and Non- Human Targets in Armed Conflicts*, Cambridge University Press 2022; *The Russian-Ukrainian Conflict and War Crimes Challenges for Documentation and International Prosecution*, Routledge 2025. She is an editor in chief of two international journals: ESIL Reflections and Journal of International Humanitarian Action.

Milan Lipovský
is lecturer and researcher at the Department of International Law, Faculty of Law, Charles University (Prague). He graduated (both Master's degree and Ph.D.) from the Charles University and focuses at international criminal law and the law of international peace and security. His Ph.D. thesis concerned the topic of the crime of aggression. He is member of the Czech Society of International Law and European Society of International Law. His latest publications include e.g., an article in the Polish Yearbook of International Law called: *What is 'a Certain International Criminal Court' and does the Choice of a Fully International or Internationalized (Hybrid) Court/Chambers Matter for the Crime of Aggression Committed Against Ukraine?* (2023).

Emil Ruffer
is a lawyer and diplomat, former Ambassador and Permanent Representative of the Czech Republic to the Council of Europe and currently a Deputy Legal Adviser and Director of International Law Department at the Ministry of Foreign Affairs of the Czech Republic. He graduated from the Charles University, Faculty of Law and also studied Law and Politics at Cardiff University and undertook research as a Visiting Fulbright Scholar at the Fordham Law School. His field of research includes public international law and the external relations law of the European Union, and he holds Ph.D. in European and International law from the Charles University. He is a member of, *inter alia*, Czech Society of International Law and International Law Association Czech Branch.

Pavel Šturma
is a Full Professor of International Law at Charles University, Faculty of Law. Graduated from Charles University in law (1985), philosophy and economics (1992), and also studied at the Institut des Hautes Études Internationales (Université Paris 2 Panthéon-Assas). Before joining the teaching staff of the Faculty of Law, he served as a staff member of the United Nations Office at Vienna and a senior research fellow at the Institute of Law of the Czech Academy of Sciences. He was a member and former chairperson of the UN International Law Commission (2012-2022), member of the Czech national group at the Permanent Court of Arbitration, Judge ad hoc of the European Court of Human Rights, and Associated member of *Institut de Droit International*. President of the Czech Society of International Law and editor-in-chief of the Czech Yearbook of Public and Private International Law. He is the author or co-author of 21 books and more than 220 articles and studies in international law. He publishes in the field of state responsibility, international criminal law, international investment law, and immunities in international law.

Jennifer Trahan
is a professor at NYU's Center for Global Affairs. She is also Convenor of The Global Institute for the Prevention of Aggression and holds various positions with the American Branch of the ILA, including as Vice President. She is additionally one of the American members of the Use of Force Committee of the ILA. She graduated from Amherst College (AB), NYU School of Law (JD) and Columbia Law School (LL.M.). Her field of research includes the International Criminal Court, and particularly the crime of aggression, as well as the veto power of the UN Security Council, and other areas of international criminal law and public international law. Her most recent book is *Legal Limits to Security Council Veto Power in the Face of Atrocity Crimes* (Cambridge U. Press 2020).

Kristýna Urbanová
is a lecturer at Faculty of Law of the Charles University (Prague), a member of the Czech Bar Association. She graduated from the Charles University (Ph.D., Mgr.) and the University of Cambridge (LL.M.). Her main focus in the research area is on international criminal law.

Renán Villacís
is the Director of the Secretariat of the Assembly of States Parties of the International Criminal Court. He studied law at the University of Cuenca, Ecuador, and international relations at the School of Advanced International Studies, Johns Hopkins University, Washington D.C. Prior to joining the Secretariat of the Assembly, he had worked as a member of the Foreign Service of Ecuador and then as a legal officer in the Codification Division of the Office of Legal Affairs of the United Nations Secretariat in New York. Since 2006 he has been the Director of the Secretariat.

Introduction

Pavel Šturma and Milan Lipovský

1 The Need for a New *ad hoc* Judicial Mechanism

As a result of the complicated negotiations in Rome in 1998, in Kampala in 2010, and in New York in 2017, there exists a jurisdictional gap in the scope of jurisdiction of the International Criminal Court (ICC) regarding the crime of aggression.[1] While under Art. 12(2) of the Rome Statute (RS),[2] the ICC may exercise jurisdiction over the other 3 core crimes (i.e., genocide as it is defined in Art. 6 RS, crimes against humanity as they are defined in Art. 7 RS, and war crimes as they are defined in Art. 8 RS) when the crimes are either committed by nationals of States Parties, or within the territory of States Parties, the same does not apply to the crime of aggression (defined in Art. 8 *bis* RS). This is because of the special conditions for the exercise of the ICC's jurisdiction in respect of the crime of aggression, adopted as a part of the negotiation package in Kampala. Due to the jurisdictional gap, the ICC's jurisdictional scope over the crime of aggression only covers cases where the crime is committed by nationals of States Parties to the Rome Statute (as amended by the Kampala definition of aggression)[3] *and* it is committed within territory of a State Party (or States Parties) of the Rome Statute (as amended by the Kampala definition of aggression). The roots of this jurisdictional gap rest in two provisions:

i) Art. 121(5) RS which applies to amendments of "definition articles", while the definition of the crime of aggression is part of an amendment adopted in 2010, and
ii) Art. 15 *bis* (5) RS.

While the jurisdictional gap may be circumvented by triggering the ICC's jurisdiction by the UN Security Council (UNSC) under Art. 15 *ter* RS, the UNSC's

1 *See e.g.,* explanation by Dannenbaum, Tom, 'Mechanisms for Criminal Prosecution of Russia's Aggression Against Ukraine' (blog *Justsecurity.org,* 10 March 2022) <https://www.justsecurity.org/80626/mechanisms-for-criminal-prosecution-of-russias-aggression-against-ukraine/> (last accessed 14 May 2025).

2 Rome Statute of the International Criminal Court (adopted 17 July 1998, entered into force 1 July 2002) 2187 UNTS 3.

3 ICC, Assembly of States Parties, Review Conference, The Crime of Aggression, Annex I, ICC Doc. RC/Res.6 (11 June 2010), available online at <https://treaties.un.org/doc/source/docs/RC-Res.6-ENG.pdf> (last accessed 14 May 2025).

 | DOI:10.1163/9789004740945_002

decision-making process regulated by Art. 27(3) of the UN Charter[4] allows for a veto of any of its permanent members, including the Russian Federation – the aggressor in the armed conflict between Russia and Ukraine.[5] Consequently, the jurisdictional gap is likely not to be overcome by political decision of the Security Council in this situation and possibly neither in other potential situations.

For those reasons, and latest since 24 February 2022, the international community, scholars, as well as laymen, commenced a debate on how to close this jurisdictional gap in general as well as how to solve the gap specifically with relation to the ICC's lack of jurisdiction over the crime of aggression committed against Ukraine till the gap is closed in general. Establishing a new judicial *ad hoc* mechanism for assessment of the individual international criminal responsibility for the crime of aggression committed against Ukraine is one of the highlights in these efforts.

And those efforts include both an amendment of the Rome Statute – the goal of which is to unify the jurisdictional regime over all four core crimes – as well as the creation of the above-mentioned special judicial mechanism for the crime of aggression committed against Ukraine.

2 The Conference at the Charles University Faculty of Law

To address the topics related to creation of the new mechanism, the Charles University Human Rights Research Centre organized a conference called "Towards accountability for the crime of aggression committed against Ukraine"[6] on 10–11 November 2023. Scholars, States' representatives, and members of the public participated in the conference and this book is the written outcome prepared by several of the speakers. As such, it is dedicated to contributing to academic research in the field and enhancing the international legal response.

However, this monograph is not just a collection of contributions from the said conference. The authors present the research in individual chapters and also follow up on the joint discussion. At the same time, the authors followed developments in the ongoing expert discussions and intergovernmental nego-

4 Charter of the United Nations (adopted 26 June 1945, entered into force 24 October 1945) 892 UNTS 119.

5 UNGA Res ES-11/1, Aggression against Ukraine (2 March 2022).

6 *See* conference webpage available online at <https://law.prf.cuni.cz/specialtribunalforaggression/> (last accessed 14 April 2025).

tiations between November 2023 and May 2025 in order to update their chapters. Also, while the book is focused on the specific situation of Ukraine and the crime of aggression, it does not end there and assesses more general issues of public international law related to the topics discussed in the chapters.

3 Addressing the Creation of the Special Judicial Mechanism for the Crime of Aggression Committed against Ukraine

This book is situated around three axes that partly intersect. The first of them is focused on the negotiation history and efforts to find a suitable mechanism for prosecuting the crime of aggression committed against Ukraine. The second axis focuses on some substantive legal and procedural prerequisites and/or obstacles for prosecuting the crime of aggression. And the third axis touches on some specific issues of legal proceedings, which may be particularly relevant in the case of prosecuting those accused of the crime of aggression against Ukraine (common knowledge of the facts and proceedings *in absentia*). Of course, the above-mentioned axes also meet. For example, the choice of the model of the special mechanism has an impact on a greater or lesser obstacle based on the immunity of prosecuted public officials.

In order to fully comprehend the complexity of the jurisdictional gap and its possible solutions, it is necessary to understand the several decades long process of negotiations that eventually climaxed in the adoption of the Rome Statute and its amendments. A historical and comparative view of older international and internationalized/hybrid criminal tribunals sheds light on the advantages and disadvantages of the various considered forms of the mechanism and the possible paths to its establishment. For that reason, **Renán Villacis** begins with statistical information about the ICC with regard to conferences in Rome and Kampala as well as the prepared review conference of 2025.

Being aware of the jurisdictional gap, the so-called Core Group of States (many members of which are also States Parties to the Rome Statute) decided to "pick up the glove" of the jurisdictional gap highlighted by the Russian war of aggression against Ukraine, and not only backed the special mechanism for the crime of aggression committed against Ukraine politically but also negotiated its establishing treaties. While the contents of the negotiations and their outcomes have not been fully disclosed yet when this book was finalized (and thus does not reflect them), on 8 May 2025, finalization of the preparatory works to establish the mechanism has been announced. Despite the continuing partial secrecy, it is a matter of public knowledge that throughout its existence, the Core Group's members' preferences of the form of the mechanism were as divided, perhaps even more, as the opinions of authors of doctrine. Two among the most discussed forms of the tribunal debated were an international form and internationalized/hybrid form. The elements of these seemingly dichotomic types are not perfectly clear but they were focused upon particularly due to the pronouncement of the International Court of Justice (ICJ) in its famous *Arrest Warrant* Case[7] that personal immunities are inapplicable before 'certain international criminal courts and tribunals'. The ICJ did not however elaborate upon the nature of such courts and tribunals in detail and thus left the door opened to various interpretations that further complicated the debates.

As establishing the special judicial mechanism is one of the many efforts contained in the vast post-2022 response of the international community to the Russian aggression, **Emil Ruffer** describes them together, with particular focus on the efforts of the Core Group of States and also upon the role of the diplomacy of the Czech Republic in that regard. Regarding the creation of the special judicial mechanism, the fruition of these efforts was achieved by the Core Group this year and as it was announced by the European Commission,[8] the tribunal's jurisdiction will be derived from Ukraine. Choosing a regional European intergovernmental organization (the Council of Europe) as a partner was one of the proposed forms of establishment of the mechanism and the consequences of such a choice were widely discussed in relation to the other proposed options. Those other options included establishing the tribunal e.g., by a universal treaty opened to all States, by a treaty between Ukraine and the United Nations represented by the Secretary General, or by establishing a tribunal under Chapters 7 or 6 of the UN Charter.

Any of the envisaged paths, including the one eventually chosen, have significant consequences in both international criminal law as well as in general international law. Because the tribunal will be established by an international treaty, the law of treaties comes into play. And the Vienna Convention on the Law of Treaties (1969)[9] contains a special provision that prevents aggressor

7 ICJ, *Arrest Warrant of 11 April 2000* (Democratic Republic of the Congo v. Belgium), Judgment of 4 February 2002, ICJ Reports 2002.

8 European Union (European Commission), International Coalition Agrees on the Establishment of the Special Tribunal for the Crime of Aggression against Ukraine (9 May 2025), available online at <https://enlargement.ec.europa.eu/news/international-coalition-agrees-establishment-special-tribunal-crime-aggression-against-ukraine-2025-05-09_en> (last accessed 14 April 2025).

9 Vienna Convention on the Law of Treaties (adopted 22 May 1969, entered into force 27 January 1980) 1155 UNTS 331.

state(s) to object to obligations imposed upon it(them) by a treaty "*in consequence of measures taken in conformity with the Charter of the United Nations with reference to that State's aggression*" even if it is not a party to such a treaty. This exception to the rule of *pacta tertiis nec nocent nec prosunt* contained in Art. 75 VCLT pointed out by **Pavel Šturma** indicates the need to comprehend general international law in order to evaluate all the possible outcomes of choosing a particular form of a tribunal. Although not utilized in the end either, the proposal of **Jennifer Trahan** to establish the tribunal pursuant to Chapter 6 of the UN Charter, could have been a way how to circumvent the veto power of the Russian Federation in the UN Security Council due to the applicability of Art. 27(3) UN Charter.

Based on the so-far publicly available information, it may be assumed that the new mechanism will most likely be much closer to an internationalized character than to an international one. Keeping that in mind, the mechanism might be unable to disregard personal immunities. Exactly for that reason, **Patrycja Grzebyk's** proposal to interpret the leadership clause of the crime of aggression broadly, in compliance with the Nuremberg scope rather than Kampala scope, might be of significant importance. She also points out the circle of persons who *prima facie* could be prosecuted for the crime of aggression, and by doing so indicates that even if the tribunal may not exercise its jurisdiction over those endowed with personal immunities, it will still have a lot of work.

The matter of applicability of personal immunities before international criminal courts and tribunals is a long-term controversy. The above-mentioned *Arrest Warrant* Judgment's interpretation as well as the interpretation of the subsequent case law of various international tribunals and opinions of authors of doctrine vary significantly. **Kristýna Urbanová** builds upon this topic and like other authors of this book highlights the need to understand general international law, including the way how international customary law is created and changed, in order to correctly evaluate specific questions.

Although the tribunal's creation is now a confirmed matter, there remain many issues of procedural law that will have to be tackled with. **Simon De Smet** dissects the concept of judicial notice of facts of common knowledge in general and suggests how it could function in any possible trial for the crime of aggression. And in the last chapter, **Milan Lipovský** proposes that proceedings *in absentia*, usually a controversial issue, often incorrectly understood as a violation of human rights, may in fact help to circumvent certain political bars to the exercise of international justice with regard to the crime of aggression.

4 Final Remarks

The book proves that the crime of aggression committed against Ukraine triggered a strong response not only in the political and sociological sphere, but also in the sphere of public international law. The paths to solving the effects of the jurisdictional gap of the ICC are certainly complex and complicated. While the contents of the agreements between Ukraine and the Council of Europe are not yet public (at the time of finalization of the book), it is clear that to guarantee that the results of the work of the new special judicial mechanism's work reach the highest possible legitimacy, it is necessary to satisfy highest general international and human rights standards as they are pointed out among others in the subsequent text of this book.

PART 1

Negotiations of the Rome Statute, the Crime of Aggression, and the Mechanism for Crime of Aggression

CHAPTER 1

The Assembly of States Parties and the Crime of Aggression: From Rome 1998 to 2025

Renan Villacis

This chapter seeks to provide a broad overview of the discussion regarding the crime of aggression (CoA) in the Rome Statute system.

1 Rome 1998

The International Law Commission (ILC) prepared the Draft Statute for an International Criminal Court at its sessions from 1990 to 1994.[1] The United Nations General Assembly then established in 1994 an *ad hoc* committee to review the ILC Draft Statute. This was then followed by a General Assembly decision to set up the Preparatory Committee on the Establishment of an International Criminal Court.

During the negotiations, there were some *red lines* set out by different groups. On the one hand, many states felt very strongly that the crime of aggression had to be included as one of the crimes over which the new Court would have jurisdiction. Without its inclusion, an agreement to establish a new international criminal court would simply not be possible. Likewise, for some other states, there could be no agreement on setting up a new international criminal court if there was an insistence on including the use of nuclear weapons as a crime.

There were enormous expectations at the time, since the end of the Cold War had ushered in the hope of the 'peace dividend': what had not been attainable before due to the divergent interests of the two superpowers with the capacity to annihilate life on the planet, was considered feasible in a world under transformation; the huge resources which used to be channeled to military forces could be redirected to satisfy other needs.

1 ILC, Draft Statute for an International Criminal Court with commentaries (1994), YILC, 1994, vol. II, Part Two. *See also* ILC Webpage available online at <https://legal.un.org/ilc/reports/reports1990.shtml> (last accessed 17 October 2024).

 | DOI:10.1163/9789004740945_003

There was total elation among the vast majority of delegates at adoption of the Rome Statute[2] on 17 July 1998. The agreement was attained after five weeks of intense negotiations,[3] the culmination of years of work, of initiatives, and dreams of many generations of believers in having an international court to hold to account individuals accused of committing the worst atrocity crimes.

The outcome was the Rome Statute establishing an international criminal court with jurisdiction over the four crimes: genocide, war crimes, crimes against humanity, and the crime of aggression. There were other crimes which different states had wanted to see included in the new statute, but these were the four crimes on which it was politically feasible then to reach an agreement. It was truly a unique moment in international criminal law; to defer the negotiations to another year would most likely have resulted in prolonging the negotiations without a concrete end in sight. Even this outcome of having the four crimes in the Rome Statute would perhaps not have been possible at a different juncture.

Although the crime of aggression was included in the Rome Statute as one of the four crimes over which the Court had jurisdiction, it is important to recall that there was no legal definition of the crime of aggression in the statute, nor any reference to the conditions for exercise of the jurisdiction of the Court over the crime of aggression. In other words, a considerable amount of negotiations was still needed. This was a matter left for discussion at the Review Conference, with some preparatory work already undertaken as of the second meeting of the Preparatory Commission for the International Criminal Court.[4]

An unexpected flurry of ratifications of the Rome Statute led to its entry into force at a date much earlier than anyone could have expected: 1 July 2002. This was also the beginning of the annual sessions of the Assembly of States Parties to the Rome Statute (ASP).

The preparations for the Review Conference then continued the unfinished discussions from Rome via a Special Working Group on the Crime of Aggression (SWGCA)[5] at the annual sessions of the Assembly. An informal but key

2 Rome Statute of the International Criminal Court (adopted 17 July 1998, entered into force 1 July 2002) 2187 UNTS 3 (Rome Statute).

3 The Rome Diplomatic Conference took place from 15 June to 17 July 1998.

4 26 July to 13 August 1999. UN Office of Legal Affairs Webpage, Preparatory Commission for the International Criminal Court, available online at <https://legal.un.org/icc/prepcomm/prepfra.htm> (last accessed 17 October 2024).

5 *See* ICC, Assembly of States Parties, Continuity of Work in Respect of the Crime of Aggression, ICC-ASP/1/Res.1 (9 September 2002), available online at <https://asp.icc-cpi.int/sites/asp/files/asp_docs/Resolutions/ICC-ASP-ASP1-Res-01-ENG.pdf> (last accessed 17 October 2024), operative para. 2 which reads:

component was the Princeton Process which, via inter-sessional meetings, greatly facilitated the process.[6]

2 Review Conference Kampala 2010

The Review Conference, which was held in Kampala for two weeks,[7] included a stocktaking exercise on four different topics, but the core of the work was the negotiations on the crime of aggression. The Conference ended with the successful adoption of the so-called Kampala amendments, which completed the unfinished work from Rome 1998.[8]

It is worth noting that, as had been the case with the Preparatory Committee, the Rome Diplomatic Conference,[9] the Preparatory Commission for the International Criminal Court, and the annual sessions of the Assembly of States Parties to the Rome Statute, there was almost universal participation in the negotiations in Kampala, including from all the permanent members of the United Nations Security Council, who participated actively in the negotiations.[10]

"*Decides* to establish a special working group on the crime of aggression, open on an equal footing to all States Members of the United Nations or members of specialized agencies or of the International Atomic Energy Agency, for the purpose of elaborating proposals for a provision on aggression in accordance with paragraph 2 of article 5 of the Statute and paragraph 7 of resolution F adopted at the United Nations Diplomatic Conference of Plenipotentiaries on the Establishment of an International Criminal Court on 17 July 1998."

6 *See, e.g.*, several ICC ASP documents at ICC ASP Webpage <https://asp.icc-cpi.int/crime-of-aggression/History-CoA> (last accessed 17 October 2024).

7 From 31 May to 11 June 2010.

8 ICC, Assembly of States Parties, Review Conference, The Crime of Aggression, ICC Doc. RC/Res.6 (11 June 2010), available online at <https://treaties.un.org/doc/source/docs/RC-Res.6-ENG.pdf> (last accessed 17 October 2024).

9 UN Office of Legal Affairs Webpage, United Nations Diplomatic Conference of Plenipotentiaries on the Establishment of an International Criminal Court. Rome, 15 June – 17 July 1998, available online at <https://legal.un.org/icc/rome/proceedings/contents.htm> (last accessed 17 October 2024). Volume II of the *Official Records* contains the list of delegations.

10 Despite being an Observer state, the United States delegation in Kampala was the second largest of all: 30 delegates. ICC ASP Webpage, Newsletter, December 2010, available online at <https://asp.icc-cpi.int/sites/asp/files/asp_docs/Publications/Newsletter-ASP-5-Web-ENG.pdf> (last accessed 17 October 2024).

The outcome from Kampala included:

a) A definition of the crime of aggression essentially based on the 1974 United Nations General Assembly Resolution 3314.[11]
b) Conditions for the exercise of the jurisdiction of the Court requiring, *inter alia*, a minimum number of ratifications of the amendments (30), and the need for an Assembly of States Parties resolution to activate the exercise of jurisdiction as of a given date.

3 Post Review Conference

The pace of ratification of the Kampala amendments, which began with Liechtenstein in May 2012, was relatively slow after 2016.

- 2012: 3
- 2013: 10
- 2014: 7
- 2015: 6
- 2016: 6
- 2017: 3
- 2018: 2
- 2019: 2
- 2020: 1
- 2021: 1
- 2022: 3
- 2023: 1
- 2024: 1
- 2025: 1

The State of Palestine submitted the 30th ratification in the summer of 2016, thus meeting one of the key conditions for the entry into force of the Kampala amendments.

At the ASP in 2017, complicated and sometimes divisive negotiations took place with an outcome where once again States Parties agreed on a text not to everyone's satisfaction, but no one was willing to not proceed with the activation resolution.

The historic Assembly resolution ICC-ASP/16/Res.5 on 14 December 2017 set 17 July 2018 (the Day of International Criminal Justice) for the activation of the jurisdiction of the Court over the crime of aggression.

11 UNGA Res 3314 (XXIX), Definition of Aggression (14 December 1974).

The total number of ratifications of the amendments on the crime of aggression stands at 47.[12] The regional breakdown is:

- Africa: 2
- Asia-Pacific: 4
- Eastern European Group: 11
- Group of Latin American and Caribbean States: 12
- Western European and other States Group: 18

4 2025 Review

The Review Conference, in resolution 6, operative para. 4, decided "to review the amendments on the crime of aggression seven years after the beginning of the Court's exercise of jurisdiction", in other words in 2025.

This would seem to require some prior discussion earlier in 2025 and perhaps even some preparatory work in 2024. What exactly a "review" entails is the primary question to be elucidated.[13]

---

12 United Nations Treaty Series Webpage, available online at <https://treaties.un.org/Pages/ViewDetails.aspx?src=TREATY&mtdsg_no=XVIII-10-b&chapter=18&clang=_en> (last accessed 28 April 2024). It is notable that on 25 October 2024 Ukraine deposited its instruments of ratification to become a party to the Rome Statute as well as to the amendments on the crime of aggression. Denmark, which deposited its instruments of acceptance of the amendments on the crime of aggression on 1 January 2025, specifically excluded the Faroe Islands and Greenland from their application.

13 The substantive discussions fall under the remit of the Working Group on Amendments, which is a New York based subsidiary body of the ASP. The text of the proposed amendments to article 15 *bis* of the Rome Statute was formally circulated by the United Nations Secretary General on 7 April 2025 (depositary communication C.N.162.2025.TREATIES-XVIII.10, available online at <https://treaties.un.org/doc/Publication/CN/2025/CN.162.2025-Eng.pdf> (last accessed 28 April 2025)). The text reads:

"*Article 15bis (4) and (5) are replaced by the following text inserted after article 15bis (3):*

4. The Court may, in accordance with article 12, exercise jurisdiction over a crime of aggression if one or more of the following States have ratified or accepted the aggression amendments, or have accepted the exercise of the jurisdiction of the Court over the crime of aggression in accordance with paragraph 5:

(*a*) *The State on the territory of which the conduct in question occurred or, if the crime was committed on board a vessel or aircraft, the State of registration of that vessel or aircraft;*

(*b*) *The State of which the person accused of the crime is a national.*

5. If the acceptance of a State that has not ratified or accepted the aggression amendments, or that is not a Party to this Statute, is required under paragraph 4, that State may, by declaration lodged with the Registrar, accept the exercise of jurisdiction by the Court over the crime of aggression in accordance with article 12, paragraph 3."

The so-called "omnibus" resolution (ICC-ASP/22/Res.3), adopted on 13 December 2023, contains in operative para. 157 the following mandate: "Recalls *the decision taken by the first Review Conference to review the amendments on the crime of aggression seven years after the beginning of the Court's exercise of jurisdiction and* notes *that this review is to be prepared ahead of 17 July 2025.*"[14]

5 Outstanding Issues for Discussing during the Review of the Kampala Amendments

The *format* has yet to be decided. The options include:
a) A format similar to the SWGCA (all States equal),
b) only States Parties,
c) only States which have ratified the amendments,
d) observers: include international organizations/entities dealing with crime of aggression/related crimes.

Venue for preparatory work: could be in New York/The Hague
a) In one venue or both (joint meetings would mean virtual meetings)
b) One facilitator/two co-facilitators
c) Perhaps a focal point for the initial preparations

Venue for Decision-Making
The Assembly of States Parties is scheduled to take place in The Hague in December 2025.[15] The venue can be an essential factor to bear in mind because of the presence in New York of all the states.

Should there be a preference for a second review conference to have the decision-making, then it is possible to consider different venues (neither New York nor The Hague). This would have the benefit of separating the discussion on the review of the crime of aggression amendments and the decision-making from the annual discussions on the budget, cooperation, comple-

14 ICC, Assembly of States Parties, Strengthening the International Criminal Court and the Assembly of States Parties, ICC-ASP/22/Res.3 (13 December 2023), available online at <https://asp.icc-cpi.int/sites/default/files/asp_docs/ICC-ASP-22-Res3-ENG.pdf> (last accessed 17 October 2024). *See also* Resolution RC/Res.6, *supra* note 8, paragraph 4.

15 According to usual triennial sequencing of Assembly venues, the next Assembly scheduled to take place in New York is in December 2026.

mentarity, elections, etc. The date for a second review conference could be sometime in 2025.

The new President of the Assembly of States Parties, Amb. Paivi Kaukoranta (Finland), and the new Bureau members assume functions on 15 December 2023 for a three-year period. They would need to begin initial consultations on these matters, perhaps even in the first months of 2024.

If any review conference is to be considered, there is a need to bear in mind possible programme budget implications by May 2024 (to include in the proposed programme budget for 2025, which is prepared in June 2024)[16] and to make at least initial arrangements with the "host state"[17] for the Review Conference.[18]

6 Other Developments

6.1 *Dual Track Approach on the Crime of Aggression*

There is a need to bear in mind that some states are advocating for what is known as a *dual track approach*, which consists of moving forward with a tribunal on the crime of aggression for Ukraine, while also trying to close what they consider the accountability gap resulting from the Kampala process.[19] The dynamics are different and thus it is difficult to see at this stage how there may be coordination between the two approaches, also because the states involved are not all parties to the Rome Statute.

---

16 *See* document ICC-ASP/23/10, available online at <https://asp.icc-cpi.int/sites/default/files/asp_docs/ICC-ASP-23-10-ENG.pdf> (last accessed 17 October 2024), para. 886, and annex XVIII.

17 A process would need to be established to see which State Party may be willing to host such a review conference. It should preferably be a State Party which has ratified the Agreement on Privileges and Immunities of the International Criminal Court.

18 After an informal consultation process held among States Parties in 2024, the Assembly decided to hold a special session in New York from 7 to 9 July 2025. ICC, Assembly of States Parties, Strengthening the International Criminal Court and the Assembly of States Parties, ICC-ASP/23/Res.1 (6 December 2024), available online at <https://asp.icc-cpi.int/sites/default/files/asp_docs/ICC-ASP-23-Res.1-ENG.pdf> (last accessed 28 April 2025). *See also* Resolution RC/Res.6, *supra* note 8, paragraph 4. The ASP approved a budget to cover the cost of holding that meeting at UN headquarters; subsequently the Invitations to the special session were sent on 29 January 2025 to all States.

19 Speech by the Federal Foreign Minister of Germany, Annalena Baerbock in The Hague entitled "Strengthening International Law in Times of Crisis" (16 January 2023), available online at <https://www.auswaertiges-amt.de/en/newsroom/news/strengthening-international-law-in-times-of-crisis/2573492> (last accessed 17 October 2024).

6.2 *The ICC and a New Crime of Aggression Tribunal for Ukraine*

It would seem necessary to have regular coordination on work undertaken, as some of the facts/evidence/situations may fall under the respective jurisdictions, so more of an operational agreement with the ICC (the Office of the Prosecutor in particular).

6.3 *Global South Views*

In recent years, there is a general perception in the so-called Global South of neglect/lack of interest in issues of primary concern to those countries, some even of an existential nature. Examples include:

a) the lack of COVID-19 vaccines for the Global South when the vaccines were first developed; states are wary of being faced with a similar situation when another pandemic breaks out,
b) the slow concrete steps to address climate change,
c) limited investments in medical treatments/vaccines, such as ones related to tropical diseases.

There is a concern that priority resources, human and financial, are directed to issues of particular interest to one group of states ("Western States" and their allies).

That concern has already been expressed in the context of the ICC budget and human resources discussions (allegedly privileging one particular situation over the rest).

Thus, paradoxically, it would seem that the Global South, which championed the crime of aggression inclusion back in Rome in 1998, is less enthusiastic in promoting the jurisdiction over the crime of aggression than was the case in Rome.

This may help to explain the limited number of participants in some of the informal groups where discussions on the crime of aggression are held, including the United Nations Security Council and the United Nations General Assembly votes and discussions. There are historical legacies, including colonial past to bear in mind, but also invasion/occupation/use of force in the 20th century, including in the post-World War II era, which constitute elements of the background for decision-makers in the Global South.

7 Final Remarks

It is vital to see the tremendous legal and political advancement made by the adoption of the Rome Statute with the inclusion of the crime of aggression, as well as the 2010 Kampala amendments and the activation by the ASP in 2017.

The rest of the chapters have yet to be written, hopefully with full participation in the discussion of all states because it is indispensable to reinforce the rule of law for the entire world community.

Since we commemorated the 25th anniversary of the Rome Statute, the author wishes to quote one of the most admired United Nations officials of his time, Kofi Annan (Campidoglio, Rome 1998): "*The establishment of the Court is still a gift of hope to future generations, and a giant step forward in the march towards universal human rights and the rule of law.*"

CHAPTER 2

United Nations, European Union, Council of Europe, and Core Group Activities in Creation of the Tribunal for the Crime of Aggression against Ukraine and the Role of the Czech Diplomacy

Emil Ruffer

1 Introduction

This chapter intends to present a concise overview of various diplomatic efforts to ensure accountability in the aftermath of Russia's aggression against Ukraine in different international organizations, such as the United Nations (UN), the European Union (EU), and the Council of Europe (CoE). After presenting this framework of different initiatives, the focus will be turned to the work of the *Core Group*, a special platform established in response to numerous calls for accountability and with the aim to discuss and develop suitable model(s) of a Special Tribunal to prosecute the crime of aggression against Ukraine. In the treatment of the subject, we shall also try to make a preliminary assessment (hopefully not too biased) of the role of Czech diplomacy in the process, given the fact that the first *Core Group* meeting took place in Prague. Finally, an attempt to take stock of the progress achieved so far will be made, as well as reflection on the way forward and challenges ahead of us.

To put this endeavor and strive for accountability in context, it needs to be stressed that we are facing a rather unprecedented situation, at least from the European perspective. All legal instruments and concepts available (including highly debated collective countermeasures)[1] are being used against an aggres-

1 For the doctrine of countermeasures, *see* Articles 49–54 of the Articles on Responsibility of States for Internationally Wrongful Acts (International Law Commission, Articles on Responsibility of States for Internationally Wrongful Acts with commentaries (2001), YILC, 2001, vol. II, Part Two) (ARSIWA), text adopted by the International Law Commission (ILC) at its fifty-third session, in 2001, and submitted to the General Assembly as a part of the ILC's report covering the work of that session. The report, which also contained commentaries on ARSIWA, appeared in the Yearbook of the International Law Commission, 2001, vol. II (Part Two). However, as regards the third-party or collective countermeasures, i.e., invoking the countermeasures doctrine by non-injured states, the ILC refrained from

 DOI:10.1163/9789004740945_004

sor state,[2] which was until recently our often difficult, but still a partner in the CoE, the pan-European human rights organization based on shared values and principles of democracy, human rights, and rule of law.[3] Furthermore, Russia is still a Participating State in the Organisation for Security and Co-operation in Europe (OSCE), and most importantly, it is a permanent member of the UN Security Council (UNSC). As such, it should fulfil the role of one of the five permanent guardians of international peace and security (at least in the letter and spirit of the UN Charter). The reality, obviously, is very different.

2 Response at the Global UN Level

Due to Russia's role and entrenched position in the UN system, the response to the act of aggression committed against Ukraine could not come from the UNSC itself, but only from the UN General Assembly (UNGA), in the form of the political condemnation of the aggression pronounced in the UNGA resolution '*Aggression against Ukraine*' from 2 March 2022, urging the Russian Federation to reverse its course of action, withdraw all of its military forces, and respect the territorial sovereignty and integrity of Ukraine within its internationally recognized borders (OP2-OP4):

> 2. [The General Assembly] Deplores in the strongest terms the aggression by the Russian Federation against Ukraine in violation of Article 2 (4) of the Charter;
> 3. Demands that the Russian Federation immediately cease its use of force against Ukraine and to refrain from any further unlawful threat or use of force against any Member State;

---

pronouncing itself on this matter and incorporated an explicit disclaimer in its commentary to ARSIWA that it did "*not purport to regulate the taking of countermeasures by States other than the injured State*" (commentary to Chapter 2, para. 8).

2 For a thorough treatment of the international law doctrine of countermeasures (incl. a possible use of collective countermeasures) to freeze Russian sovereign assets in order to secure payment of war reparations by Russia to fulfil its responsibility for the damage caused by its aggression against Ukraine, *see* Hathaway, Oona A., Mills, Maggie M., Poston, Thomas M., 'War Reparations: The Case for Countermeasures' (2024) Stanford Law Review, vol. 76, no. 5, <https://ssrn.com/abstract=4548945> (last accessed 9 October 2024).

3 The Russian Federation was expelled from the CoE on 16 March 2022, by the decision of the Committee of Ministers' Deputies, for the breach of fundamental principles of the Statute of the Council of Europe (Statute of the Council of Europe (adopted 5 May 1949, entered into force 3 August 1949) ETS No. 1), incl. its Art. 3.

> 4. Also demands that the Russian Federation immediately, completely and unconditionally withdraw all of its military forces from the territory of Ukraine within its internationally recognized borders.[4]

Altogether eight resolutions by UNGA, relevant for our topic, were adopted so far in the framework of the eleventh emergency special session, including '*Suspension of the rights of membership of the Russian Federation in the Human Rights Council*' from 7 April 2022,[5] '*Furtherance of remedy and reparation for aggression against Ukraine*' from 14 November 2022,[6] '*Principles of the Charter of the United Nations underlying a comprehensive, just and lasting peace in Ukraine*' from 23 February 2023, as a reminder of one year passing since the beginning of Russia's full-scale attack against Ukraine,[7] as well as the most recent one '*Advancing a comprehensive, just and lasting peace in Ukraine*' from 24 February 2025.[8]

In the UNGA resolution from 23 February 2023, there was a reference (although rather vague and opaque) to a special tribunal (OP9), which was repeated verbatim in the most recent UNGA resolution from 24 February 2025 (OP5):

> Emphasizes the need to ensure accountability for the most serious crimes under international law committed on the territory of Ukraine through appropriate, fair and independent investigations and prosecutions at the national or international level, and ensure justice for all victims and the prevention of future crimes.

---

4 UNGA Res ES-11/1, Aggression against Ukraine (2 March 2022); 141 votes in favor / 5 votes against / 35 abstentions.

5 UNGA Res ES-11/3, Suspension of the Rights of Membership of the Russian Federation in the Human Rights Council (7 April 2022); 93 votes in favor / 24 votes against / 58 abstentions.

6 UNGA Res ES-11/5, Furtherance of Remedy and Reparation for Aggression against Ukraine (14 November 2022); 94 votes in favor / 14 votes against / 73 abstentions.

7 UNGA Res ES-11/6, Principles of the Charter of the United Nations Underlying a Comprehensive, Just and Lasting Peace in Ukraine (23 February 2023); 141 votes in favor / 7 votes against / 32 abstentions.

8 UNGA Res ES-11/7, Advancing a Comprehensive, Just and Lasting Peace in Ukraine (24 February 2025); 93 votes in favor / 18 votes against / 65 abstentions. During the same session, a competing resolution was adopted (proposed by the United States of America), UNGA Res ES-11/8, The Path to Peace (25 February 2025); 93 votes in favor / 8 votes against / 73 abstentions. This latter resolution is remarkable for its brevity and does not mention accountability at all.

This is, *cum grano salis*, as far as it went at the level of the UN and the international community at large. However, for the sake of completeness, a UNSC resolution adopted on 24 February 2025 should not be omitted, the only one adopted by the UNSC since the start of Russia's full-scale invasion against Ukraine in 2022. The UNSC expresses "*Mourning the tragic loss of life*" and in the sole operative paragraph "[i]*mplores a swift end to the conflict and further urges a lasting peace between Ukraine and the Russian Federation.*"[9] Regrettably, it fails to refer to and condemn the Russia's aggression against Ukraine, and thus does not constitute a major breakthrough in the (lack of) UNSC response to the ongoing Russia's war of aggression.

3 Response of the Regional Actors: The Council of Europe and European Union

At the regional level, the CoE has been at the forefront of the debates on the establishment of an *ad hoc* tribunal for the crime of aggression. Parliamentary Assembly of the CoE (PACE) passed a resolution already on 28 April 2022, calling to "*urgently set up an ad hoc international criminal tribunal, which should* [...] *receive a mandate to investigate and prosecute the crime of aggression allegedly committed by the political and military leadership of the Russian Federation.*"[10] The Committee of Ministers' Deputies (CMD)[11] followed later by a (slightly less ambitious) decision from 15 September 2022, in which it merely "*noted with interest the Ukrainian proposals to establish an ad hoc special tribunal for the crime of aggression ... .*"[12]

However, since then there has been a number of discussions / exchanges of views on the topic both at the political level in the CMD and at the expert level

---

9 UNSC Res 2774 (2025), Mourning the Tragic Loss of Life (24 February 2025); 10 votes in favor / 5 abstentions.

10 Council of Europe (Parliamentary Assembly) 'The Russian Federation's Aggression against Ukraine: Ensuring Accountability for Serious Violations of International Humanitarian Law and Other International Crimes' (28 April 2022), resolution 2436 (2022), para. 11.6.

11 Format of the Committee of Ministers at the level of Ambassadors / Permanent Representatives (i.e., Deputies), which usually meets at the headquarters of the CoE in Strasbourg every Wednesday.

12 Council of Europe (Committee of Minister's Deputies) 'Consequences of the Aggression of the Russian Federation against Ukraine – Accountability for International Crimes' (15 September 2022), decision CM/Del/Dec(2022)1442/2.3.

in GR-J[13] and CAHDI.[14] A major political impetus to these efforts was given in the Reykjavík Declaration, which stated:

> We welcome international efforts to hold to account the political and military leadership of the Russian Federation for its war of aggression against Ukraine and the progress towards the establishment of a special tribunal for the crime of aggression as highlighted at the Summit of the Special Tribunal's Core Group chaired by President Zelenskyy. The Council of Europe should participate, as appropriate, in relevant consultations and negotiations and provide concrete expert and technical support to the process.[15]

The first series of CMD decisions as a follow-up to implement the Reykjavík Declaration was adopted on 5 July 2023, in which the Deputies

> invited their competent rapporteur groups to examine the implementation of the Reykjavík Declaration, in accordance with the indications that appear in CM/Del/Dec(2023)1471/1.6-app, with a view to reporting back to them for the first time by their 1478th meeting (18 October 2023) at the latest, and subsequently on a regular basis so as to enable the Deputies to prepare a comprehensive report on the implementation of the Reykjavík Declaration to be submitted to the 133rd Session of the Committee of Ministers (Strasbourg, May 2024).[16]

The CMD further "*agreed to remain seized of the issue of the accountability of the Russian Federation for its continued war of aggression against Ukraine in flagrant violation of international law*", which gave the clear task to the GR-J group to continue its focus on accountability issues, including the establishment of the Special Tribunal for the Crime of Aggression against Ukraine and

13 Group of Rapporteurs on Legal Cooperation, in the relevant period (2022–2024) chaired by Ambassador Petr Válek, Permanent Representative of the Czech Republic to the Council of Europe.

14 Committee of Legal Advisers on Public International Law, expert intergovernmental committee bringing together Legal Advisers for the respective Ministries of Foreign Affairs of the CoE member States.

15 Council of Europe, 'United Around Our Values, Declaration of 4th Summit of Heads of State and Government of the Council of Europe', Reykjavík (16–17 May 2023).

16 Council of Europe (Committee of Minister's Deputies), 4th Summit of Heads of State and Government of the Council of Europe (Reykjavík, Iceland, 16–17 May 2023) – Follow-up (5 July 2023), CM/Del/Dec(2023)1471/1.6.

the possible role for the CoE. These efforts then culminated, for the time being, in the adoption of the CMD decision authorizing the Secretary General (through the competent services of the CoE Secretariat)[17] to participate and play an active role in the *Core Group*. To this end, the Deputies

> 1. authorised the Secretary General to prepare any necessary documents to contribute to consultations within the Core Group on a possible draft Agreement between the Council of Europe and the Government of Ukraine on the Establishment of a Special Tribunal for the Crime of Aggression of the Russian Federation against Ukraine, including its Statute, and on a possible draft enlarged partial agreement governing the modalities of support to such a Tribunal, its financing and other administrative matters;
> 2. requested the Secretary General to report regularly to the Deputies on the progress of work and of these consultations;
> 3. agreed to consider any possible next steps in this process, as and when appropriate, taking account of any proposals that may be made by the Secretary General.[18]

Further in the European arena, the EU has also been vocal on the accountability issue, albeit gradually. In the European Council (EUCO) Conclusions of 25 Mar 2022, we find just the following sentence: "*These war crimes must stop immediately. Those responsible, and their accomplices, will be held to account in accordance with international law*."[19] Almost a year later, on 19 January 2023, the European Parliament adopted a resolution calling for the creation of an international tribunal to investigate and prosecute the crime of aggression.[20] In one of the more recent EUCO Conclusions of 26–27 October 2023, there is already a much clearer message:

17 The competent service in this case is the Directorate for Legal Advice and Public International Law (DLAPIL).

18 Council of Europe (Committee of Minister's Deputies) '*Core Group* on the Establishment of a Special Tribunal for the Crime of Aggression of the Russian Federation against Ukraine' (30 April 2024) CMD CM/Del/Dec(2024)1497/10.2.

19 European Union (European Council), European Council Meeting (24 and 25 March 2022) – Conclusions, EUCO 1/2022, para. 1.

20 European Union (European Parliament), Resolution 2022/3017(RSP) on the Establishment of a Tribunal on the Crime of Aggression against Ukraine (19 January 2023), Official Journal of the EU 2023/C 214/10.

> Russia and its leadership must be held fully accountable for waging a war of aggression against Ukraine and other most serious crimes under international law. The European Council calls for work to continue, including in the Core Group, on efforts to establish a tribunal for the prosecution of the crime of aggression against Ukraine that would enjoy the broadest cross-regional support and legitimacy, and towards the establishment of a future compensation mechanism. Moreover, the European Council expresses its support for the work of the International Criminal Court and condemns the Russian attempts to undermine its international mandate and functioning.[21]

Finally, in the EUCO Conclusions of 20 March 2025, the EU Heads of State or Government endorsed the progress in establishing the Special Tribunal within the CoE framework:

> The European Council reaffirms the EU's strong commitment to ensuring full accountability for war crimes and the other most serious crimes committed in connection with Russia's war of aggression against Ukraine. In this context, the progress made on establishing a Special Tribunal for the Crime of Aggression against Ukraine, within the framework of the Council of Europe, is an important step.[22]

4 The Birth of the *Core Group*

This brings us finally to the inception of the *Core Group*, a format established by Ukraine with a group of like-minded states and inaugurated at its first meeting in Prague on 26 January 2023. It functioned as a confidential / closed discussion platform, with no decision-making powers, where representatives of states discussed various legal issues and options relevant to the establish-

21 European Union (European Council), European Council Meeting (26 and 27 October 2023) – Conclusions, EUCO 14/2023, para. 7.

22 European Union (European Council), European Council Meeting (20 March 2025) – Conclusions, EUCO 11/2025, para. 11. It is worth noting, however, the 'disclaimer' attached: "*The text set out in this document was firmly supported by 26 Heads of State or Government.*" This was due to Hungary's opposition to the text of the draft EUCO Conclusions on Ukraine, therefore the formal EUCO Conclusions (document EUCO 1/2025 of 20 March 2025) merely mentioned in Part 1. a debate on Ukraine, and referred to the document EUCO 11/2025, supported by 26 EU Member States, with the exception of Hungary.

ment of the Special Tribunal, in particular its possible models and related legal, procedural, and practical aspects. There were 14 meetings of the *Core Group* altogether, before the conclusion of its work, and they took place at regular intervals approx. every two months, with a possibility to convene an online Working Group in-between.[23]

When joining the *Core Group*, the Government did not commit to support any specific kind of model for the establishment of the Special Tribunal. The only commitment was to support the idea of ensuring accountability for the crime of aggression against Ukraine, the establishment of an appropriate justice mechanism for it, and to actively participate in the work of the *Core Group*. Governments participating in the work of the *Core Group* were represented by Legal Advisers / Directors for Public International Law of the respective Ministries of Foreign Affairs.

The *Core Group* consisted of around 41 states,[24] along with representatives of international organizations, namely the EU (represented by the Legal Services of the European External Action Service and the European Commission), the CoE (which participated through the Directorate for Legal Advice and Public International Law), and Organisation of American States (OAS). Altogether 25 EU Member States participated in the *Core Group* and all G7 members[25] were included, thus ensuring wide and cross-regional representation of important stakeholders.

There was a wide consensus in the *Core Group* on the need to ensure accountability and to establish some sort of a Special Tribunal, as a matter of priority and urgency. There was also a common understanding on some legal and procedural aspects (e.g., that functional immunities should not prevent prosecution for the crime of aggression, as well as shared concerns about chal-

---

23 This was the busy itinerary of the *Core Group*: 26 January 2023 in Prague, 21–22 March 2023 in Strasbourg, 12 May 2023 in Tallinn, 30 June 2023 in Warsaw, 22 September 2023 in The Hague, 16 November 2023 in Berlin, 19 January 2024 in Luxembourg, 7 March 2024 in Vienna, 10 May 2024 in Vilnius, 28 June 2024 in Bucharest, 17 September 2024 in Vienna (*back to back* with the CAHDI meeting from 18 to 20 September 2024), 22 October 2024 in Riga, 3–4 February 2025 in Brussels and the final concluding meeting on 19–21 March 2025 in Strasbourg (once again *back to back* with the CAHDI meeting taking place from 17 to 18 March 2025).

24 Unfortunately, the full and up-to-date list of all participating states (the number slightly increased / varied over time) is not available in the public domain and the confidentiality of the work of the *Core Group* needs to be respected.

25 The Group of Seven (G7) is an intergovernmental political and economic forum dating back to 1973, consisting of Canada, France, Germany, Italy, Japan, the United Kingdom, and the United States, with the European Union as the 'non-enumerated member'. Not to be confused with 'The Magnificent Seven'.

lenges and potential lack of legitimacy of *trials in absentia*). Regrettably, there was much less consensus on the model of the tribunal (so-called *international* model based on UNGA resolution vs. *internationalized / hybrid* model based on national jurisdiction). The G7 states publicly expressed their preference for a hybrid model ("*an internationalized tribunal based in Ukraine's judicial system*"),[26] whereas some other states (incl. the Czech Republic) publicly stated their inclination to explore the international model:

> The crime of aggression can only be committed by a person who is in a position effectively to exercise control over or to direct the political or military action of the aggressor State(s). In order to be fully effective, this judicial mechanism should allow for the prosecution of the most senior leadership of such aggressor State(s).
>
> We believe that an international tribunal, before which the immunities granted by international law to the most senior leadership of a state do not apply, is best placed to deliver the above described objectives. We therefore call on the international community to actively engage in discussions on the establishment of such a tribunal, in particular through decisions of the United Nations General Assembly.[27]

To overcome these differences, a rather creative and innovative *third option* had been brought into equation, which would have encompassed the transfer of criminal proceedings in the most serious / high profile cases from the Ukrainian territorial jurisdiction to the Special Tribunal. In addition, based on the CMD decision of 30 April 2024, a complementary option involving the CoE concluding a bilateral agreement with Ukraine on the establishment of the Special Tribunal, including its Statute, has been put forward, whereas the management and financing of the Special Tribunal would be regulated in the Enlarged Partial Agreement, adopted by the participating states as a particular form of co-operation within the CoE in the form of the CMD resolution. This

26 G7 Japan 2023 Foreign Ministers' Communiqué (18 April 2023) Karuizawa, Nagano, available online at <https://www.gov.uk/government/publications/g7-japan-2023-foreign-ministers-communique/g7-japan-2023-foreign-ministers-communique-18-april-2023-karuizawa-nagano> (last accessed 9 October 2024).

27 Joint Statement by Albania, Belgium, Costa Rica, Czech Republic, Estonia, Guatemala, Latvia, Liechtenstein, Lithuania, Luxembourg, Marshall Islands, North-Macedonia, and Poland on the Accountability for the Crime of Aggression Committed on the Territory of Ukraine (17 April 2023), available online at <https://un.mfa.ee/joint-statement-on-the-accountability-for-the-crime-of-aggression-committed-on-the-territory-of-ukraine/> (last accessed 9 October 2024).

last option then served as the basis for the final compromise and adoption of the texts of the three above mentioned instruments at the technical level of Legal Advisers,[28] at the last meeting of the Core Group held on 21 March 2025 (symbolically) in Strasbourg.[29] However, no matter how interesting it might be to explore and compare these options in more detail, it is not possible at this stage, since the discussions in the *Core Group* were confidential, in order to ensure frank and open exchanges among the participating states and their representatives, and their outcomes have not been made public yet.[30]

The *Core Group* met, by default, at the level of Legal Advisers, i.e., senior civil servants from the Ministries of Foreign Affairs with the necessary legal expertise. However, as an exception to this rule and to give the political impetus to the deliberations, an online summit of the Heads of State and Government of the *Core Group* was held on 9 May 2023 and a Joint statement on efforts to establish a tribunal on the crime of aggression against Ukraine was adopted, aptly expressing the overall aim and purpose of the *Core Group* and its role as the main platform for collective endeavor with the widest possible participation:

> We [the representatives of participants of the Core Group] reaffirm that those responsible for committing the crime of aggression against Ukraine must not go unpunished, and call on the international community to consider appropriate actions, including through the establishment of an appropriate justice mechanism to ensure effective accountability for the crime of aggression, which is of concern to the international community as a whole.
>
> We therefore support exploring the creation of a tribunal to ensure effective accountability for the crime of aggression against Ukraine.

---

28 *See* the statement by the CoE Secretary General, H.E. Mr Alan Berset, of 21 March 2025, available online at <https://www.coe.int/en/web/portal/-/special-tribunal-for-ukraine-secretary-general-welcomes-completion-of-technical-discussions> (last accessed 22 April 2025).

29 The possibility to reach a consensual outcome in Strasbourg was greatly facilitated by the 2-day meeting in Brussels (3–4 February 2025) and the commitment and dedication of the Legal Services of the EEAS and the Commission's services.

30 For a useful and comprehensive overview of different positions and preferences, based on thorough research of publicly available sources, *see* Butchard, Patrick, 'Conflict in Ukraine: A Special Tribunal on the Crime of Aggression' (*House of Commons Library Research Briefing*, 27 August 2024) <https://commonslibrary.parliament.uk/research-briefings/cbp-9968/#:~:text=Two%20years%20after%20Russia's%20full-scale%20invasion> (last accessed 9 October 2024).

> We underline the importance of the Core Group as the main platform for developing an effective mechanism for exploring the legal and technical issues involved in creation of such a tribunal and call on other states and international organizations to join our collective work.[31]

To conclude this section, it is interesting and worthwhile to turn again to the PACE, which on several occasions reflected on the involvement of the CoE in the establishment of the Special Tribunal and adopted a resolution outlining its preference for such mechanism.[32] The essential features should be as follows:

- its jurisdiction should be limited to the crime of aggression committed against Ukraine and should extend *ratione temporis* to such aggression starting in February 2014;
- its jurisdiction should include the role and complicity of the leaders of Belarus;
- its statute should contain a definition of the crime of aggression fully in line with Article 8bis of the ICC Statute, which reflects customary international law;
- personal immunities of key suspects shall not apply before the special tribunal; its statute should leave the issue of personal immunities to the interpretation of the judges of the special tribunal, having regard to the practice of other international criminal tribunals and the precedents in international law;
- functional immunities shall not apply before the special tribunal;
- its statute should contain a list of fair trial rights of the accused, in line with international human rights law;
- its statute could foresee the possibility of *in absentia* proceedings before the trial stage, for instance hearings for the confirmation of charges in the absence of the suspect;
- its role should be complementary to the ICC's jurisdiction and its statute should regulate the co-operation and sharing of evidence between the special tribunal and the ICC;

31 Core Group, Joint Statement on Efforts to Establish a Tribunal on the Crime of Aggression against Ukraine (9 May 2023). The complete text of the Joint Statement is available online at <https://www.president.gov.ua/en/news/spilna-zayava-stosovno-zusil-zi-stvorennya-tribunalu-shodo-z-82785> (last accessed 9 October 2024).

32 Council of Europe (Parliamentary Assembly) 'Legal and Human Rights Aspects of the Russian Federation's Aggression against Ukraine' (26 June 2024), resolution 2556 (2024).

– its statute should contain rules regarding co-operation with participating and other states, which could be complemented with specific co-operation agreements.[33]

It is apparent that some of these features are rather straightforward and non-controversial (fair trial guarantees, complementarity, and cooperation with the ICC), whereas other are more contentious and were subject to thorough debates and carefully balanced solutions had to be reached (such as the personal immunities of some of the top suspects). In any case, the active involvement of the CoE, positively acknowledged and supported by the PACE,[34] gave a new impetus to the discussions and brought the *Core Group* closer to a consensual outcome of its work.

Following the conclusion of the *Core Group* work, the PACE revisited the issue once again and made the following statement:

> In this context, the Assembly welcomes the successful outcome of the Core Group's meeting in Strasbourg between 19 and 21 March 2025 and the finalisation of the necessary legal documents for the establishment of the Special Tribunal for the Crime of Aggression within the framework of the Council of Europe, after almost two years of consultations. The agreed texts include a draft bilateral agreement between Ukraine and the Council of Europe, the Special Tribunal's draft statute and a draft enlarged partial agreement on the management of the Special Tribunal. The three documents have now been submitted for political consideration in Ukraine and in the States participating in the Core Group. Participation in the enlarged partial agreement will be open to non-member States, therefore ensuring cross-regional support and international legitimacy. The Assembly considers that the model of the tribunal envisaged by the Core Group, with the participation of international judges and the application of international law, contains features that make it sufficiently international. By establishing such a tribunal, the Council of Europe will not only support its member State, Ukraine, in its efforts to ensure accountability, but will also uphold the international legal order, on the premise that the pursuit of peace based on justice and inter-

33 Ibid, para. 13.9.

34 Council of Europe (Parliamentary Assembly) 'European Commitment to a Just and Lasting Peace in Ukraine' (30 January 2025), resolution 2588 (2025), paras. 8.7. and 11.5.

> national co-operation is vital for the preservation of human society and civilisation, as recalled in the Preamble to its Statute (ETS No. 1).[35]

The PACE went further to make certain comments on immunities, the definition of the crime of aggression, trials *in absentia* and the temporal scope of jurisdiction, assuming that the documents finalized by the *Core Group* did not fully reflect the preferences outlined by the PACE on previous occasions:

> The Assembly expresses its hope that the final texts on the Special Tribunal will address some of its demands stated in previous resolutions, including with regard to functional immunities, the definition of the crime of aggression, trials in absentia, fair trial rights and co-operation with the ICC. With regard to the temporal scope of its jurisdiction, the Assembly refers to its Resolution 2482 (2023) and Resolution 2556 (2024) and reiterates that the full-scale invasion launched on 24 February 2022 constitutes a continuation of the war of aggression by the Russian Federation against Ukraine that began on 20 February 2014. Any compromise reached on other issues should be understood as not undermining the ability of the Special Tribunal to effectively investigate and punish the crime of aggression and should be without prejudice to the current state and future development of international law. The Assembly stresses that the Special Tribunal's jurisdiction should extend to the alleged crimes of aggression committed by the so-called Belarusian leadership as well as the military and political leadership of North Korea.[36]

In any case, there are still several important steps foreseen in order to achieve the establishment of the Special Tribunal within the CoE framework:

i. States and international partners that have participated in the *Core Group* need to reach a final political agreement on the draft texts (the draft bilateral Agreement between Ukraine and the CoE, the draft Statute and the draft Enlarged Partial Agreement);
ii. following an official request from Ukraine to launch the process and upon completion of internal proceedings within the CoE, the CMD will

---

35 Council of Europe (Parliamentary Assembly) 'Russian War of Aggression against Ukraine: the Need to Ensure Accountability and Avoid Impunity' (9 April 2025), resolution 2598 (2025), para. 9.

36 Ibid, para. 10.

need to authorize (if need be, by a two-thirds majority vote)[37] the Secretary General to conclude the bilateral Agreement with Ukraine;

iii. the Enlarged Partial Agreement will need to be negotiated and adopted in the CMD by participating States, to provide for the necessary financial resources and management structures (it will be opened for joining also for non-member States of the CoE and the EU).

5 The Role of Czech Diplomacy

Finally, as regards the role of Czech diplomacy (and the Foreign Minister personally), it has been supportive to the accountability initiatives from the very outset. During the Czech Presidency of the EU Council in 2022, a thematic COJUR Working Party meeting on the Special Tribunal was organized and the Czech Republic was among the first states to join the *Core Group*. The preference of the Czech Republic, advocated by the Ministry of Foreign Affairs as the responsible authority for international criminal justice, has been towards the international model, while expressing openness to discuss all possible options in a constructive manner. At the same time, due to the long-standing support to the International Criminal Court (ICC), the Czech Republic wishes to protect the integrity of the international criminal justice system and ensure complementarity and cooperation between the ICC and the Special Tribunal. All the activities and efforts of Czech diplomacy in this area aim at creating a tribunal with a sound legal basis, international legitimacy, and acceptable to the Ukrainian partners as an instrument to achieve just and lasting peace, while bringing the perpetrators of the most serious crime of aggression to justice.

6 Conclusion

The *Core Group* has no doubt proved its usefulness and added value in streamlining efforts to ensure accountability for the crime of aggression. It operated in a difficult context, with the conflict in Ukraine having entered its fourth year and any prospect of a just, lasting and sustainable peace solution still quite distant. At this stage of the conflict, it seems crucial to provide Ukraine with military support in order to exercise its right of self-defense in

37 *See* Articles 15.a and 20.d of the Statute of the Council of Europe.

accordance with the UN Charter. However, the conflict must end one day, and it is hardly imaginable that the post-war reconciliation could be achieved without making the perpetrators of the crime of aggression fully accountable. This is why the efforts and outcomes of the *Core Group* to fill in the accountability gap are so important, as a significant contribution to gradually making progress in overcoming difficulties and differences on this long and winding road to international justice.

Note: The author is the Director of the International Law Department at the Ministry of Foreign Affairs of the Czech Republic and participated in the *Core Group* meetings. The views expressed in this chapter are, nevertheless, attributable solely to the author and neither represent an official position of the Ministry of Foreign Affairs nor bind this institution in any manner.

PART 2

Structure and Alternatives of the Mechanism

CHAPTER 3

Possible Ways to the Creation of the Special Tribunal for the Crime of Aggression

Pavel Šturma

1 Introduction

Although international criminal justice has become part of the mainstream of international law theory over the past 30 years, the international community has never faced the challenge of creating a tribunal to prosecute the crime of aggression during this period. Indeed, all of the international or mixed criminal tribunals that have been established since the first half of the 1990s have had their subject matter jurisdiction limited to the crime of genocide, crimes against humanity, and war crimes, or only some of them, or also to certain other serious crimes under international or domestic law. By contrast, the crime of aggression, under the older name the crime against peace, was first and last tried internationally before the international military tribunals at Nuremberg and Tokyo, established immediately after World War II. According to the opinion of the Nuremberg Tribunal, "*those who wage aggressive war are doing that which is equally illegal, and of much greater moment than a breach of one of the rules of the Hague Convention*".[1] It is interesting that the Nuremberg definition of the crime against peace includes the term "war of aggression" but it was left completely undefined, despite the effort of Justice Robert Jackson in London.[2]

It is also significant that the permanent International Criminal Court, established under the Rome Statute (1998),[3] originally had no jurisdiction over the crime of aggression at all. Although the Kampala Amendment (2010) added, in Article 8*bis*, the definition of the crime of aggression and modified the specific conditions for exercising jurisdiction (as will be explained below), given the

1 International Military Tribunal (Nuremberg), Judgment and Sentences, (1947) 41 *American Journal of International Law* 172, 218–219.

2 *See* Clark, Roger S., 'Nuremberg and the Crime Against Peace' (2007) 6 *Washington University Global Studies Law Review* 527, 529–530.

3 Rome Statute of the International Criminal Court (adopted 17 July 1998, entered into force 1 July 2002) 2187 UNTS 3 (Rome Statute).

 | DOI:10.1163/9789004740945_005

conditions, it has never dealt with this crime and is unlikely to do so in the future. It seems paradoxical that while the crime against peace (or aggression) was considered to constitute "*the supreme international crime*",[4] its definition and, in particular implementation, proved to be extremely complicated.

In view of the aggression of the Russian Federation against Ukraine, which has been ongoing since 24 February 2022, the idea of a possible *ad hoc* tribunal for the crime of aggression in Ukraine has attracted the interest of the expert community. This proposal appeared shortly after the start of the Russian aggression thanks to an article written by Prof. Philip Sands.[5] Subsequently, the Government of Ukraine has taken up the idea, with some other states gradually joining in. However, this is still not a majority of the UN membership. Furthermore, it is not clear what form such a special tribunal should take and what legal route or form should be taken to achieve its creation.

This chapter will attempt not only to formulate the following questions but also offer preliminary answers. Why is the International Criminal Court not enough, or could its statute be modified? Should a possible special tribunal be purely international or a mixed criminal tribunal? Can the choice of the type of tribunal affect the legal form of its establishment (statute)? What good can the recently considered UN General Assembly resolution do? What is the significance of the form of the statute of a future special tribunal in terms of legitimacy and legality? What are the other legal obstacles (especially immunities) to the prosecution of those responsible for the crime of aggression?

The questions of the need, feasibility and modalities of the creation of a special tribunal have been discussed in the literature for some time. This publication builds on the debate, both by looking historically at possible models of international and hybrid tribunals, and by taking into account recent developments and the possibilities of applying accountability for the crime of aggression against Ukraine.[6]

---

4 *See e.g.*, International Nuremberg Principles Academy, Nuremberg Declaration on the Crime of Aggression (8 May 2023), available online at <https://crimeofaggression.info/wp-content/uploads/Nuremberg_Declaration_on_the_Crime_of_Aggression.pdf> (last accessed 28 April 2025).

5 *See* Sands, Philippe, 'Putin's Use of Military Force is a Crime of Aggression' *Financial Times* (28 February 2022) <https://www.ft.com/content/cbbdd146-4e36-42fb-95e1-50128506652c> (last accessed 13 October 2024).

6 *See e.g.*, Dannenbaum, Tom, 'A Special Tribunal for the Crime of Aggression' (2022) 20:4 *Journal of International Criminal Justice* 859; Grigaite-Daugirde, Gabija, 'Crime of Aggression against Ukraine: Legality and Legitimacy of Domestic Prosecutions in Third States' (2023) 43 *Polish Yearbook of International Law* 299; Korynevych, Anton, Sanatorova Oksana, Shepitko, Mykhaylo, 'Prosecution of the Crime of Aggression in International and Ukrainian Jurisdiction: Challenges and Prospects', (2023) 43 *Polish Yearbook of International Law* 367; Kulaga,

To answer these questions, however, it is first necessary to recall the past development of international criminal tribunals from the Nuremberg Tribunal to the present day, to show the forms of their establishment and also the differences between international and mixed criminal tribunals.

2 Development of International Criminal Tribunals

2.1 *International Military Tribunals after World War II*

Efforts to punish crimes against international law and to establish an international criminal court have quite a long history.[7] The first truly functioning court was the International Military Tribunal based in Nuremberg (IMT), established by the Agreement on the Prosecution and Punishment of the Principal War Criminals of the European Axis (London Agreement, 1945) with an attached Charter.[8] In January 1946, a similar Charter was adopted for the International Military Tribunal for the Far East (IMT for the Far East) in Tokyo.[9] Both were *ad hoc* international courts of an extraordinary, military nature.

The Nuremberg Tribunal was, and still is, largely highly regarded as an instrument of international justice. Its significance is not only seen in the trial and punishment of war criminals, but also – from today's perspective above all – in the confirmation and development of the rules of international law. Specifically, it concerns the rules relating to the prohibition of the most serious crimes against peace, against humanity, and against the laws and customs of war, in

Lukasz, 'Domestic and International Criminal Jurisdiction in the Context of the Initiative for a Special Tribunal for the Crime of Aggression', (2023) 43 *Polish Yearbook of International Law* 339; McDougall, Carrie, 'Why Ukraine Needs an International – not Internationalised – Tribunal to Prosecute the Crimes of Aggression Committed Against It', (2023) 12:2 *Polish Review of International and European Law* 65.

7 *See* Bassiouni, M. Cherif, 'Introduction to the History of Establishing an International Criminal Court' in Bassiouni, M. Cherif (ed.), *International Criminal Law, vol. III, Enforcement* (Transnational Publ. Inc., Dobbs Ferry, N.Y., 1986), 181; Friedlander, Robert A., 'Problems of Enforcing International Criminal Law', in Bassiouni, M. Cherif (ed.), *International Criminal Law, vol. III, Enforcement* (Transnational Publ. Inc., Dobbs Ferry, N.Y., 1986), 13 ff.

8 Agreement by the Government of the United Kingdom of Great Britain and Northern Ireland, the Government of the United States of America, the Provisional Government of the French Republic and the Government of the Union of Soviet Socialist Republics for the Prosecution and Punishment of the Major War Criminals of the European Axis (adopted and entered into force 8 August 1945) 82 UNTS 279.

9 Charter of the International Military Tribunal for the Far East in Tokyo, proclaimed at Tokyo, *T.I.A.S.* No. 1589; *see* Glaser, Stefan, *Droit international pénal conventionnel* (Bruxelles: Bruylant, 1970), 225–230.

particular the clear establishment of the individual criminal responsibility of the perpetrators of these crimes under international law. On the other hand, however, there are objections that this was more about the exercise of the law of the victors over the vanquished than about genuine international criminal justice. However, it differed from the traditional courts of occupying states in that (a) it was composed of judges from different states and (b) it judged according to the rules of international law. In terms of the composition of the court and the law applied, it was therefore the first international criminal tribunal, although otherwise it could appear as a judicial body of occupying states.[10]

The transfer of territorial sovereignty to the authorities of the Allied Powers following the unconditional surrender of Germany and Japan superseded the consent of these states to the jurisdiction of the IMT and the IMT for the Far East. It is therefore not decisive that Germany was not among the parties to the London Charter, a multilateral treaty, nor that the statute of the Tokyo Tribunal was adopted in the form of a declaration by the Supreme Commander of the Allied occupation forces in Japan, General MacArthur. This is also why this model is not transferable to the current situation.

The International Military Tribunals at Nuremberg and Tokyo were unique institutions in their establishment and functioning and had no direct successors. As far as the crime against peace (today's crime of aggression) is concerned, they remain to this day the only international tribunals that have prosecuted this crime. Nevertheless, the principles contained in their statutes and judgments have greatly enriched international law, both substantive (the catalogue of crimes under international law) and the principle of individual criminal responsibility under international law, with the result that the individual has become entrenched in international law as its subject, albeit with partial to marginal competence. Since then, however, the development of international law has not stopped, although for many years (notably the Cold War period) it slowed down considerably in the institutional sphere.

---

10 *See* Hobza, Antonín, *Přehled mezinárodního práva válečného. Dodatek: Trestání válečných zločinů* [Survey of International Law of War. Punishment of War Crimes] (Praha: Všehrd, 1946), 158; cf also Jílek, Dalibor, 'Přemítání o založení Mezinárodního tribunálu pro stíhání osob odpovědných za závažná porušení mezinárodního práva humanitárního spáchaná na území bývalé Jugoslávie od roku 1991 [Reflections on the Establishment of an International Tribunal for the Prosecution of Persons Responsible for Serious Violations of International Humanitarian Law Committed on the Territory of the Former Yugoslavia Since 1991]' (1996) *Časopis pro právní vědu a praxi* 1, 56–57.

2.2 *Ad Hoc International Criminal Tribunals Established by the UN*

The breakthrough was brought about only by the international community's frustration with the mass killings, "ethnic cleansing" and other crimes committed on the territory of the former Yugoslavia in the conflicts that arose after its break-up. The response was the establishment of the International Tribunal for the Prosecution of Persons Responsible for Serious Violations of International Humanitarian Law Committed on the Territory of the Former Yugoslavia since 1991 (ICTY). However, this tribunal, with limited jurisdiction in terms of place and time, was not established by an international treaty, but by a decision of the Security Council (UNSC or SC) acting under Chapter 7 of the UN Charter.[11] This enabled its rapid establishment. Similarly, the International Criminal Tribunal for Rwanda (ICTR) was established by Security Council resolution in 1994.[12] The subject-matter jurisdiction of these tribunals covers the crime of genocide, crimes against humanity, and serious violations of international humanitarian law applicable in international and internal armed conflict, in the case of the ICTR only in an internal conflict.

In terms of the regulation of the exercise of criminal jurisdiction, the military tribunals after World War II differed from the tribunals for the former Yugoslavia and Rwanda. At that time, the principle of territoriality was applied to the prosecution of war criminals, in the sense that ordinary war criminals should be, and were, prosecuted and punished in the countries where they committed their acts. The International Military Tribunal, on the other hand, was created to try major war criminals whose crimes could not be particularly geographically located. Therefore, one can speak of a divided jurisdiction. In contrast, the ICTY and ICTR are based on the principle of concurrent jurisdiction. An example of this arrangement is Article 9 of the Statute of the International Criminal Tribunal for the former Yugoslavia, which established the priority of the International Tribunal in the competition between the jurisdiction of the Tribunal and that of national courts. Unlike the post-war military tribunals, these were purely international bodies, not only in their composition but also in the manner of their establishment and functioning.

These tribunals did not have the *de facto* power of an occupation administration behind them but had to rely on the cooperation of the respective territorial sovereigns. Thanks to UNSC resolutions, the obligation to cooperate

---

11 *See* UNSC Res 808 (1993) (19 February 1993) and UNSC Res 827 (1993) (25 May 1993) with annex "Report of the Secretary-General pursuant to paragraph 2 of the Security Council Resolution 808 (1993)", Doc. S/2504 (3 May 1993).

12 *See* UNSC Res 955 (1994) (8 November 1994).

applied to all member states. Under their respective statutes, the two International Tribunals had the power to issue binding orders and requests for cooperation to states in all areas (arrest warrants, summoning witnesses, surrender of persons, etc.) where the cooperation of national authorities was necessary for the purposes of criminal proceedings. The only exception is the execution of sentences, which relies on the willingness of a small number of states which have concluded specific agreements with the Tribunals for the execution of sentences imposing deprivation of liberty on their territory.

2.3 *Mixed (Hybrid) Criminal Tribunals*

Following the creation of the ICTY, the ICTR, and the adoption of the Rome Statute, the turn of the millennium saw the emergence of mixed (or internationalized) tribunals. In some respects, the first example is the Special Court for Sierra Leone. These also include the Special Panels in East Timor, United Nations Interim Administration in Kosovo's (UNMIK) efforts to establish a similar system in Kosovo, and the Extraordinary Chambers for the Prosecution of Crimes in Cambodia (ECCC), the Extraordinary African Chambers, and the Special Tribunal for Lebanon. The War Crimes Chamber of the State Court of Bosnia and Herzegovina may also be added for completeness.

2.3.1 Special Court for Sierra Leone

The Statute of the Special Court for Sierra Leone (SCSL), which takes the form of a bilateral treaty between the UN and the government of the West African country,[13] has certain specificities. This form was chosen as an alternative to the originally intended establishment of an international tribunal by a UN Security Council resolution, but the latter instead asked the Secretary-General to negotiate an agreement with the Government of Sierra Leone.[14] It had jurisdiction to prosecute not only crimes under international law (crimes against humanity and serious violations of international humanitarian law) but also certain crimes under Sierra Leonean law.

The Special Court for Sierra Leone is considered to be the first of the so-called mixed (or internationalized) tribunals, as its subject matter jurisdiction covers not only crimes under international law but also certain crimes under Sierra Leonean law, and the composition of the court is also mixed. Yet, by most features on the notional scale of mixed tribunals, this tribunal appears to

---

13 Agreement between the United Nations and the Government of Sierra Leone on the Establishment of a Special Court for Sierra Leone (adopted 16 January 2002, entered into force 12 April 2002) 2178 UNTS 137.

14 UNSC Res 1315 (2000) (14 August 2000).

be the one with the most international elements. This was also reflected in the Charles Taylor judgment, where the SCSL refused to recognize the immunity of the Head of State (the President of Liberia) precisely on the grounds that the proceedings were not before a domestic court but before an international tribunal where the immunities of heads of state against foreign criminal jurisdiction did not apply.[15]

2.3.2 Special Panels in Timor-Leste

The Special Panels in Timor-Leste are among the oldest of the so-called mixed tribunals. They were established to prosecute crimes committed in the country during 1999, when the country was seeking an end to the Indonesian occupation since 1975 and independence. Most of the crimes were committed after the referendum held on 30 October 1999, in which 75.5% of the population voted in favor of independence. The ensuing unrest, to which Indonesia made a significant contribution, was only brought to an end by the deployment of the international UN force INTERFET, which was tasked by the Security Council in Resolution 1264 with restoring peace and security, facilitating humanitarian aid and protecting the UN civilian mission.[16] The presence of the international force on the island led to a calming of the situation and enabled the Security Council to establish the United Nations Transitional Administration in East Timor (UNTAET), headed by a Special Representative of the Secretary-General.[17]

An important function of UNTAET was to establish an effective judicial system in East Timor.[18] Even though the creation of an *ad hoc* tribunal modeled after the ICTY was considered, or SC for Sierra Leone,[19] this idea was abandoned in favor of strengthening the national penalty. Finally, UNTAET issued Regulation 2000/11 on the Organization of Courts in East Timor, which gave the Dili District Court exclusive jurisdiction over crimes of genocide, war crimes, crimes against humanity, murder, torture, and sexual crimes committed between 1 January and 25 October 1999. Special Panels, composed of East Timorese and international judges, were created to prosecute them.

---

15 SCSL, *Prosecutor v Taylor* (Decision on Immunity from Jurisdiction) SCSL-2003-01-I, ACh (31 May 2004), 19–20, paras. 38–40.

16 *See* UNSC Res 1264 (1999) (15 September 1999).

17 *See* UNSC Res 1272 (1999) (25 October 1999).

18 *Cf., e.g.*, Fitzpatrick, Daniel, 'Developing a Legal System in East Timor: Some Issues of UN Mandate and Capacity' (2000) 5 *Austrian Review of International and European Law*, 5–29.

19 *See* Report of the International Commission of Inquiry on East Timor to the Secretary General, UN Doc. A/54/726, S/2000/59 (2000), para. 153.

The panels are composed of two international and one East Timorese judge, respectively three and two judges in particularly serious cases.[20] The applicable law under which the Panels decide under Regulation 2000/15 is the Indonesian criminal law in force at the time of the commission of the crimes, insofar as it is compatible with international law and regulations issued by UNTAET. The definition of genocide was taken from the Convention against Genocide (1948),[21] crimes against humanity, and war crimes from the Rome Statute, and torture from the UN Convention against Torture and Other Cruel, Inhuman or Degrading Treatment or Punishment (1984).[22] In terms of jurisdiction *ratione personae*, the Panels are not limited by any condition of citizenship.

2.3.3 Extraordinary Chambers of the Courts of Cambodia

During the reign of the so-called Khmer Rouge led by Pol Pot (1975–1979), at least 1.7 million people (20% of the population) were exterminated in Cambodia. Although this regime was overthrown by the Vietnamese army in January 1979, during the Cold War the representatives of the overthrown government retained a seat in the UN, and consideration of punishment for crimes did not occur until the 1990s. At the request of the Cambodian government, a UN Group of Experts was commissioned in 1997 to examine the appropriate legal basis and feasibility of the processes. Although the experts' report recommended an *ad hoc* international tribunal under the auspices of the United Nations among possible options,[23] the Cambodian government rejected this option and the United Nations finally agreed to a compromise solution, according to which the tribunal would be part of Cambodia's legal system and consist of national and international judges.

Despite the temporary suspension of negotiations between the UN and Cambodia, the Cambodian Senate approved on 23 July 2001 the law on the establishment of Extraordinary Chambers in the courts of Cambodia for the

20 Under the regulation UNTAET/REG/2000/15 (6 June 2000). *See* Ascensio, Hervé, Lambert Abdelgawad, Elisabeth., Sorel, Jean-Marc, *Les juridictions pénales internationalisées*, CERDIN (Université de Paris 1/SLC, Paris, 2006), 321 ff.

21 (UN) Convention on the Prevention and Punishment of the Crime of Genocide (adopted 9 December 1948, entered into force 12 January 1951) 78 UNTS 277.

22 *See* (UN) Convention against Torture and other Cruel, Inhuman or Degrading Treatment or Punishment (adopted 10 December 1984, entered into force 26 June 1987) 1465 UNTS 85.

23 *See* Report of the Group of Experts for Cambodia, UN Doc. A/53/850 – S/1999/231, para. 129. Cf. also Ratner, Steven R. 'The United Nations Group of Experts for Cambodia' (1999) 93 *American Journal of International Law* 948, 948.

prosecution of crimes committed during the Khmer Rouge rule. Although essentially domestic Cambodian courts, the Extraordinary Chambers have international elements: (1) they include several foreign judges in addition to domestic judges, (2) all international judges and prosecutors are selected from a list prepared by the UN Secretary-General, (3) their jurisdiction is criminal offenses both under the 2001 Act and under international law, and (4) the UN is to contribute to the activity from a special fund. On the basis of General Assembly resolution 57/228 (2002), an agreement between the UN and the government of Cambodia was negotiated in 2003.[24] After the ratification of this agreement on 19 October 2004, the aforementioned law was changed.[25]

The Extraordinary Chambers have jurisdiction *ratione materiae* over the crimes of murder, torture, and religious persecution under the Criminal Code of Cambodia 1956, as well as over crimes defined under international law: genocide under the Genocide Convention (1948), crimes against humanity taken from the ICTR Statute, grave breaches of the Geneva Conventions from 1949, destruction of cultural property according to the Convention for the Protection of Cultural Property in the Event of Armed Conflict (1954), and crimes against internationally protected persons according to the Convention on the Prevention and Punishment of Crimes against Persons Enjoying International Protection, including Diplomatic Representatives (1973). The nationality of the offender is not a condition for the exercise of jurisdiction.

2.3.4 Kosovo Specialist Chambers (KSC)

After the ethnic conflict between Albanians and Serbs in Kosovo and NATO's military intervention against the Federal Republic of Yugoslavia (FRY), an agreement was reached between NATO states and the FRY on the withdrawal of Yugoslav armed forces. This paved the way for the adoption of Security Council Resolution 1244 (1999), which authorized the Secretary-General to establish the United Nations Interim Administration in Kosovo (UNMIK). One of UNMIK's tasks is to stabilize the legal system and administer criminal justice in Kosovo. On the basis of Regulation (Regulation) UNMIK 1999/1 as amended by Regulation 1999/24, the applicable law in Kosovo consists of

---

24 *See* UNGA Res 57/228 B, Khmer Rouge Trials (22 May 2003).

25 Cambodia, Law on the Establishment of Extraordinary Chambers in the Courts of Cambodia for the Prosecution of Crimes Committed During the Period of Democratic Kampuchea, with inclusion of amendments as promulgated on 27 October 2004, NS/RKM/1004/006. *See* Ascensio, Lambert-Abdel and Sorel, *supra* note 20, 368 ff. Cf. Martineau, Anne-Charlotte, *Les juridictions pénales internationalisées: un nouveau modèle de justice hybride?* (Paris: Pedone, 2007), 32–35.

all UNMIK legal instruments and the law that was valid in Kosovo on 22 March 1989 (the day when Kosovo's autonomy within the FRY was abolished). Unlike the situation in Timor-Leste, UNMIK did not establish special panels for the trial of war and ethnic crimes, although this option was considered.[26] Instead, UNMIK merely adopted Regulation 2000/64, which allowed for the creation of mixed chambers, with the participation of international judges and prosecutors.[27]

Later, however, the Kosovo Specialist Chambers and the Specialist Prosecutor's Office were actually created. This happened as a result of the report of the committee of the Parliamentary Assembly of the Council of Europe on the inhumane treatment of people and the illegal trafficking of human organs in Kosovo (2011). Subsequently, the EU Mission for the Rule of Law in Kosovo (EULEX Kosovo) launched a preliminary investigation and set up a Special Investigation Team. In April 2014, the President of Kosovo sent a letter to the EU High Representative for Foreign and Security Policy, in which he expressed interest in the establishment of specialized chambers within the judicial system of Kosovo, staffed by international EULEX staff. Based on a positive response, i.e., an exchange of letters, an international agreement was concluded, which was then ratified by law in April 2014 in the Assembly of the Republic of Kosovo.[28] Subsequently, the Constitution of Kosovo was amended and a law was passed (2015), which enabled the creation of specialized chambers with jurisdiction over crimes against humanity, war crimes, and other crimes under Kosovo law.[29]

Despite this substantive jurisdiction and staffed by international experts, Kosovo's specialized chambers represent internationalized national courts rather than an international tribunal. Despite the possibility of relatively quick establishment, they are of limited importance as a model for a special tribunal for Ukraine (for the crime of aggression).

26 Martineau, *supra* note 25, 24.

27 UNMIK/REG/2000/64 (15 December 2000), on Assignment of International Judges / Prosecutors and/or Change of Venue, as amended by UNMIK/REG/2001/34 (15 December 2001).

28 Kosovo, Assembly, Law No. 04/L-274, On Ratification of the International Agreement Between the Republic of Kosovo and the European Union on the European Union Rule of Law Mission in Kosovo.

29 Kosovo, Assembly, Amendment of the Constitution of the Republic of Kosovo, Amendment no. 24, No.05-D-139, 3 August 2015; Kosovo, Assembly, Law No.05/L-053, On Specialist Chambers and Specialist Prosecutor's Office, 3 August 2015.

2.3.5 Special Tribunal for Lebanon

Another milestone in the development of international criminal tribunals was the adoption on 30 May 2007 of UN Security Council Resolution 1757 (2007) with the attached Agreement between the UN and the Republic of Lebanon on the establishment of the Special Tribunal for Lebanon, to which the Statute of the Special Tribunal for Lebanon is attached.[30] This is the latest case of the establishment of an international *ad hoc* tribunal, which combines on the one hand certain features of previous international and mixed tribunals, but on the other hand contains completely unique and unprecedented features. Among other things, it is a tribunal that is not intended to prosecute crimes under international law (such as genocide, crimes against humanity, or war crimes), but acts of terrorism, or specific terrorist attacks.

The legal basis for the Special Tribunal for Lebanon consists of three interrelated documents: (1) Resolution 1757 (2007), annexed (2) Agreement between the United Nations and the Republic of Lebanon on the Establishment of the Special Tribunal for Lebanon, finally annexed (3) Statute of the Special Tribunal for Lebanon. The Special Tribunal consists of chambers, the prosecutor, the court office (Registry) and the defense office. The panels consist of one investigating judge (Pre-Trial Judge), a trial panel and an appeal panel. With the exception of the position of investigating judge, the composition of the chambers follows the model tried at the Special Court for Sierra Leone, i.e., a combination of international and national (Lebanese) judges. In the case of the Investigating Judge, this post is filled by an international judge, the Trial Chamber consists of one Lebanese and two international judges, and the Appeals Chamber consists of two Lebanese and three international judges.

The basic definition of the Tribunal's jurisdiction in Article 1 of the Statute coincides with the definition in Article 1(1) of the Agreement. The tribunal was established to prosecute "*those responsible for the attack on 14 February 2005 leading to the death of former Lebanese Prime Minister Rafiq Hariri and the death or injury of others.*" However, the law applicable to the prosecution and punishment of the crimes referred to in Article 1 is not international law, but rather (a) the provisions of the Lebanese Criminal Code relating to acts of terrorism, crimes and offenses against life and personal integrity, illegal associations and non-reporting of crimes, as well as provisions regarding material elements of a crime, criminal participation and conspiracy and (b) Articles 6 and 7 of the Lebanese Law of 11 January 1958 on increasing the

30 *See* UNSC Res 1757 (2007) (30 May 2007).

penalties for sedition, civil war and fighting between followers of different faiths (Article 2).

2.3.6 Extraordinary African Chambers

Another of the mixed criminal tribunals created outside the UN framework are the Extraordinary African Chambers.[31] They were created in February 2013 to prosecute international crimes committed in Chad between 7 June 1982 and 1 December 1990. The most famous case to reach the Extraordinary African Chambers, which may have led to the creation of this mixed tribunal, is the prosecution of former Chadian President Hissène Habré, accused of crimes against humanity, torture, and war crimes. Efforts to prosecute the crimes of the former Chadian president have been going on since 2000, when a group of victims filed a petition, on the basis of which a Senegalese judge accused H. Habré of torture, crimes against humanity, and other "barbaric acts". However, appeals courts stayed the prosecution on the grounds that Senegalese courts do not have jurisdiction to try crimes committed abroad. Other victims, including three Belgian citizens of Chadian origin, turned themselves to judicial authorities in Belgium in 2000. After four years of investigation, Belgian authorities charged Habré with crimes against humanity, war crimes, and torture. In 2005, they asked Senegal to extradite him, but a Senegalese court ruled that it did not have jurisdiction to rule on extradition requests.

Only after the judgment of the International Court of Justice (ICJ), to which Belgium appealed, did the development change. On 20 July 2012, the ICJ issued a judgment ruling that Senegal had breached its obligations under the Convention Against Torture and ordered Senegal to prosecute Habré without further delay unless they extradited him.[32] The ICJ ruling led to the resumption of negotiations between Senegal and the African Union (AU), which ended in an agreement to create Extraordinary African Senates. On the basis of the treaty, the National Assembly of Senegal adopted a law on the establishment of special senates (17 December 2012). According to the Statute, the Extraordinary African Chambers of the Courts of Senegal are established with the following composition: one investigation chamber within the regional court (*Tribunal*

---

31 *See* Statute of the Extraordinary African Chambers (2012), *International Legal Materials*, vol. 52, 2013, 1020–1036. Cf. also Šturma, Pavel, 'Povinnost aut dedere aut judicare a nový smíšený trestní tribunál pro stíhání zločinů podle mezinárodního práva [Obligation Aut Dedere Aut Judicare and a New Mixed Criminal Tribunal for Prosecution of Crimes under International Law]' (2014) 4 *Jurisprudence*, 12–16.

32 ICJ, *Questions Relating to the Obligation to Prosecute or Extradite* (Belgium v Senegal) Judgment of 20 July 2012, ICJ Reports 2012, para. 121.

Regional Hors Classe) in Dakar, one indictment chamber at the Dakar Court of Appeal, one trial chamber and one appeal chamber at the same court of appeal (Art. 2). According to Article 3, the Extraordinary African Chambers have the power to prosecute and try those most responsible for crimes and serious violations of customary international law and international treaties ratified by Chad, committed between 7 June 1982 and 1 December 1990. Subject matter jurisdiction is regulated in Articles 4 to 8 of the Statute. It includes the crime of genocide (Art. 5), crimes against humanity (Art. 6), war crimes (Art. 7) and torture (Art. 8).

The composition of the Extraordinary African Chambers reflects the mixed nature of the tribunal as well as the fact that Senegal's legal system is based on French law. The investigative panel is composed of 4 investigating judges and 2 substitutes of Senegalese jurisdiction, proposed by the Senegalese Minister of Justice and appointed by the Chairperson of the AU Commission. The Indictment Chamber is composed of 3 judges and one alternate of Senegalese jurisdiction, proposed by the Senegalese Minister of Justice and appointed by the Chairperson of the AU Commission. In addition to the President, the Judicial Chamber has 2 judges and 1 alternate of Senegalese jurisdiction, proposed by the Senegalese Minister of Justice and appointed by the President of the AU Commission. The president of the panel must be a judge from another AU Member State. The same applies to the composition of the appeal panel. The structure of the tribunal further includes the Office of the Prosecutor and an office composed of Senegalese citizens.

3 Searching for a Suitable Model of a Special Tribunal for Ukraine

3.1 *Obstacles to the Use of the International Criminal Court*

The main reason for considering the establishment of a special tribunal for Ukraine is the limited jurisdiction of the International Criminal Court. Although Article 5 of the Rome Statute (1998) established the subject-matter jurisdiction of the ICC in relation to four categories of crimes: genocide, crimes against humanity, war crimes, and the crime of aggression, the last of these was not defined in the original statute and the jurisdiction of the ICC was deferred. Therefore, as a compromise, the Statute envisaged the extension of the Court's jurisdiction to this crime as well, as soon as the relevant provision is supplemented in accordance with the UN Charter at the review conference, which was to be held seven years after the entry into force of the Statute (Article 5(2)). It is true that at the conference in Kampala, 2010 amendments to the Rome Statute were adopted, especially the definition of the crime of aggression (Article 8*bis*) and special conditions for the exercise of the ICC's jurisdiction in relation to this crime (Article 15*bis* and Article 15*ter*), but still the ICC has never opened an investigation into the crime of aggression and is unlikely to do so in the future.

Unlike other crimes in the Rome Statute, the Court cannot exercise jurisdiction over the crime of aggression committed on the territory or by nationals of a state that is not a party to the Rome Statute.[33] This rule does not apply to a situation where an investigation is requested by the UN Security Council under Chapter 7 of the UN Charter.[34] Furthermore, this amendment provides that a citizen of a party to the Rome Statute, which would not be a party to the amendment on the crime of aggression, may be tried by the ICC for the crime of aggression committed on the territory of the party under the definition of the crime of aggression, unless that state has previously submitted to the Secretary-General of the United Nations an "opt out" statement that it was not bound by the definition of the crime of aggression.

In the case of Russian aggression against Ukraine, it is therefore obvious (despite Ukraine's accession to the Rome Statute), when Russia is not a contracting party to the Rome Statute (and of course not the Kampala Amendments), that the International Criminal Court cannot deal with this situation from the point of view of possible prosecution of the crime of aggression. On the other hand, based on the initiative of 43 parties to the Rome Statute, the International Criminal Court also began to deal with the situation in Ukraine regarding crimes other than the crime of aggression. The other crimes are independent from the crime of aggression. With respect to them, the ICC has its jurisdiction based on Article 12 of the Statute.[35] As early as March 2022, the ICC Prosecutor's Office started an investigation, including the dispatch of investigators to Ukraine, where, in cooperation with local authorities, they secure

33 *See* Art. 15*bis*, para. 5, of the Rome Statute: "*In respect of a State that is not a party to this Statute, the Court shall not exercise its jurisdiction over the crime of aggression when committed by that State's nationals or on its territory.*" On the "aggression gap", see also Dannenbaum, *supra* note 6, 860–863.

34 Because of the special jurisdictional conditions set in Art. 15*ter*.

35 In the absence of ratification of the Rome Statute by Ukraine, the ICC has first established its jurisdiction based on the Ukrainian declaration of 8 September 2015 according to Art. 12, para. 3. Subsequently, on 25 October 2024, Ukraine deposited its instrument of ratification of the Rome Statute, which officially entered into force on 1 January 2025. See webpage available online at <https://www.icc-cpi.int/situations/ukraine> (last accessed 28 April 2025). Since the consent expressed by ratification does not have retroactive effects, the ICC's jurisdiction over crimes committed prior to 2025 can still rely on the Ukrainian declaration.

evidence regarding war crimes, or crimes against humanity. This is necessary so that specific individuals can be charged and warrants issued in the future. While it is not certain that all those responsible (especially those at the highest levels of military and political command) will be brought before the International Criminal Court in The Hague, the very risk of arrest and rendition will always accompany them. At the same time, it should be remembered that crimes under international law are not statute-barred.

If only the ICC should remain (no new tribunal will be created), two paths are possible. There is a possibility of a revision of the Rome Statute, which would change the special (and very restrictive) conditions for the exercise of jurisdiction of the ICC in relation to the crime of aggression.[36] However, such a proposal has not yet been submitted. But even if the proposal were officially submitted, it is not certain whether or when such a change to the Rome Statute would be accepted by the Assembly of States Parties and enter into force. We certainly cannot expect a quick adoption, after all, even the change contained in the Kampala amendment from 2010 was the result of negotiations lasting over ten years. In addition, the Rome Statute has rather complex amendment rules; ratification or acceptance by 7/8 of the parties to the Rome Statute would be required for such a revision to enter into force.[37] In addition, the question of retroactivity must be taken into account, which would probably prevent the application of more liberal conditions for the exercise of jurisdiction of the ICC against Russian officials responsible for the crime of aggression against Ukraine, committed on 24 February 2022. This is

---

36 On the issue of an amendment to the ICC regime, *see* Dannenbaum, *supra* note 6, 869–871.

37 *See* Art. 121 of the Rome Statute:

1. After the expiry of seven years from the entry into force of this Statute, any State Party may propose amendments thereto. The text of any proposed amendment shall be submitted to the Secretary-General of the United Nations, who shall promptly circulate it to all States Parties.
2. No sooner than three months from the date of notification, the Assembly of States Parties, at its next meeting, shall, by a majority of those present and voting, decide whether to take up the proposal. The Assembly may deal with the proposal directly or convene a Review Conference if the issue involved so warrants.
3. The adoption of an amendment at a meeting of the Assembly of States Parties or at a Review Conference on which consensus cannot be reached shall require a two-thirds majority of States Parties.
4. Except as provided in paragraph 5, an amendment shall enter into force for all States Parties one year after instruments of ratification or acceptance have been deposited with the Secretary-General of the United Nations by seven-eighths of them.

also why there is no need to examine the risk of competing jurisdictions here. Under the current wording of the Rome Statute, possible jurisdictional conflicts between the ICC and the Special Tribunal for the Crime of Aggression are virtually excluded. The ICC can prosecute genocide, crimes against humanity and war crimes, whereas the Special Tribunal would have its jurisdiction limited to the crime of aggression committed by Russia against Ukraine.

The second option is to completely give up the effort to investigate the crime of aggression and bring before the international court the Russian officials responsible for this crime, but to concentrate only on the prosecution of the numerous war crimes and crimes against humanity committed in Ukraine as a result of Russian aggression, which is within the jurisdiction of the International Criminal Court. On the other hand, the crime of aggression is by its nature (violation of the rules of *jus ad bellum*) different from other categories of crimes under international law, where it is a violation of international humanitarian law (*jus in bello*) or human rights. Already at the time of the Nuremberg Tribunal, the preparation and launching of an offensive war (then a crime against peace) was considered a more serious crime than individual violations of the laws and customs of war (i.e., war crimes). Moreover, aggression remains the most serious crime in itself, even if the rules of international humanitarian law (IHL) were not violated during the course of the armed conflict. This is because the aggression starts an armed conflict (war) and thus creates a situation in which killing people and destroying property is legitimate if a party to the conflict does not transgress the applicable rules of IHL.

There is also a difference in the circle of possible perpetrators, which in the case of the crime of aggression can only be high-ranking representatives of the state, whose position allows them to effectively exercise control over the state or direct its political or military actions.

3.2 *Possible Overcoming of the Limitations of the Rome Statute without Its Revision*

As in the case of the creation of a new, special tribunal for the crime of aggression (see below), the best and legally indisputable way to use the existing International Criminal Court would be through a decision of the UN Security Council. This is because it can refer the situation regarding the crime of aggression to the ICC by its resolution, in accordance with Article 15*ter* of the Rome Statute as amended by the Kampala Amendments. In doing so, the aforementioned restrictive jurisdictional conditions may not be met.

In the current situation, however, the possibility of adopting a UNSC resolution is completely unrealistic due to the condition of unanimity of permanent members (at least due to Russia's veto). However, the question arises whether the decision of the Security Council could be replaced by a resolution of the General Assembly. There is a need to return to UNGA Resolution 377(V) "Uniting for Peace", which is the basis for convening an emergency special session of the General Assembly and adopting recommendations in cases of SC inaction. According to this resolution, which was adopted at the time of the Korean War and is now considered part of customary international law,[38]

> if the Security Council, because of the lack of unanimity of the permanent members, fails to exercise its primary responsibility for the maintenance of international peace and security in any case where there appears to be a threat to the peace, a breach of the peace, or an act of aggression, the General Assembly shall consider the matter immediately with a view to making appropriate recommendations to Members for collective action, including, in the event of a breach of the peace or act of aggression the use of armed force when necessary, to maintain or restore international peace and security.[39]

After all, on the basis of this provision, an emergency special session of the UN General Assembly was convened in March 2022, which adopted a resolution condemning Russian aggression against Ukraine.[40] As part of the renewed meetings of that emergency special session, the GA then adopted several other resolutions, the last of which also mentions responsibility in a general way.[41] It is therefore possible that if the General Assembly, under Resolution 377(V), may even recommend the use of armed force, it should be able to recommend the creation of a special tribunal,[42] or to refer the situation regarding the crime of aggression to the ICC.[43]

---

38 Corten, Olivier, *The Law against War* (2nd edn., Oxford: Hart Publ., 2021), 335–341.

39 UNGA Res 377, Uniting for Peace (3 November 1950).

40 UNGA Res ES-11/1, Aggression against Ukraine (2 March 2022).

41 UNGA Res ES-11/6, Principles of the Charter of the United Nations Underlying a Comprehensive, Just and Lasting Peace in Ukraine (23 February 2023).

42 *See* Corell, Hans, 'A Special Tribunal for Ukraine on the Crime of Aggression – The Role of the U.N. General Assembly' (blog *Justsecurity.org*, 14 February 2023) <www.justsecurity.org/85116/a-special-tribunal-for-ukraine-on-the-crime-of-aggression-the-role-of-the-u-n-general-assembly/> (last accessed 13 October 2024).

43 *See* Corten, Olivier, Koutroulis, Vaios, *Tribunal for Crime of Aggression against Ukraine – a Legal Assessment.* In-depth Analysis (Brussels: EU, December 2022), 20–21.

However, there is the extensive literature arguing that the Uniting for Peace Resolution cannot be used for enforcement purposes.[44] According to this reading, the GA can make recommendations for collective action including the use of armed force only in the event of a breach of the peace or act of aggression and when necessary, but this use of force is justified by the collective self-defense. This would not be case in other situations (such as response to genocide or other serious international crimes that may constitute a threat to the peace). It is significant that the GA never recommended such collective forcible measures. Instead, the GA recommended, in several cases, the use of measures without armed force.[45] It is important to note that even UN peacekeeping operations (such as the UN Operation in the Congo, UNUC (1960) are not the coercive use of force. This was confirmed by the International Court of Justice in its *Certain Expenses* Advisory Opinion of 1962.[46] Therefore, it is plausible to argue that the GA can recommend the creation of or the reference of the given situation to an international criminal tribunal, which constitutes a measure short of the armed force.[47]

The first option (i.e., a new tribunal) raises a number of questions regarding the form and method of creating a special tribunal, so it will be the subject of further analysis. Regarding the possibility of transferring the situation to the ICC on the basis of a resolution of the UN General Assembly, it can be briefly noted that such a resolution may be adopted along the lines of "Uniting for Peace", but it does not guarantee that the ICC will begin to deal with the situation. The ICC is bound by the express wording of the Rome Statute, which both in the general provision of Article 13(b) and in the special regulation of jurisdiction for the crime of aggression (Article 15*ter*) for referral explicitly requires a resolution of the Security Council acting under Chapter 7 of the UN Charter. Thus, it is likely that the Court would not have to accept the handover and open an investigation. If they had done so, their decision would likely

44 *See e.g.*, Franck, Thomas M., *Recourse to Force: State Action Against Threats and Armed Attacks* (Cambridge University Press, 2001); Johnson, Larry D., '"Uniting for Peace": Does it still serve any useful purpose?' (2014) 108 *AJIL Unbound* 106; Tomuschat, Christian, *Uniting for Peace*, UN Audiovisual Library of International Law (2008).

45 *See* Johnson, *supra* note 44, 110–112.

46 ICJ, *Certain Expenses of the United Nations (Article 17, paragraph 2, of the Charter)* Advisory Opinion, ICJ Reports 1962, at 151, 166.

47 *Cf. in particular*, the legal qualification provided by the ICTY in *Prosecutor v Tadić* (Decision on the Defence Motion for Interlocutory Appeal on Jurisdiction) IT-94-1-AR 72, ACh, (2 October 1995), para. 35.

have been challenged for lack of jurisdiction. Although it is therefore unlikely that the ICC will deal with the crime of aggression in general and against Ukraine in particular in the foreseeable future, it is still appropriate to explore the possibilities of such modifications of the Rome Statute that would allow this.

3.3 *Ways to Create a Special Tribunal for Ukraine*

Due to the problems with the limited jurisdiction of the ICC, the main considerations and discussions, conducted not only at the academic level, but also at the intergovernmental level, are focused on the possibility of creating a special tribunal for Ukraine to prosecute the crime of aggression. Even here, however, there is not one reliable way, but rather a number of variants that have their own advantages and disadvantages.

The existing practice of *ad hoc* criminal tribunals, which was the subject of the previous parts, shows a number of examples of tribunals, although the crime of aggression (crime against peace) was included, if we do not count the Rome Statute of the ICC, only in the Nuremberg IMT and Tokyo IMT statutes. Given that the political conditions enabling the creation of the tribunals of that time are not given at the present time, more recent examples of international and mixed criminal tribunals should be taken into account. It is the choice between the model of a purely international and a mixed tribunal that plays a crucial role. It is then followed by the selection of legal instruments applicable to the establishment of such a special tribunal. It can be a multilateral treaty, a bilateral treaty, a resolution of the Security Council or the General Assembly, or a combination of several of the above instruments.

3.3.1 Model of an International Criminal Tribunal

From the above analysis, it is clear that the fastest and legally cleanest way to create a special tribunal for Ukraine (as an international tribunal) would ideally be through a UN Security Council resolution, as was the case with the ICTY and ICTR. However, due to Russia's (and probably also China's) veto, this path is currently excluded. Therefore, other options need to be explored, which is the creation of a special tribunal directly by a resolution of the General Assembly, or by a treaty between states, or by a treaty between the UN and Ukraine, for which the necessary authorization (recommendation) would be provided by the UNGA resolution.

3.3.1.1 *Tribunal Established by a Resolution of the General Assembly?*

Although the adoption of the UNGA resolution is generally considered an important element of the legitimacy of the established special tribunal, it does not appear that such a resolution alone is sufficient for its creation. There are some arguments in favor of this solution, based on both the "Uniting for Peace" resolution and past practice. It is true that, according to the famous Resolution 377(V), the General Assembly can recommend certain collective measures to UN members, which can also include the creation of a special tribunal.[48] In the same way, we can point to the practice of the UN General Assembly, which established the UN Administrative Tribunal (UNAT) in 1949.[49] The legality of its establishment was later recognized by the International Court of Justice.[50]

The key argument for rejecting this path (UNGA resolution only) is that it is only a recommendation. While "Uniting for Peace" expanded the General Assembly's mandate into an area where the Security Council should otherwise exercise its primary responsibility, nothing changed about its powers, which are to issue recommendations rather than legally binding acts. This may be sufficient for an administrative tribunal to adjudicate employee disputes with the Organization, since the UNGA was thus exercising the power under the Charter to regulate the (labor) relations of employees. On the other hand, it would be something else to create a special tribunal for Ukraine, which would have a criminal nature and try citizens of one of the UN Member States.[51]

Even if it is necessary to reject the resolution of the UNGA as an independent basis for a special tribunal, nevertheless, efforts to negotiate and adopt it are of considerable importance in connection with the possible creation of this tribunal by means of a treaty, concluded on universal or regional level.

3.3.1.2 *A Tribunal Established by an International Treaty?*

An international criminal tribunal can be governed by a treaty, namely a multilateral treaty concluded by member states (ideally on the recommendation of the UNGA). Another way could be a bilateral treaty between the UN and Ukraine, but a similar model has so far only been applied to create a mixed tribunal (see below).

A multilateral treaty, if it had a sufficiently large number of contracting parties, also undoubtedly has the advantage that all parties will be obliged to

48 *See* Corell, *supra* note 42, 2.

49 UNGA Res 351 A(IV), Establishment of a United Nations Administrative Tribunal (24 November 1949).

50 ICJ, *Effect of Award of Compensation by the United Nations Administrative Tribunal*, Advisory Opinion, ICJ Reports 1954, 53.

51 *See* Corten and Koutroulis, *supra* note 43, 15–16.

cooperate with the tribunal, including the handover of accused persons. The situation would be more problematic in terms of the legitimacy and effectiveness of the tribunal if a larger number of states, especially larger states and great powers, remained outside such a treaty. The main problem, however, is that Russia, over whose nationals (including prominent officials) the tribunal should have jurisdiction to prosecute, cannot be expected to become a contracting party.

The obstacle is the classic rule of *pacta tertiis nec nocent nec prosunt*, which is codified in Articles 34 and 35 of the Vienna Convention on the Law of Treaties (1969).[52] In other words, the principle of relative effects of treaties means that a treaty does not create rights or obligations for a third state without its consent. This would generally mean that without Russia's consent, which, of course, cannot be assumed, the treaty concluded between Ukraine and other states (regardless of their number) would constitute *res inter alios acta*, therefore no obligation would arise from it for Russia.

However, there is an almost forgotten provision of Article 75 of the Vienna Convention, which has the nature of a saving clause allowing to break the above-mentioned principle in the case of an aggressor state.[53] The purpose of this article is to remind that the aggressor state cannot invoke the Vienna Convention to absolve itself of the obligations it has incurred as a result of its responsibility for aggression. The vagueness of the adopted text, as also follows from the commentary of the International Law Commission, is rather intentional (formulated in entirely general terms) so that all possible situations are covered.[54] In particular, the aggressor cannot invoke Article 52 on the invalidity of a treaty imposed on them, for example the peace treaties concluded after the end of the Second World War with the satellites of Nazi

52 *See* Vienna Convention on the Law of Treaties (adopted 22 May 1969, entered into force 27 January 1980) 1155 UNTS 331: Art. 34 General rule regarding third States

A treaty does not create either obligations or rights for a third State without its consent.

Art. 35 Treaties providing for obligations for third States

An obligation arises for a third State from a provision of a treaty if the parties to the treaty intend the provision to be the means of establishing the obligation and the third State expressly accepts that obligation in writing.

53 *See* Art. 75 Case of an aggressor State

The provisions of the present Convention are without prejudice to the obligation in relation to a treaty which may arise for an aggressor State in consequence of measures taken in conformity with the Charter of the United Nations with reference to that State's aggression.

54 *See* YILC, 1966, vol. II, 268, para. 5.

Germany (Italy, Bulgaria, Finland, Hungary, and Romania).[55] Similarly, referring to Article 34, the aggressor cannot reject obligations that it did not accept by consent, for example for Germany in the case of the Potsdam Declaration.[56]

It is worth noting that the draft provision that eventually became Article 75 of the Vienna Convention was not in the original draft articles of the International Law Commission. It only got there during the second reading, based on comments from four governments (Hungary, the Soviet Union, the USA, and Ukraine). Therefore, the Special Rapporteur Waldock proposed a new provision (paragraph 2 of the then draft article 58), which was the basis for a later separate article.[57] During further discussion within the Commission, there was some opposition to the proposal based on the belief that legal consequences for the aggressor have their basis in the rules of State responsibility and the UN Charter, not in the law of treaties.[58] Due to the fact that some issues were expressly excluded from the codification of the law of treaties, even the mention of responsibility was dropped in the final version.[59]

In the light of the coercive mechanism established by the Charter, which rests on the system of collective security with the primary responsibility of the Security Council (if it is also capable of action), the aforementioned contractual forms of realization of responsibility for aggression may appear to be outdated. However, the clause in Article 75 of the Vienna Convention is a certain insurance, both for previously negotiated peace treaties and agreements to the detriment of the aggressor, as well as for possible future use. Even in the case of the functional coercive mechanism used against Iraq as a result of its annexation of Kuwait (1990–1991), one can see in a modified form the linkage of the binding Security Council Resolution 687 (1991), which established certain requirements for the end of allied military coercive action (disarmament, compensation, etc.) that Iraq had to accept, with the expression its

55 *Cf.* Šturma, Pavel, Čepelka, Čestmír and Balaš, Vladimír, *Právo mezinárodních smluv* [Law of International Treaties] (Plzeň: Aleš Čeněk, 2011), 196–197.

56 Report of the Conference of the Heads of Governments of Great Britain, the United States and USSR (Potsdam, 2 August 1945), *American Journal of International Law*, vol. 39 (1945), Suppl., 245.

57 *See* YILC, 1966, vol. II, 69, para. 4: *"Nothing in the present article or article 58 precludes a provision in a treaty from being binding on an aggressor State, not a party to the treaty, without its consent if such provision is imposed on it in accordance with the law of State responsibility and with the principles of the Charter of the United Nations."*

58 *See* Fitzmaurice, Malgosia, 'Third Parties and the Law of Treaties' (2002) 6 *Max Planck Yearbook of United Nations Law*, 62–63; Villiger, Mark E., *Commentary on the 1969 Vienna Convention on the Law of Treaties* (Leiden: Nijhoff, 2009), 913–918.

59 *See* YILC, 1966, vol. II, 268.

consent.[60] This leads part of the doctrine to compare this well-known resolution with the institution of a peace treaty.[61]

All the more, a treaty form is offered in a situation where the Security Council system is blocked by the veto of one of the permanent members. But as the Commission pointed out in its commentary on the provision that later became Article 75 of the Vienna Convention, the reference to measures taken in accordance with the UN Charter is essential to avoid the danger of one state unilaterally labeling another as an aggressor. However, with regard to the practice based on the resolution "Uniting for Peace", this requirement can also be met by a resolution of the General Assembly, which called the act an aggression and recommended that states take certain measures.

In the case of the establishment of a special tribunal for Ukraine on the basis of a treaty, the related UNGA resolution is not only a politically significant legitimizing element, but also a condition of legality, or the legal effects of obligations from such a treaty for a third country.

3.3.2 Model of a Hybrid Criminal Tribunal

However, for many of the states that even consider establishing a special tribunal for the crime of aggression, a hybrid (mixed) criminal tribunal appears to be a more feasible and preferred option. This option has its advantages, but also disadvantages. Above all, in the last two decades there has been a greater number of mixed (hybrid) tribunals that can serve as an example.

The advantage is that such a tribunal could be created by a bilateral treaty between the government of Ukraine and the UN, and relatively quickly. Such a treaty could be signed on behalf of the UN by its Secretary-General. In most cases, they are authorized to negotiate a treaty by a Security Council resolution, which is not an option for the establishment of a special tribunal for Ukraine. However, there is also a precedent where a mixed tribunal (ECCC) was established by a bilateral treaty that preceded a recommendation in a General Assembly resolution.[62] A similar procedure could be applied to the establishment of a special tribunal for Ukraine.[63] However, the resolution of

60 UNSC Res 687 (1991) (3 April 1991), para. 33: "[…] *upon official notification by Iraq* […] *of its acceptance of the above provisions, a formal cease-fire is effective* […]."

61 *See* Combacau, Jean, Sur, Serge, *Droit international public* (8e éd., Paris: LGDJ, 2008), 652: "*La résolution 687, longue et complexe, constitue un véritable traité de paix imposé à l'Iraq.*"

62 *See* UNGA Res 57/228, Khmer Rouge Trials (22 May 2003).

63 *See* Hathaway, Oona A., 'The Case for Creating an International Tribunal to Prosecute the Crime of Aggression Against Ukraine (Part I)' (blog *JustSecurity.org*, 20 Septem-

the General Assembly itself was not then, nor can it be now, the legal basis of such a tribunal. This was precisely the bilateral treaty (2003) combined with the Law on Extraordinary Chambers adopted by Cambodia in 2001. If this path were chosen, the jurisdiction of the Special Tribunal would be derived from that of domestic courts.[64]

What was a certain advantage in the case of the ECCC, however, could be more of a disadvantage for the Special Tribunal for Ukraine, which should have exclusive subject-matter jurisdiction over the crime of aggression. If it were part of the judicial system of Ukraine, even with some international elements, one can have doubts about its international nature. If Ukrainian criminal law were to be applied, there could be a problem with the inconsistency between the factual basis and the definition of the crime in Article 8*bis* of the Rome Statute of the ICC (according to the Kampala amendments), especially with regard to the so-called leadership clause. In addition, Cambodia's Extraordinary Chambers tried its own citizens for crimes against humanity, genocide, and war crimes, while the Special Tribunal for Ukraine is supposed to have jurisdiction over the crime of aggression committed by Russian officials. This raises the issue of the immunity of state officials of a foreign state, which the ECCC and most other mixed tribunals have not had to deal with. It is the ECCC model as a tribunal with relatively weak international elements that does not guarantee an exemption from *immunity ratione personae* for the highest state representatives of Russia, which would be given before an international criminal court or tribunal.[65]

Moreover, the government of Ukraine, which seeks to establish a purely international tribunal, is not in favor of the option of a mixed tribunal. One of the reasons is the obstacle to the participation of international judges in Ukrainian courts, where only citizens of Ukraine can sit without amending the constitution.[66]

---

ber 2022) <https://www.justsecurity.org/83117/the-case-for-creating-an-international-tribunal-to-prosecute-the-crime-of-aggression-against-ukraine/> (last accessed 13 October 2024).

64 Dannenbaum, Tom, 'Mechanisms for Criminal Prosecution of Russia's Aggression Against Ukraine' (blog *Justsecurity.org*, 10 March 2022) <https://www.justsecurity.org/80626/mechanisms-for-criminal-prosecution-of-russias-aggression-against-ukraine/> (last accessed 13 October 2024).

65 ICJ, *Arrest Warrant of 11 April 2000* (Democratic Republic of the Congo v Belgium), ICJ Reports 2002, para. 61. Cf. Šturma, Pavel, Chovancová, Katarína, Šmigová, Katarína, Větrovský, Jaroslav, *Immunities of States and Their Officials in Contemporary International Law* (Passau-Berlin-Prague: RW&W Science & New Media, 2017), 112–120.

66 Art. 127, Ukraine, Constitution of Ukraine (1996), available online at <https://rm.coe.int/constitution-of-ukraine/168071f58b> (last accessed 13 October 2024).

In addition, it is currently not clear that the majority of UN Member States would support the negotiation of a treaty between the UN and Ukraine leading to the establishment of such a tribunal. Today, this scenario looks rather unlikely. Therefore, it is advisable to consider the possibility of establishing a tribunal with the help of a regional organization.

3.3.3 Regional Solution for a Special Tribunal for the Crime of Aggression

Since there is not much hope for the creation of an international or hybrid tribunal at the universal level (through the UN), regional solutions are also beginning to be considered. One such regional organization that could play a role in the establishment of the Special Tribunal is the Council of Europe. This regional organization has started to work on it.[67] There are, of course, arguments both in favor and against the establishment of such a tribunal within or with the help of a regional organization. Although most of the international or hybrid criminal tribunals to date have been established by the UN (by Security Council resolutions or by a treaty between the UN and the relevant state), there are also examples of tribunals established at the regional level.

An example of the establishment of a criminal tribunal by a regional organization, in this case the African Union, is the Malabo Protocol. This document is the Protocol on Amendments to the Protocol of the Statute of the African Court of Justice and Human Rights (2014) that provides for a criminal chamber of the African Court of Justice and Human Rights (ACJHR). However, the Malabo Protocol has not yet entered into force.[68] Other examples of regional tribunals are the Extraordinary African Chambers, established by a treaty between the AU and Senegal (see above Section 2.3.6) or the Kosovo Specialist Chamber, established by the exchange of letters between the representatives of Kosovo and the EU High Representative for Foreign and Security Policy (see above Section 2.3.4).

However, in the case of the tribunal foreseen by the Malabo Protocol and the Extraordinary African Chambers, the AU established tribunals designed to prosecute citizens of AU Member States. In the case of the KSC, although Kosovo is outside the EU, the jurisdiction of the KSC is derived from the jurisprudence of Kosovo's domestic courts, which the EU rather provides support for. The establishment of the Special Tribunal for the Crime of Aggression, which should prosecute the representatives of Russia, by the Council of Europe, of

---

67 For the role of the Council of Europe, *see* chapter by Emil Ruffer, 17–19.

68 *See* Werle, Gerhard, Vormbaum, Moritz, *The African Criminal Court. A Commentary on the Malabo Protocol* (Springer, 2017).

which Russia is no longer a member, would be somewhat more complicated but not impossible.

It is therefore necessary to assess whether the Council of Europe has the authority to negotiate an international treaty, the content of which would be the establishment of an international or hybrid criminal tribunal. As far as the possibility of organizing the negotiations of international agreements is concerned, it results from the international legal entity of the Council of Europe. This is similar to the case of the UN, where this authority is not explicitly stated in the Charter but can be inferred as an implied power.[69]

To make it clear, the Council of Europe has the power to conclude international treaties, but such agreements must remain within the scope of its mandate as it is set by its Statute. It is a general rule regarding the capacity of international organizations to conclude treaties that was codified in Article 6 of the Vienna Convention on the Law of Treaties between States and International Organizations or between International Organizations (1986).[70]

However, it does not mean that any international organization may conclude a treaty on any subject-matter. The International Court of Justice pointed out that international organizations do not, unlike states, possess a general competence, but are governed by the *principle of specialty*, that is to say, they are invested by the states which create them with powers, the limits of which are a function of the common interests whose promotion those states entrust to them.[71]

This implies that if the Council of Europe does not possess a competence to organize international criminal justice, it will not be able to establish, by way of a treaty, an international tribunal competent to prosecute the crime of aggression. The Statute and the existing activities of the Council of Europe do not suggest that it could establish an international tribunal, even less the

---

69 *Cf.* ICJ, *Reparation for Injuries Suffered in the Service of the United Nations*, Advisory Opinion, ICJ Reports 1949, 179; ICJ, *Certain Expenses of the United Nations (Article 17, paragraph 2, of the Charter)* Advisory Opinion, ICJ Reports 1962, 167–168.

70 *See* Art. 6: "*The capacity of an international organization to conclude treaties is governed by the rules of that organization.*" Official Records of the United Nations Conference on the Law of Treaties between States and International Organizations or between International Organizations, vol. II.

71 ICJ, *Legality of the Use by a State of Nuclear Weapons in Armed Conflict*, Advisory Opinion, ICJ Reports 1996, para. 24. Cl. also Akande, Dapo, 'The Competence of International Organizations and the Advisory Jurisdiction of the International Court of Justice' (1998) 9 *European Journal of International Law*, 437–467; Faix, Martin, *The Law of International Organizations* (Olomouc: Palacký University, 2012), 79–80.

tribunal competent to try crimes committed by representatives of a non-member state.

However, the situation seems to be less clear when it comes to the scenario of a hybrid criminal argument. One can argue that the inter-state cooperation in criminal matters comes within the competence of the Council of Europe. The long list of (224) conventions of the Council of Europe includes various examples, such as the European Convention on Extradition (1957), the European Convention on Mutual Assistance in Criminal Matters (1959), the European Convention on the International Validity of Criminal Judgments (1970), the European Convention on the Transfer of Proceedings in Criminal Matters (1972), the European Convention on the Non-Applicability of Statutory Limitations to Crimes against Humanity and War Crimes (1974), the European Convention on the Suppression of Terrorism (1977) etc. Among more recent instruments, treaties such as the Convention on Action against Trafficking in Human Beings (2005) or the Budapest Convention on Cybercrime (2001) should be mentioned. The last two conventions are open also to non-member states.

This suggests that even if the Council of Europe as such does not have the competence to combat the crime of aggression and to establish an international tribunal, it may facilitate the cooperation between the like-minded Member States and non-member states leading to the negotiation of a treaty, statute of a hybrid criminal tribunal. It may be concluded in the form of a multilateral or bilateral treaty. Such a tribunal would have its jurisdiction derived from the jurisdiction of individual Member States, in particular that of Ukraine.

Nevertheless, there are two caveats regarding this scenario. First, the analysis of feasibility of a treaty instrument concluded on universal level holds true, *mutatis mutandis*, for the regional instrument. For the sake of legitimacy of such treaty instrument, the involvement of the United Nations is useful, at least in the form of the GA resolution. Second, the envisaged scenario involves the risk that the hybrid tribunal established by the Council of Europe or its member states with Ukraine would be more an internationalized domestic court than a genuine international tribunal. This may have negative consequences regarding its capacity to overcome the immunity *ratione personae* of the high-level officials of the Russian Federation. However, as there is no universal model of a hybrid tribunal, the level of internationalization of a tribunal depends rather on the number and strength of elements contributing to its international character. These elements include, *inter alia*, the composition of the tribunal (predominantly international judges), the definition of the crime of aggression under international law (preferably modelled on Article 8*bis* of the Rome Statute of the ICC), and the seat of the tribunal outside the territory of Ukraine. In other words, it is possible to imagine a strong hybrid tribunal with high degree of internationalization that may serve the same purpose as an international criminal tribunal.

Anyway, any model of a special criminal tribunal would have some advantages and disadvantages.[72]

4 Conclusion

Any reflection on the possibilities of creating a special tribunal to prosecute the crime of aggression in Ukraine should begin by recalling and comparing the existing international and mixed criminal tribunals, as well as the International Criminal Court. Against this background, in addition to resigning, of course, to the international punishment for the crime of aggression, three basic options are offered. The first of them is based on the existence of a permanent International Criminal Court, which would ideally be the most appropriate forum. Due to the special, very restrictive regulation of the conditions for the exercise of jurisdiction over the crime of aggression in the Rome Statute, this is not possible today. At least for the foreseeable future, a revision or extensive interpretation of the Rome Statute does not appear to be a realistic path, but that does not mean that it is entirely out of the question.

The other two options envisage the creation of a new, special tribunal for Ukraine, which would fill the current gap in the jurisdiction of the ICC. The essential difference and ongoing debate concern whether it would be a purely international tribunal or a mixed (hybrid) tribunal. While it is not easy to create one with the UN Security Council blocked, there are alternative ways to do it. In both cases, it could rely on a combination of a General Assembly resolution and an international treaty. It is not only an obvious question of the legitimacy of the special tribunal established in this way, but also of its legality. Although generally an international treaty does not create obligations for a third state without its consent, Article 75 of the Vienna Convention (1969) provides an exception for obligations that may arise for an aggressor state as a result of measures taken under the UN Charter.

From the point of view of overcoming problems with the immunity of high-ranking state officials, the proposal to establish an international tribunal seems better, even if it is still associated with a number of political and legal

72 *Cf.* Dannenbaum, *supra* note 6, 873.

difficulties. The legal basis could be a multilateral treaty concluded by as many states as possible, including Ukraine, on the basis of recommendations in a General Assembly resolution. Without reaching a resolution, supported by a large majority of UN Member States, there is no point in negotiating such a treaty.

The second possibility is the establishment of a hybrid criminal tribunal based on a bilateral treaty. Although it seems simpler to negotiate a bilateral treaty between the UN (represented by the Secretary-General) and the Government of Ukraine that would create a mixed criminal tribunal, this option is not ideal for a special tribunal to prosecute the crime of aggression. In addition, it is currently not clear that the majority of UN Member States would support the negotiation of a treaty between the UN and Ukraine leading to the establishment of such a tribunal. Therefore, regional solutions should also be considered. One such regional organization that could play, and started to play, a role in the establishment of the Special Tribunal is the Council of Europe. Even if the Council of Europe as such does not have the competence to combat the crime of aggression and to establish an international tribunal by its unilateral act, it may contribute to the creation and financing of a hybrid criminal tribunal on the basis of the bilateral treaty with Ukraine.

CHAPTER 4

Can States Find a Third Way to Structure a Crime of Aggression Tribunal for the Situation of Ukraine?

Jenniffer Trahan

1 Introduction

In the wake of Russia's February 2022 invasion of the territory of Ukraine, a core group of states has committed to ensuring the creation of an aggression-specific tribunal to investigate and prosecute the crime of aggression being committed against Ukraine. This approach is necessitated because the jurisdiction of the International Criminal Court (ICC) over the crime of aggression is unduly restrictive so that the ICC cannot investigate or prosecute the crime in the current situation, even though it possesses jurisdiction over the ICC's other core crimes if committed in the territory of Ukraine. As of this writing, the core group of states[1] has faced significant deadlock in their proposals for a tribunal, although they may be on the cusp of overcoming them.

This deadlock began when approximately half of the states within the core group supported the establishment of a Special Tribunal on the Crime of Aggression (STCoA) to be created by agreement between the UN and Ukraine, upon the recommendation of the UN General Assembly.[2] Ukraine supported this approach.[3] By contrast, the other half of states in the core group, including

1 This chapter was written in fall 2023 with minor updates made in spring 2025. As of this writing, there are approximately forty states in the core group. Labuda, Patryk, 'Making Counter-Hegemonic International Law: Should a Special Tribunal for Aggression Be International or Hybrid?' (blog *Justsecurity.org*, 19 September 2023) <https://www.justsecurity.org/88373/making-counter-hegemonic-international-law-should-a-special-tribunal-for-aggression-be-international-or-hybrid/> (last accessed 11 October 2024) (listing, at that time, thirty-eight). *See also* chapter by Emil Ruffer.

2 Observations of a participant in the negotiations. This proposal is discussed in Section 3.1.

3 President of Ukraine, Volodymyr Zelenskyy, Official website, President: Ukraine Stands against Hybrid Formats of Tribunal for Russian Crime of Aggression, 4 May 2023, available online at <https://www.president.gov.ua/en/news/ukrayina-vistupaye-proti-gibridnih-formativ-tribunalu-shodo-82669> (last accessed 11 October 2024).

 | DOI:10.1163/9789004740945_006

members of the G7 group of states,[4] proposed utilizing a Ukrainian domestic court with some internationalized elements.[5] The deadlock persisted for several months, without either side showing signs of acquiescing to the other side's position. Subsequently, similar deadlock developed within the core group – but over the form a tribunal could take if established by agreement between the Council of Europe and Ukraine.[6]

This chapter commences by considering, in Section 2, the reasons why the ICC's jurisdiction over the crime of aggression is so truncated and whether that is a rational and justifiable approach. The chapter, in Section 3, then explores what had been the two dominant competing proposals for establishing a freestanding aggression-specific tribunal. Namely, Section 3.1. explores what had been the proposal to have the UN General Assembly recommend the establishment of the tribunal, with it formed by agreement between the UN and Ukraine, while Section 3.2. explores what had been the proposal to establish an internationalized Ukrainian chamber. The chapter then, in Section 4, suggests other possibilities for structuring the tribunal. Specifically, Section 4.1 explores the potential of the UN Security Council recommending the establishment of the tribunal under a Chapter VI resolution, admittedly an approach that failed to attract significant interest. Section 4.2 explores the potential to establish a regionally backed tribunal formed by agreement between Ukraine and the Council of Europe, which is the current path being pursued. The chapter ultimately argues both for establishing an aggression-specific tribunal for the situation of Ukraine – but one that is able to overcome personal immunities that otherwise risk shielding high-level leaders from prosecution – and fixing the ICC's jurisdiction over the crime of aggression to cover future similar situations.

2 How the ICC's Jurisdiction over the Crime of Aggression Came to Be So Truncated

The international community has primarily decided against creating new international or hybrid tribunals every time a mass atrocity situation arises;

4 The Group of Seven (G7) consists of Canada, France, Germany, Italy, Japan, the United Kingdom, and the United States.

5 Observations of a participant in the negotiations. This proposal is discussed in Section 3.2.

6 *See* Council of Europe (Parliamentary Assembly), 'Legal and Human Rights Aspects of the Russian Federation's Aggression against Ukraine' (26 January 2023), resolution 2482 (2023) (recommending the establishment of a tribunal). This proposal is discussed in Section 4.2.

instead, it chose to create one standing institution, the ICC.[7] Thus, initially one might be puzzled why the international community would seemingly go back in time to create an aggression-specific tribunal for only one situation. Clearly, such an approach is hardly ideal and detractors can easily level accusations of selectivity – why should aggression against Ukraine be prosecuted, and not in other situations?

The answer is that it must be prosecuted in both, and, ideally, the crime should be prosecuted, at least in the future, before the ICC. This was always the assumption under the Rome Statute.[8] Thus, already in 1998, Article 5(1) of the Rome Statute provided that there were four crimes within the jurisdiction of the court.[9] It was also the assumption that the crime would be prosecuted before the ICC when the crime of aggression amendments were negotiated[10] and later adopted at the ICC Review Conference in Kampala, Uganda, in 2010.[11] And, it was the assumption when the ICC's jurisdiction over the crime was activated in 2017, by resolution of the ICC's Assembly of States Parties (ASP), effective 17 July 2018.[12] (The definition of the crime and conditions for the ICC's exercise of jurisdiction over it were not contained in the original Rome Statute that was finalized in 1998, but had to be completed through a later process.)[13]

---

7 Certain exceptions exist – primarily in situations where the ICC would lack jurisdiction – the Special Tribunal for Lebanon (which tried the crime of terrorism committed in Lebanon), the Kosovo Specialist Chambers (KSC) and Specialist Prosecutor's Office (trying crimes committed prior to the Rome Statute's entry into force), and the Extraordinary African Chambers in the Courts of Senegal (the same) – or to supplement the ICC's work, as with the Special Criminal Court in the Central African Republic.

8 Rome Statute of the International Criminal Court (adopted 17 July 1998, entered into force 1 July 2002) 2187 UNTS 3 (as amended) (Rome Statute).

9 Article 5(1) states: "*The jurisdiction of the Court shall be limited to the most serious crimes of concern to the international community as a whole. The Court has jurisdiction in accordance with this Statute with respect to the following crimes: (a) The crime of genocide; (b) Crimes against humanity; (c) War crimes; (d) The crime of aggression.*" Ibid, Art. 5(1).

10 From 1999 through 2002, negotiations took place during meetings of the Preparatory Commission for the Establishment of an International Criminal Court. From 2003 through 2009, negotiations continued before the Special Working Group on the Crime of Aggression (SWGCA).

11 ICC, Assembly of States Parties, Review Conference, The Crime of Aggression, Annex I, ICC Doc. RC/Res.6 (11 June 2010), available online at <https://treaties.un.org/doc/source/docs/RC-Res.6-ENG.pdf> (Review Conference Resolution) (last accessed 11 October 2024).

12 ICC, Assembly of States Parties, Activation of the Jurisdiction of the Court over the Crime of Aggression, ICC-ASP/16/Res.5 (14 December 2017) (Activating Resolution).

13 *See* note 10 *supra*. Rome Statute Article 5(2) stated: "*The Court shall exercise jurisdiction over the crime of aggression once a provision is adopted in accordance with articles 121 and*

Yet, the ICC's jurisdiction over the crime of aggression is based on a different jurisdictional regime than the ICC's jurisdiction over its other three crimes. This divergence in approach was permitted under the Rome Statute, which expressly allowed a different jurisdictional regime to be created for the crime of aggression.[14] The truncation of jurisdiction occurred in Kampala, Uganda, in 2010, at the ICC Review Conference, when certain states, led primarily by the United States, insisted that aggression committed by the nationals of, or on the territory of, non-States Parties should be completely exempt from ICC jurisdiction.[15] This became memorialized in Article 15*bis*(5).[16] Then, given that approach, States Parties also negotiated an *opt out* provision, whereby they could opt out of the court's jurisdiction *vis-à-vis* the crime of aggression. This became memorialized in Article 15*bis*(4).[17] A further dispute as to how to read the jurisdiction that was agreed on in Kampala later erupted and further limitations on the crime of aggression's jurisdictional regime occurred in 2017, or arguably occurred then, because it is unclear if the attempted modifications are effective.[18]

What matters for present purposes is the carve-out found in Article 15*bis*(5), the exemption for the nationals of non-States Parties. It is that provision that has now carved Russian political and military leaders out of the ICC's jurisdiction as to the investigation and prosecution of the crime of aggression in the

---

123 defining the crime and setting out the conditions under which the Court shall exercise jurisdiction with respect to this crime. Such a provision shall be consistent with the relevant provisions of the Charter of the United Nations." Rome Statute, *supra* note 8, Art. 5(2). That text was agreed to be deleted. *See* Review Conference Resolution, *supra* note 11, Annex I.

14 Rome Statute, *supra* note 8, Art. 5(2).

15 For details of the negotiations, *see* Trahan, Jennifer, 'Negotiating the Amendment on the Crime of Aggression: Proceedings at the Kampala Review Conference on the International Criminal Court' (2011) 11 *International Criminal Law Review* 49.

16 It states: "*In respect of a State that is not a party to this Statute, the Court shall not exercise its jurisdiction over the crime of aggression when committed by that State's nationals or on its territory.*" Rome Statute, *supra* note 8, Art. 15*bis*(5).

17 It states: "*The Court may, in accordance with article 12, exercise jurisdiction over a crime of aggression, arising from an act of aggression committed by a State Party, unless that State Party has previously declared that it does not accept such jurisdiction by lodging a declaration with the Registrar. The withdrawal of such a declaration may be effected at any time and shall be considered by the State Party within three years.*" Ibid, Art. 15*bis*(4).

18 *See* Activating Resolution, *supra* note 12. For an argument about the invalidity of the modification made in the Activating Resolution of the amendment text agreed on in Kampala, *see* Trahan, Jennifer, 'From Kampala to New York – The Final Negotiations to Activate the Jurisdiction of the International Criminal Court over the Crime of Aggression' (2018) 18 *International Criminal Law Review* 197.

situation of Ukraine. Despite Ukraine having initially accepted the ICC's jurisdiction by executing two Article 12(3) declarations,[19] these only enable the ICC to investigate and prosecute the ICC's other three crimes (genocide, crimes against humanity, and war crimes). As a result of the application of Article 15*bis*(5), there is no ICC jurisdiction over the crime of aggression occurring in the territory of Ukraine committed by the nationals of a non-State Party, such as the leaders of the Russian Federation (and Belarus).[20] The same is true now that Ukraine has ratified the Rome Statute.[21]

This leads to the obvious question of whether the ICC's jurisdiction over the crime of aggression should not be fixed – by the ASP adopting an amendment to the Kampala crime of aggression amendments. The author firmly believes this should occur. Germany, as well as a fair number of additional states, have shown an interest in pursuing such an amendment.[22] The non-governmental organization The Global Institute for the Prevention of Aggression (GIPA), of which the author serves as Convenor, has proposed a model amendment

19 Webpage of the International Criminal Court, Ukraine, Situation in Ukraine, available online at <https://www.icc-cpi.int/situations/ukraine> (last accessed 11 October 2024).

20 For a list of States Parties, *see* webpage of the International Criminal Court, The States Parties to the Rome Statute, available online at <https://asp.icc-cpi.int/states-parties> (last accessed 11 October 2024). Having permitted Russian forces to use its territory as a staging ground, the leaders of Belarus also face potential criminal responsibility for the crime of aggression. *See* Rome Statute, *supra* note 8, Art. 8*bis*(2)(f) (including as an act of aggression, "[t]*he action of a State in allowing its territory, which it has placed at the disposal of another State, to be used by that other State for perpetrating an act of aggression against a third State*").

21 On 25 October 2024, Ukraine deposited its instrument of ratification with the Secretary-General of the United Nations, meaning its ratification became effective 1 January 2025. President of Ukraine, Official Website: On January 1, 2025, Ukraine Will Become the 125th Member State of the International Criminal Court, 25 October 2024, available online at <https://www.president.gov.ua/en/news/z-1-sichnya-2025-roku-ukrayina-stane-125-yu-derzhavoyu-uchas-94061> (last accessed 28 October 2024). As part of its ratification package, Ukraine has also purported to invoke Rome Statute Article 124 (which permits a state to opt out of the ICC's jurisdiction regarding war crimes for a period of seven years), but only insofar as Ukrainian nationals are concerned. That is, Ukraine is attempting to leave in place the ICC's jurisdiction regarding war crimes committed by Russian nationals. It is unclear whether such a one-sided opt out would be effective; there are strong arguments for rejecting such selectivity.

22 *See* Speech by Foreign Minister Annalena Baerbock at the Commemoration of the 25th Anniversary of the Adoption of the Rome Statute of the International Criminal Court, 17 July 2021, available online at <https://www.auswaertiges-amt.de/en/newsroom/news/-/2609126> (last accessed 11 October 2024). Approximately thirty to forty states have joined Germany in endorsing the need to amend the ICC's crime of aggression jurisdiction.

text.[23] Moreover, not only does the invasion of Ukraine (and lack of ICC jurisdiction over the crime of aggression) shine a spotlight on the undue restrictions on the ICC's jurisdiction over the crime, but the ASP's review of the crime is mandated. The Kampala Review Conference resolution called for review of the crime of aggression seven years after activation of the ICC's jurisdiction over the crime;[24] the review accordingly falls due in 2025. Thus, there is an upcoming opportunity for the ASP to amend the Rome Statute to fix the ICC's jurisdiction over the crime of aggression.[25]

States Parties should amend the Rome Statute (i.e., amend the Kampala amendments on the crime of aggression) by eliminating the exceptional approach taken regarding the crime's jurisdiction. Specifically, States Parties should delete Article 15*bis*(4) and 15*bis*(5) and, *in lieu*, spell out how Article 12 applies, thereby returning the crime of aggression to the default jurisdictional rules in the Rome Statute.[26] Thus, in the future, if this amendment were effectuated, aggression committed by nationals of a non-State Party (such as Russia), in the territory of a State Party or state that has accepted the ICC's jurisdiction (such as Ukraine), would be subject to the ICC's jurisdiction, just as

---

23 For the amendment proposal, *see* webpage of the GIPA, available online at <https://crimeofaggression.info/wp-content/uploads/GIPA-model-amendment-proposal.pdf> (last accessed 11 October 2024). *See also* GIPA's reasons for the proposed amendment, available online at <https://crimeofaggression.info/wp-content/uploads/GIPA-Proposal-Short.pdf> (last accessed 11 October 2024); Trahan, Jennifer, 'Amending the Kampala Amendments: Proposal to Harmonize the ICC's Jurisdiction over the Crime of Aggression with its Jurisdiction over its Other Core Crimes' (blog *Opinionjuris.org*, 2 November 2023) <https://opiniojuris.org/2023/10/02/amending-the-kampala-amendments-a-proposal-to-harmonize-the-iccs-jurisdiction/> (last accessed 11 October 2024). *See also* Letter to the Permanent Representatives of States Parties to the Rome Statute from the Permanent Missions of Costa Rica, Sierra Leone, Vanuatu, Germany and Slovenia to the United Nations, Mandated Review of the Kampala Amendments on the Crime of Aggression, dated 8 November 2024, available online at <https://crimeofaggression.info/wp-content/uploads/Letter-to-all-ICC-SPs_distribution-of-discussion-paper-on-review-of-Kampala-Amendments-on-the-Crime-of-Aggression_Nov-2024.pdf> (last accessed 14 April 2025).

24 Review Conference Resolution, *supra* note 11 ("*decides to review the amendments on the crime of aggression seven years after the beginning of the Court's exercise of jurisdiction*"). Activation occurred in 2017. *See* Activating Resolution, *supra* note 12.

25 There was no reason to wait until 2025 to consider the issue; yet, only recently have states begun the legwork needed for the ASP to be in a position to adopt the amendment.

26 GIPA's amendment proposal takes the view that it is preferable to detail how Article 12 would apply, by quoting its text, rather than simply referencing Article 12. *See* GIPA amendment proposal, *supra* note 23.

jurisdiction exists in that situation regarding the Rome Statute's other three crimes.

Yet, the negotiations are predicted to be difficult, complex[27] and expansion of jurisdiction may be bitterly opposed by some of the same states that truncated it in 2010 and sought to further truncate it in 2017.[28] Due to the uncertain outcome of the amendment negotiations – when they might be concluded, what the substantive outcome will be, and when any resulting amendment would enter into force – it is unclear whether the amendment, which presumably will not apply retroactively, would come in time and/or be of a scope to cover the aggression occurring against Ukraine. For this reason, the preferable approach involves two steps: to establish an aggression-specific tribunal for the situation of Ukraine and pursue amending the Rome Statute to cover future similar situations.

3 The Initial Dominant Proposals for an Aggression-Specific Tribunal

Two dominant competing proposals for creating an aggression-specific tribunal for the situation of Ukraine emerged by the summer of 2022 and early 2023: (1) the UN General Assembly recommending the establishment of the tribunal; and (2) Ukraine establishing an internationalized chamber within its court system.

3.1 *The UN General Assembly Recommending the Establishment of the Tribunal*

As to the first approach, in June 2022, a fairly detailed proposal for structuring an aggression-specific tribunal was presented at the Yale Club, in New York City, in a meeting sponsored by the Permanent Mission of Liechtenstein to the UN and the Permanent Mission of Latvia to the UN.[29] The proposal was for

27 *See* Reisinger Coracini, Astrid, 'Is Amending the Rome Statute the Panacea Against Perceived Selectivity and Impunity for the Crime of Aggression Committed Against Ukraine?' (blog *Justsecurity.org*, 21 March 2023) <https://www.justsecurity.org/85593/is-amending-the-rome-statute-the-panacea-against-perceived-selectivity-and-impunity-for-the-crime-of-aggression-committed-against-ukraine/> (last accessed 11 October 2024).

28 Those efforts in 2017 were led by the United Kingdom and France.

29 *See* Letter dated 12 August 2022 from the Representatives of Latvia, Liechtenstein and Ukraine to the United Nations Addressed to the Secretary-General, UN Doc. A/ES-11/7-S/2022/616 (17 August 2022), available online at <https://www.justsecurity.org/wp-content/uploads/2022/09/unsc-Letter-12-August-2022.pdf> (last accessed 11 October 2024).

the tribunal to be created by agreement between the United Nations and Ukraine, upon the recommendation of the UN General Assembly.[30]

The establishment of the tribunal through the United Nations was a central element of the proposal. Due to Russia's veto before the UN Security Council, establishing a tribunal under the Security Council's Chapter VII powers – the method by which the International Criminal Tribunal for the former Yugoslavia (ICTY) and the International Criminal Tribunal for Rwanda (ICTR) were established[31] – was seen as not possible.

Under the internationally accepted definition of the crime of aggression found in Rome Statute Article 8*bis*[32] – which was the product of negotiations open to *all states* (not just Rome Statute States Parties)[33] – the crime is a *leadership crime*. That is, it only applies to leaders who planned, prepared, initiated, or executed an act of aggression and were "*in a position effectively to exercise control over or to direct the political or military action of a State*."[34]

It thus came to be seen by many states, including, importantly, Ukraine, that a key feature of the tribunal needed to be the ability to overcome personal immunities that otherwise could attach to the so-called 'troika' – the President, Minister of Foreign Affairs, and Head of Government.[35] It is clear from

30 Ibid. *See also* Frequently Asked Questions (FAQ), Endorsed by Albania, Belgium, Estonia, Guatemala, Latvia, Liechtenstein, Lithuania, Luxembourg, Marshall Islands, North Macedonia, Poland and Ukraine, available online at <https://www.justsecurity.org/wp-content/uploads/2023/01/FAQ_Special-Tribunal-for-the-Crime-of-Aggression.pdf> (last accessed 11 October 2024). For additional details, *see* Blog Series: The Case for Creating an International Tribunal to Prosecute the Crime of Aggression against Ukraine (Parts I, II, III, IV), blog series *Justsecurity.org*, available online at <https://www.justsecurity.org/tag/prosecuting-the-crime-of-aggression-against-ukraine/> (posts of Oona Hathaway, Astrid Reisinger Coracini, Jennifer Trahan, and David J. Scheffer) (last accessed 11 October 2024).

31 UNSC Res 827 (1993) (25 May 1993) (establishing the ICTY); UNSC Res 955 (1994) (8 November 1994) (establishing the ICTR).

32 The Article 8*bis* definition was adopted by consensus of all the States Parties to the Rome Statute. *See* Review Conference Resolution, *supra* note 11.

33 *See* Grover, Leena, 'Interpreting the Crime of Aggression' in Kreβ, Claus, Barriga, Stefan (eds.), *The Crime of Aggression: A Commentary* (Cambridge University Press, 2016), 388 (the definition was the product of negotiations that were open to *all* states). Russia, for example, attended the SWGCA negotiations.

34 Rome Statute, *supra* note 8, Art. 8*bis*(1).

35 ICJ, *Arrest Warrant of 11 April 2000* (Democratic Republic of the Congo v Belgium), Judgment of 4 February 2002, ICJ Reports 2002, paras. 51, 61 ("*holders of high-ranking office in a State, such as the Head of State, Head of Government and Minister for Foreign Affairs, enjoy immunities from jurisdiction in other States*" but may be prosecuted before *certain international courts* such as the ICTY, ICTR, or ICC). In the case of Russia, the

the case law of the International Court of Justice (ICJ) in its *Yerodia* (Arrest Warrant) decision,[36] the Special Court for Sierra Leone's *Charles Taylor* decision,[37] and the ICC's decision regarding Jordan's failure to arrest then President Bashir of Sudan,[38] that such immunities do not attach when prosecution of an international crime occurs before an international tribunal established under international law.[39] As Professor Astrid Reisinger Coracini and I demonstrate elsewhere, an international tribunal is one established under international law, that prosecutes crimes under international law, where the tribunal's establishment represents the will of the international community as a whole.[40]

While the ICJ in the *Yerodia* (Arrest Warrant) case listed the ICTY, ICTR, and ICC as *international tribunals* to which such personal immunities would not attach,[41] it did not limit itself to those tribunals. For example, the Special Court for Sierra Leone detailed why that tribunal (despite hybrid features) was also an *international* one where such immunities would not apply:

---

positions of the troika are held by President Vladimir Putin, Prime Minister Mishustin, and Foreign Minister Lavrov.

36 *Arrest Warrant Judgment, supra* note 35.

37 SCSL, *Prosecutor v Taylor* (Decision on Immunity from Jurisdiction) SCSL-2003-01-I, ACh (31 May 2004).

38 ICC, *Prosecutor v Al-Bashir* (Judgment in the Jordan Referral re Al-Bashir Appeal) ICC-02/05-01/09 OA2, ACh (6 May 2019). The ICTY also confirmed the indictment against former President Slobodan Milošević of the Federal Republic of Yugoslavia and transmitted his arrest warrant to all UN Member States at a time when Milošević was still a sitting Head of State. ICTY, *Prosecutor v Milošević* (Decision on Review of Indictment and Application for Consequential Orders) IT-99-37-I (24 May 1999).

39 For details, *see* Reisinger Coracini, Astrid, Trahan, Jennifer, 'The Case for Creating a Special Tribunal to Prosecute the Crime of Aggression Committed Against Ukraine (Section 4): On the Non-applicability of Personal Immunities' (blog *Justsecurity.org*, 8 November 2022) <https://www.justsecurity.org/84017/the-case-for-creating-a-special-tribunal-to-prosecute-the-crime-of-aggression-committed-against-ukraine-part-vi-on-the-non-applicability-of-personal-immunities/> (last accessed 11 October 2024).

40 *See ibid.* The Appeals Chamber of the Special Court for Sierra Leone explained the reason for the distinction between national and international courts:

"A reason for the distinction, [...] between national courts and international courts, though not immediately evident, would appear due to the fact that the principle that one sovereign state does not adjudicate on the conduct of another state; the principle of state immunity derives from the equality of sovereign states and therefore has no relevance to international criminal tribunals which are not organs of a state but derive their mandate from international community."

Prosecutor v. Taylor, supra note 37, para. 51.

41 *Arrest Warrant Judgment, supra* note 35, para. 61.

a. The Special Court is not part of the judiciary of Sierra Leone and is not a national court.
b. The Special Court is established by treaty and has the characteristics associated with classical international organisations (including legal personality; the capacity to enter into agreements with other international persons governed by international law; privileges and immunities; and an autonomous will distinct from that of its members).
c. The competence and jurisdiction *ratione materiae* and *ratione personae* are broadly similar to that of ICTY and the ICTR and the ICC, including in relation to the provisions confirming the absence of entitlement of any person to claim of immunity.
d. Accordingly, there is no reason to conclude that the Special Court should be treated as anything other than an international tribunal or court, with all that implies for the question of immunity for a serving Head of State.[42]

The same would be true of a STCoA established upon the recommendation of the UN General Assembly and by agreement between the UN and Ukraine.[43]

Other key features of the proposed STCoA were that it would only prosecute the crime of aggression, would only do so in the situation of Ukraine, would be located in The Hague, Netherlands, and would utilize the definition of the crime found in Article 8*bis*.[44] It would also possess the full panoply of fair trial protections to ensure the tribunal operates in full compliance with due process requirements.[45] As former US War Crimes Ambassador David

42 *Prosecutor v. Taylor, supra* note 37, para. 41.

43 That is: (1) it would not be part of the judiciary of Ukraine, and thus not a national court; (2) it would be established by treaty and have the characteristics associated with classical international organizations (including legal personality, the capacity to enter into agreements with other international persons governed by international law, privileges and immunities, and an autonomous will distinct from that of its members); (3) and it would have the competence and jurisdiction *ratione materiae* and *ratione personae* broadly similar to that of the ICTY and the ICTR and the ICC, including in relation to the provisions confirming the absence of entitlement of any person to a claim of immunity. Thus, it would be an international court or tribunal, with all that implies for the question of immunity for a serving Head of State and other members of the troika.

44 *See* Yale Club write-up, *supra* note 29; Blog series, *supra* note 30.

45 *See ibid*; *see also* International Covenant on Civil and Political Rights (adopted 16 December 1966, entered into force 23 March 1976) 999 UNTS 171, Art. 14 (fair trial rights). Such fair trial rights/due process protections can be found in Article 21 of the ICTY Statute (adopted 25 May 1993, as amended); Article 20 of the ICTR Statute (adopted 8 November 1994, as amended); Article 17 of the SCSL Statute (adopted 16 January 2002); and Articles 55, 66, and 67 of the Rome Statute (*supra* note 8).

J. Scheffer has explored elsewhere, the STCoA would additionally need to work cooperatively with the ICC,[46] which has already been gathering evidence of war crimes and crimes against humanity committed on the territory of Ukraine, and, to date, issued several arrest warrants.[47]

Yet another reason for establishing the tribunal through the United Nations was that the crime of aggression is simultaneously inflicting horrific harm on the people of Ukraine[48] – as well as causing mass fatalities of combatants on both sides[49] – and is an offense against the international legal order. That is, it is a violation of the core norm found in the UN Charter against the use the force, Article 2(4).[50] Additionally, because the crime has not been prosecuted at the international level since the prosecutions before the International Military Tribunal (IMT) at Nuremberg[51] and the International Military Tribunal

46 *See* Scheffer, David J., 'Forging a Cooperative Relationship Between International Criminal Court and a Special Tribunal for Aggression Against Ukraine' (blog *Justsecurity.org*, 25 October 2022) <https://www.justsecurity.org/83757/forging-a-cooperative-relationship-between-intl-crim-court-and-a-special-tribunal-for-russian-aggression-against-ukraine/> (last accessed 11 October 2024).

47 *See, e.g.*, Webpage of the International Criminal Court, Press Release, Situation in Ukraine: ICC Judges Issue Arrest Warrants against Vladimir Vladimirovich Putin and Maria Alekseyevna Lvova-Belova (17 March 2023), available online at <https://www.icc-cpi.int/news/situation-ukraine-icc-judges-issue-arrest-warrants-against-vladimir-vladimirovich-putin-and> (last accessed 11 October 2024).

48 For civilian casualties, *see* webpage of the United Nations High Commissioner for Human Rights, available online at <https://www.ohchr.org/en/news/2023/09/ukraine-civilian-casualty-update-24-september-2023> (last accessed 11 October 2024).

49 Gadzo, Mersiha, 'Record High Deaths in the Russia-Ukraine War: What You Should Know', *AL JAZEERA* (16 October 2024) <https://www.aljazeera.com/news/2024/10/16/russia-ukraine-wartime-deaths> ("[A]bout one million Ukrainians and Russians have been killed or wounded since the war began. The majority of dead are soldiers on both sides … ."). It is not a war crime during a state of an international armed conflict to target combatants. *See* Rome Statute, *supra* note 8, Arts. 8(2)(b)(i) (war crime of attacking the civilian population – not attacking combatants).

50 Article 2(4) states: "*All Members shall refrain in their international relations from the threat or use of force against the territorial integrity or political independence of any state, or in any other manner inconsistent with the Purposes of the United Nations.*" Charter of the United Nations (adopted 26 June 1945, entered into force 24 October 1945) 892 UNTS 119. It is complemented by the allowance of Security Council authorized interventions and the ability of a state to exercise individual and collective self-defense. *See* UN Charter, Chapter VII, Art. 51.

51 *See* (London) Charter of the International Military Tribunal, Annexed to the Agreement by the Government of the United Kingdom of Great Britain and Northern Ireland, the Government of the United States of America, the Provisional Government of the French

for the Far East (Tokyo),[52] the tribunal should be established in the most legitimate way possible. The thinking was that, if one wished to potentially deter other future would-be aggressors from other regions or future additional Russian aggression, nothing less than a fully legitimate tribunal, backed by the weight of the international community, would do. Moreover, one could not fully create such deterrence unless the tribunal would be able to prosecute the top-level leaders who decided to initiate the aggression – which the STCoA would have been able to achieve.

3.2 *The Competing Proposal of Establishing an Internationalized Ukrainian Chamber*

While various different approaches have been proposed,[53] what emerged during 2023 as the dominant competing proposal was to utilize a Ukrainian chamber with international elements. The United States,[54] United Kingdom,[55] and

Republic and the Government of the Union of Soviet Socialist Republics for the Prosecution and Punishment of the Major War Criminals of the European Axis (adopted and entered into force 8 August 1945) 82 UNTS 279, Art. 6(a) (jurisdiction over crimes against peace).

52 *See* International Military Tribunal for the Far East, Special Proclamation by the Supreme Commander for the Allied Powers at Tokyo, 19 January 1946 Art. 5(a) (jurisdiction over crimes against peace).

53 For the different proposals, *see* Trahan, Jennifer, 'Proposals for the Formation of a Crime of Aggression Tribunal for the Situation of Ukraine' in Dutton, Yvonne, Scharf, Michael, Sterio, Milena, William, Paul (eds.) *Ukraine, Accountability, and the New Global Order* (Routledge, forthcoming).

54 Ambassador Beth Van Schaack, on behalf of the United States, called for the establishment of "*an internationalized court that is rooted in Ukraine's judicial system, but that also includes international elements* [...]." She explained that such a court could have "*significant international elements – in the form of substantive law, personnel, information sources, and structure*", and might be located elsewhere in Europe than Ukraine. *See* Hansler, Jennifer, 'US Announces It Supports Creation of Special Tribunal to Prosecute Russia for 'Crime of Aggression' in Ukraine' *CNN* (28 March 2023) <https://edition.cnn.com/2023/03/28/politics/us-support-special-tribunal-crime-of-aggression/index.html> (last accessed 11 October 2024).

55 UK Government Press Release, UK Joins Core Group Dedicated to Achieving Accountability for Russia's Aggression against Ukraine, 20 January 2023, available online at <https://www.gov.uk/government/news/ukraine-uk-joins-core-group-dedicated-to-achieving-accountability-for-russias-aggression-against-ukraine> (last accessed 11 October 2024).

Germany[56] publicly announced their support for this approach, which subsequently evolved into the G7 position.[57]

Two initial concerns quickly emerged with this proposal. The first was that due to the leadership nature of the crime,[58] it was problematic to utilize a Ukrainian chamber. That is, even if there were some internationalized elements, it would still be a domestic court. This would mean that under the case law discussed above,[59] personal immunities would attach to the 'troika'.[60] For this reason, the approach was quickly denounced, particularly by the Government of Ukraine.[61] The concern was that it made little sense to prosecute a *leadership crime*[62] and yet immunize the top-level leaders, allowing them to pin responsibility on those in levels below in the hierarchy. Such a result could even *embolden* top-level leaders, by entrenching impunity – allowing them to escape individual criminal responsibility for a full-scale invasion of a neighboring state.

A second concerning feature was that Ukraine's Constitution prohibits the formation of 'special' or 'extraordinary' chambers while the country is in a state of martial law or a state of emergency, as it is currently.[63] This would have meant that such an internationalized Ukrainian court could only have

56 Strengthening International Law in Times of Crisis – *Rede von Außenministerin Annalena Baerbock in Den Haag,* 16 January 2023, available online at <https://www.auswaertiges-amt.de/de/newsroom/strengthening-international-law-in-times-of-crisis/2573384> (last accessed 11 October 2024).

57 *See* "'Hybrid Tribunal'": Does Not Give an Answer on How to Punish the Leaders of the Russian Federation", *Kuleba,* 9 September 2023, available online at <https://www.eurointegration.com.ua/news/2023/09/9/7169055/> (last accessed 11 October 2024) (Ukrainian Minister of Foreign Affairs Dmytro Kuleba stating that "*the position of the G7 is inclined towards a 'hybrid tribunal.'*").

58 *See* note 34 *supra* and accompanying text (leadership clause).

59 *See* notes 35–39 *supra* and accompanying text (case law).

60 *Arrest Warrant Judgment, supra* note 35, paras. 51, 61.

61 President of Ukraine, Volodymyr Zelenskyy, *supra* note 3 ("*'We understand who gave the orders. These people must not be untouchable. This is very important for us, this is one of the fundamental issues,' Volodymyr Zelenskyy said.*").

62 *See* note 34 *supra* and accompanying text (leadership clause).

63 Article 125 of the Ukrainian Constitution states that the "[e]*stablishment of extraordinary and special courts is not permitted*" and Article 157 states that "[t]*he Constitution of Ukraine shall not be amended in conditions of martial law or a state of emergency.*" Ukraine, Constitution of Ukraine, adopted at the Fifth Session of the Verkhovna Rada of Ukraine on 28 June 1996, as amended, available online at <https://www.refworld.org/legal/legislation/natlegbod/1996/en/42875> (last accessed 11 October 2024).

been established once martial law or the state of emergency was lifted.[64] Thus, essentially, one would have needed to wait until the conflict was over before the tribunal could have been established. Since it was quite unclear when the conflict will come to an end, such a delay could have potentially lasted years.

After several core group meetings, it became clear, as mentioned above, that about half of the states preferred the international approach and the other half preferred the Ukrainian chamber.[65] This was the dynamic for several meetings,[66] with little movement in either direction; neither side seemed willing to give in to the other side's approach.

The position of Ukraine in support of an international tribunal that would be able to overcome personal immunities was understandable. For the Ukrainians, prosecuting at the highest leadership level was seen as imperative.[67]

For the G7, not only did there seem to be a lack of concern about the inability to prosecute at the highest levels, one suspects that at least some of these states may actually *prefer not* to have a tribunal capable of prosecuting at the highest levels due to the precedent it could set. The negotiations, of course, are taking place against the backdrop of the US and UK having in 2003 entered into the war in Iraq based on a fairly flimsy legal theory.[68] It seems to an outside observer to the negotiations[69] as if some of the more powerful states in the G7 desire the ability to engage in future military interventions of uncertain legality, without facing difficult questions about the rule of law applying to them and their high-level leaders.

---

64 Komarov, Alexander, Hathaway, Oona A., 'Ukraine's Constitutional Constraints: How to Achieve Accountability for the Crime of Aggression' (blog *Justsecurity.org*, 5 April 2022) <https://www.justsecurity.org/80958/ukraines-constitutional-constraints-how-to-achieve-accountability-for-the-crime-of-aggression/> (last accessed 11 October 2024).

65 Observations of a participant in the negotiations.

66 The impasse lasted from summer 2023 through fall 2023.

67 *See supra* note 3 (Volodymyr Zelenskyy).

68 The UK ultimately opened an inquiry into how it became embroiled in the war, known as the Chilcot Inquiry. *See* UK House of Commons Library, Briefing Paper, *Chilcot Inquiry*, No. CBP 6215, 1 July 2016, available online at <https://researchbriefings.files.parliament.uk/documents/SN06215/SN06215.pdf> (last accessed 11 October 2024). The United States and United Kingdom *did* have a legal theory for the 2003 military intervention in Iraq; it was just not a strong one. It relied on an open-ended force authorization from Gulf War I that was still argued to be in effect years later to the extent that Iraq continued to engage in *hostile or provocative* action. *See* Law Society of Scotland, Iraq: A Basis in Law?, available online at <https://www.lawscot.org.uk/members/journal/issues/vol-61-issue-08/iraq-a-basis-in-law/> (last accessed 11 October 2024).

69 The author has not been part of the core group negotiations.

While this topic warrants more-in-depth discussion than is possible here, the author believes these concerns to be misplaced. The crime of aggression only criminalizes conduct related to an act of aggression that rises to the level of a *manifest* violation of the UN Charter, measured by its *character, gravity, and scale.*[70] This manifest threshold requires a clear violation of sufficient gravity that does not fall within any debatable theory of *jus ad bellum* law.[71] While Russia's invasion seems unsupported by any legal theory (nothing plausible has yet been articulated),[72] and it certainly meets the threshold in terms of gravity and scale, one can only hope that G7 states would not follow suit in the future. If future military interventions are in a 'gray area' of legality or *de minimis* in scale, the text of Article 8*bis* and negotiating history of the crime of aggression[73] make clear that the intervention would not have the required *character, gravity, and scale* to constitute a *manifest* UN Charter violation.[74] This should provide G7 countries with enough comfort. Even a legal theory that other states dispute (such as the 'unwilling or unable' the-

70 Article 8*bis*(1) states: For the purpose of this Statute, "crime of aggression" means the planning, preparation, initiation or execution, by a person in a position effectively to exercise control over or to direct the political or military action of a State, of an act of aggression which, *by its character, gravity and scale, constitutes a manifest violation of the Charter of the United Nations.* Rome Statute, *supra* note 8, Art. 8*bis*(1) (emphasis added).

71 Thus, for example, a June 2008 report of the SWGCA explains: "*Delegations supporting this threshold clause noted that it would appropriately limit the Court's jurisdiction to the most serious acts of aggression under customary international law, thus excluding cases of insufficient gravity and falling within a grey area* [in terms of legality]". Report of the Special Working Group on the Crime of Aggression, ICC-ASP/6/20/Add.1, Annex II, (June 2008), para. 68. Carrie McDougall explains: "*the threshold was intended at least by some, to exclude two types of acts from the jurisdiction of the Court: acts of insufficient seriousness and acts of questionable legal status.*" McDougall, Carrie, *The Crime of Aggression under the Rome Statute of the International Criminal Court* (2nd edn, Cambridge University Press, 2021), 155. A Handbook produced by the Permanent Mission of Liechtenstein to the UN states that the *manifest* requirement "*ensures that only* very serious and unambiguously illegal *instances of a use of force by a State can give rise to individual criminal responsibility of a leader of that State under the Statute.*" *Handbook, Ratification and Implementation of the Kampala Amendments to the Rome Statute of the ICC: Crime of Aggression, War Crimes* (November 2012), 8 (emphasis added).

72 *See, e.g.*, Green, James, Henderson, Christian, Ruys, Tom, 'Russia's Attack on Ukraine and the *Jus ad Bellum*' (2022) 9(4) *Journal on the Use of Force and International Law* 4.

73 Negotiation history may be resorted to in order to confirm the meaning of treaty language. *See* Vienna Convention on the Law of Treaties (adopted 22 May 1969, entered into force 27 January 1980) 1155 UNTS 331, Art. 32.

74 *See supra* note 71.

ory)[75] would provide enough legitimacy that an intervention based on it would not constitute a *manifest* UN Charter violation.[76] In this way, the crime of aggression is quite conservative,[77] and interventions that fall within truly debated areas of the *jus ad bellum* do not fall within the definition of the crime of aggression.[78]

While the author feels strongly that, for a multitude of reasons, the first approach – establishing an international tribunal through the UN – would have been the right one, the deadlock needed to be resolved.

4 Finding a Third Way to Form an Aggression-Specific Tribunal for the Situation of Ukraine

Because there did not appear to be a middle ground between forming an international tribunal and the G7 approach – either the tribunal would be international in its establishment or not[79] – the core group shifted to explor-

75 "[T]*he Obama administration* (*and subsequent administrations*) *argued that Syria was 'unable or unwilling' to counter the threat posed by* IS *and* [al-Qaeda]". Bridgeman, Tess, Rosen, Brianna, 'Still at War: The United States in Syria' (blog *Justsecurity.org*, 29 April 2022) <https://www.justsecurity.org/81313/still-at-war-the-united-states-in-syria/> (last accessed 11 October 2024). "*The scope and content of this* [...] *theory* [...] *remain deeply contested.*" Bridgeman, Tess, 'When Does the Legal Basis for U.S. Forces in Syria Expire?' (blog *Justsecurity.org*, 14 March 2018) <https://www.justsecurity.org/53810/legal-basis-u-s-forces-syria-expire/> (last accessed 11 October 2024).

76 *See* Kreβ, Claus, The State Conduct Element, in Kreβ, Claus, Barriga, Stefan (eds.), *The Crime of Aggression: A Commentary* (Cambridge University Press, 2016), 461 (discussing the 'unwilling or unable' theory and concluding that "*the whole scenario, at this moment in time, constitutes a grey area of the right of self-defence.*").

77 The 'manifest' criterion "*will make proceedings for a crime of aggression an exceptional event.*" Kreß, Claus, 'Time for Decision: Some Thoughts on the Immediate Future of the Crime of Aggression: A Reply to Andreas Paulus' (2009) 20 *European Journal of International Law* 1129, 1142.

78 Claus Kreβ, a member of the German delegation during the crime of aggression negotiations, explains that the definition excludes "*seriously controversial cases* [...] *in order not to decide major controversies about the content of primary international rules of conduct through the back door of international criminal justice.*" Ibid.

79 The question of hybridity is a different one. That is, one could have a tribunal with hybrid features that is international in its establishment, such as the Special Court for Sierra Leone, established by agreement between the UN and Sierra Leone, or one could have a tribunal with hybrid features established within a domestic court system, such as the Extraordinary Chambers in the Courts of Cambodia (ECCC) formed as a chamber within Cambodia's legal system. *Compare* Agreement between the United Nations and the Government of Sierra Leone on the Establishment of a Special Court for Sierra Leone

ing alternative possibilities.[80] This final section will discuss two possible approaches. The first, establishing the tribunal on the basis of a Chapter VI UN Security Council resolution was not pursued, but potentially could have been, and is worth considering as a possible future model. As of this writing, support has coalesced around establishing the tribunal through the Council of Europe (the second approach discussed below).

4.1 *Establishment Based on a Security Council Chapter VI Resolution*

As of late fall 2023, one idea that was being proposed was to have the tribunal created based on a UN Security Council resolution under Chapter VI of the UN Charter.[81] As previously mentioned, a Chapter VII resolution establishing the tribunal would have faced a near-certain Russian veto. The same, however, could not be said if the tribunal were recommended by the Security Council in a resolution under Chapter VI.

According to Article 27(3) of the Charter, obligatory abstention of a party to a dispute must apply to Security Council voting under Chapter VI. Specifically, Article 27(3) states:

> Decisions of the Security Council on all other matters [other than procedural ones] shall be made by an affirmative vote of nine members including the concurring votes of the permanent members; provided that, *in decisions under Chapter VI,* and under paragraph 3 of Article 52, *a party to a dispute shall abstain from voting.*[82]

Application of this language would have required that if a resolution recommending the establishment of an aggression-specific tribunal for the situation of Ukraine came to a vote before the Security Council under a Chapter VI resolution, the Russian Federation – clearly, a party to the dispute – would have been required to abstain from voting.

(adopted 16 January 2002, entered into force 12 April 2002) 2178 UNTS 137 *with* Cambodia, Law on the Establishment of the Extraordinary Chambers, with inclusion of amendments as promulgated on 27 October 2004, NS/RKM/1004/006, available online at <https://www.eccc.gov.kh/sites/default/files/legal-documents/KR_Law_as_amended_27_Oct_2004_Eng.pdf> (last accessed 11 October 2024).

80 Observations of a participant in the negotiations.

81 Ibid.

82 UN Charter, Art. 27(3) (emphasis added).

Moreover, a Chapter VI Security Council resolution has already been used to initiate the creation of a tribunal – the Special Court for Sierra Leone.[83] Based on the Security Council's request made in a Chapter VI resolution, the UN entered into negotiations and ultimately concluded an agreement with the Government of Sierra Leone to establish the Special Court.[84] Following this same precedent, the Security Council, based on a Chapter VI resolution, could have recommended the establishment of a special tribunal on the crime of aggression for the situation of Ukraine, with the tribunal created by agreement between the UN and Government of Ukraine.

The Chapter VI approach had obvious advantages in that – as with a Special Tribunal on the Crime of Aggression established after the recommendation of the General Assembly[85] – it too would overcome personal immunities; accordingly, investigations and prosecutions could proceed, even against the troika. Here, the ruling of the Special Court for Sierra Leone in the Charles Taylor case that Taylor's indictment was valid, even though issued *while* he was a sitting Head of State of a neighboring country,[86] would be directly on point. Even though the Special Court, as mentioned, possessed hybrid features (for example, benches of judges appointed both internationally and by Sierra Leone),[87] the Appeals Chamber ruled that, having been formed by agreement between the UN and Sierra Leone, its formation made it an international tribunal that could overcome personal immunities.[88] Thus, the Appeals Cham-

83 UNSC Res 1315 (2000) (14 August 2000), para. 1 ("*Requests* the Secretary-General to negotiate an agreement with the Government of Sierra Leone to create an independent special court consistent with this resolution."). There is no reference to Chapter VII contained in the resolution.

84 Agreement on the Establishment of a Special Court, *supra* note 79.

85 *See* Section 3.1.

86 *Prosecutor v. Taylor, supra* note 37, para. 53.

87 Agreement on the Establishment of a Special Court, *supra* note 79, Art. 2 (composition of the Special Court and appointment of judges).

88 *See* analysis in the text accompanying note 42 *supra*. The Appeals Chamber also focused on Security Council Resolution 1315 that initiated the establishment of the Court. *Prosecutor v. Taylor, supra* note 37, para. 37, citing UNSC Res 1315. It found that the "*Security Council acts on behalf of the members of the United Nations.*" Ibid, para. 38. It therefore concluded: "*The Agreement between the United Nations and Sierra Leone is thus an agreement between* all *members of the United Nations and Sierra Leone. This fact makes the Agreement an expression of the will of the international community. The Special Court established in such circumstances is truly international.*" Ibid. The same reasoning would have applied to an aggression-specific tribunal created upon the recommendation of either the UN Security Council or the UN General Assembly – the subsequent agreement between the UN and Ukraine would represent the will of the international com-

ber of the Special Court for Sierra Leone ruled that even though Charles Taylor was President of Liberia at the time of his indictment, "*the official position of the Applicant as an incumbent Head of State at the time when these criminal proceedings were initiated against him* [was] *not a bar to his prosecution by this court.*"[89] This ruling would have been directly applicable regarding proceedings against President Putin and other members of the troika before a tribunal created between the UN and Ukraine after a Chapter VI Security Council resolution.[90]

Additionally, because a tribunal created after a Chapter VI resolution and established by agreement between the UN and Ukraine would not be a tribunal within the Ukrainian system, there would be no need to amend Ukraine's Constitution. Thus, there would be none of the time delays associated with establishing an internationalized Ukrainian chamber.[91]

Establishing the tribunal through the UN, and specifically through the UN Security Council – which is charged under the UN Charter with primary responsibility for the maintenance of international peace and security[92] – would have additionally represented an *extremely strong* statement against the illegal use of force in contravention of Article 2(4) of the UN Charter and the need for international criminal responsibility to follow when a flagrant violation appears to have been committed.[93] It also would have created an appropriately strong precedent for the enforcement of the rule of law, even against leaders of a permanent members of the UN Security Council.

While states within the G7 had shown discomfort at the UN General Assembly's playing a role in the establishment of an aggression-specific tribunal,[94] the question remained whether they would have been open to the Security Council's doing so. G7 states had earlier articulated a concern as to

munity. Just as the Security Council acts on behalf of the members of the UN, so too does the UN General Assembly, which is composed of the members of the UN.

89 Ibid, para. 53.

90 The same reasoning would have also applied *vis-à-vis* a tribunal created by agreement between the UN and Ukraine after a UN General Assembly resolution, the approach discussed in Section 3.1. above.

91 *See* notes 63–64 and accompanying text (timing issues).

92 UN Charter, Art. 24(1).

93 In any criminal proceeding, that the UN Charter was violated (i.e., that there was an act of aggression) would need to be proven beyond a reasonable doubt. It cannot be presumed, and the General Assembly's resolutions to that effect would not suffice to establish it.

94 Observations of a participant in the negotiations.

whether the UN General Assembly could, as a legal matter, recommend the establishment of such an international tribunal.[95] While the author, as well as others, believe that there is solid foundation for the General Assembly making such a recommendation,[96] going through the UN Security Council would have negated that concern since the exact process of establishing a tribunal after a Security Council Chapter VI resolution was utilized to create the Special Court for Sierra Leone.

Admittedly, a few concerns existed with the Chapter VI approach. First was whether G7 states (particularly the United States, United Kingdom, and France) would have agreed to it; one likely would have needed the backing of these states, and they appear wary of establishing any precedent that involves the prosecution of high-level leaders for the crime of aggression. A second concern was that China (not a party to the dispute), would not be subject to Article 27(3) abstention; thus, its veto could have blocked the endeavor. G7 states would also need to have been willing to use their persuasive powers to convince China not to veto. A third concern would have been how to achieve Russia's abstention, given past inconsistent application of obligatory abstention from voting under Chapter VI.[97] If Russia were to cast

95 Statement of Ambassador Van Schaack.

96 *See, e.g.*, Corell, Hans, 'A Special Tribunal for Ukraine on the Crime of Aggression – The Role of the U.N. General Assembly' (blog *Justsecurity.org*, 14 February 2023) <https://www.justsecurity.org/85116/a-special-tribunal-for-ukraine-on-the-crime-of-aggression-the-role-of-the-u-n-general-assembly/> (last accessed 11 October 2024); Hathaway, Oona A., Mills, Maggie, Zimmerman, Heather, 'The Legal Authority to Create a Special Tribunal to Try the Crime of Aggression Upon the Request of the UN General Assembly' (blog *Justsecurity.org*, 5 May 2023) <https://www.justsecurity.org/86450/the-legal-authority-to-create-a-special-tribunal-to-try-the-crime-of-aggression-upon-the-request-of-the-un-general-assembly/> (last accessed 11 October 2024).

97 *See* Security Council Report, Article 27(3) and Parties to a Dispute: An Abridged History, available online at <https://www.securitycouncilreport.org/atf/cf/%7B65BFCF9B-6D27-4E9C-8CD3-CF6E4FF96FF9%7D/article_27_3_and_parties_to_a_dispute.pdf> (last accessed 11 October 2024) (listing twelve situations where abstention occurred, with the last being in 1960 with the abstention of Argentina related to the Eichmann question); *but see ibid* (listing fourteen situations where the question of abstention was either raised or considered without success); Milano, Enrico, 'Russia's Veto in the Security Council: Whither the Duty to Abstain under Art. 27(3) of the UN Charter?' *Max-Planck-Institute* (2015) <https://www.zaoerv.de/75_2015/75_2015_1_a_215_232.pdf> (last accessed 11 October 2024), 217 (noting 16 instances of non-compliance with the rule), citing Blum, Y.Z., *Eroding the United Nations Charter* (Brill Nijhoff, 1993), 307. *See also* Malloy, Katy, 'Ukraine v. Russia: A Case for Change in International Enforcement' (2024) 65(5) *William*

a veto of a Chapter VI resolution, this would trigger discussion of the veto within the General Assembly.[98] The General Assembly might then consider passing a resolution stressing the need to apply the plain language of Article 27(3) on obligatory abstention, or it could request an Advisory Opinion from the ICJ as to whether the plain language of the Charter should be applied. With a positive answer that it should be, or a General Assembly resolution to the same effect, unfortunately Russia would still need to have been persuaded to abstain from voting, since both General Assembly resolutions and ICJ Advisory Opinions are non-binding.[99] Admittedly, establishment of an aggression-specific tribunal based on a Security Council Chapter VI resolution poses some complications. As mentioned, it is not being pursued, although it might be a model worth consideration in the future.

4.2 *A Regionally Established Tribunal through the Council of Europe*

Another proposal that is being suggested (currently the dominant proposal as of this writing and one which may become the method by which the tribunal is established) is for the Council of Europe to form the tribunal through an agreement with Ukraine. Additional states could also potentially endorse the

---

& Mary Law Review 1231, 1256 (the abstention obligation, "*clear on its face, has been largely ignored for most of its history, and nearly non-existent in the twenty-first century.* [footnote omitted] *Even in the few instances in which the abstention obligation was cited specifically, states have only done so in vague and non-committal language.* [footnote omitted]"); Chappell, John Ramming and Svoboda, Emma, 'Must Russia Abstain on Security Council Votes Regarding the Ukraine Crisis?' (blog Lawfare, 11 February 2022) <https://www.lawfaremedia.org/article/must-russia-abstain-security-council-votes-regarding-ukraine-crisis> (last accessed 14 April 2025) ("[S]*cholars have questioned whether consistent noncompliance has weakened the obligatory nature of 27(3), under a principle of treaty interpretation that allows 'subsequent practice ... which establishes the agreement of the parties' to modify the meaning of a text. However, continued statements by Security Council members appealing to mandatory abstentions, as well as the ICJ's silence on the issue of Article 27(3) noncompliance in Namibia, leave the legal status of the abstention obligation ambiguous.*") (also discussing the distinction between "disputes" and "situations").

98 UNGA Res 76/262, Standing Mandate for a General Assembly Debate When a Veto is Cast in the Security Council (26 April 2022).

99 Sloan, F. Blaine, 'The Binding Force of a 'Recommendation' of the General Assembly of the United Nations' (1948) 25 *British Book of International Law* 1, 31 ("*As a general rule, resolutions, for lack of intention or mandatory power, in the* [General] *Assembly, do not create binding obligations in positive law.*"); webpage of the International Court of Justice, available online at <https://icj-cij.org/how-the-court-works> (last accessed 11 October 2024).

tribunal's establishment (and one might even imagine the General Assembly endorsing the tribunal's establishment, although as of the date of this writing that is not being pursued). One could envision the tribunal being funded by the Council of Europe, as well as additional states, including ones beyond Europe. The Kosovo Specialist Chambers (KSC) and Specialist Prosecutors Office, for example, are funded by the EU, Canada, Norway, Switzerland, Turkey, and the United States.[100]

If the proposal were to follow the model of the KSC, which was established under the law of Kosovo,[101] the concern would be that personal immunities would still apply. That is, funding by a variety of sources, or even utilizing all internationally appointed judges, as the KSC does,[102] would not make the tribunal an international one. An international tribunal must be created by an international agreement – and this part could be achieved by forming the tribunal by agreement between Ukraine and the Council of Europe. However, a tribunal must also represent the will of the international community to be an *international* one[103] – and a regionally backed tribunal (absent more) probably could not be said to do so.

Notwithstanding, there could be ways to sufficiently internationalize a regional tribunal so as to overcome personal immunities. For instance, one could imagine states from other regions supporting the establishment of the tribunal. Reflect that the London Charter that established the IMT at Nuremberg was initially agreed on by the four Allied Powers (the United States, United Kingdom, USSR and, France),[104] who exercised their combined legisla-

100 Webpage of the Kosovo Specialist Chambers, Background, available online at <https://www.scp-ks.org/en/background> (last accessed 11 October 2024).

101 "*The Specialist Chambers and Specialist Prosecutor's Office have jurisdiction over crimes against humanity, war crimes and other crimes* under Kosovo law." Ibid. (emphasis added).

102 Webpage of the Kosovo Specialist Chambers, Chambers, available online at <https://www.scp-ks.org/en/specialist-chambers/chambers> (last accessed 11 October 2024). The staff, Prosecutor, and Registrar are internationally appointed as well. Webpage of the Kosovo Specialist Chambers, available online at <https://www.scp-ks.org/en> (last accessed 11 October 2024).

103 The Sierra Leone Special Court found that the bilateral agreement between the UN and Sierra Leone was "*an agreement between all members of the United Nations and Sierra Leone*", which made it "*an expression of the will of the international community*" as a whole; therefore, the court was "*truly international*". *Prosecutor v. Taylor, supra* note 37, para. 38.

104 London Charter, *supra* note 51.

tive powers[105] as Occupying Powers. Nineteen additional states additionally adhered to, or seceded to, the Charter.[106]

This raises the question of how many states would need to support the endeavor – in one way or another – for the tribunal to be said to represent the will of the international community. Note that the ICC's Rome Statute provides for the absence of immunity for persons acting in an official capacity, including as Head of State or Government. Article 27(1) states:

> This Statute shall apply equally to all persons without any distinction based on official capacity. In particular, official capacity as a Head of State or Government, a member of a Government or parliament, an elected representative or a government official shall in no case exempt a person from criminal responsibility under this Statute [...].[107]

And, the Rome Statute entered into force upon the ratification or accession of sixty states.[108] This suggests that a treaty-based tribunal that is endorsed by at least sixty states would represent the will of the international community – although one would also like to see cross-regional diversity in the states endorsing.[109] However, a concern arises that a regional tribunal without some level of multilateral and cross-regional buy-in likely would not constitute an international tribunal capable of overcoming personal immunities.

---

105 The Judgment of the IMT stated that "[t]*he making of the Charter was the exercise of the sovereign legislative power by the countries to which the German Reich unconditionally surrendered; and the undoubted right of these countries to legislate for the occupied territories* [...]." IMT, 'Judgment of 1 October 1946' in *The Trial of German Major War Criminals. Proceedings of the International Military Tribunal sitting at Nuremberg, Germany, Part* 22 (22 August 1946 to 1 October 1946), 443. It continued: "*The signatory Powers* [four Allies] *created this Tribunal,* [...] *and* [i]*n doing so, they have done together what any one of them might have done singly.*" Ibid. *See also* Lippman, Matthew, 'Nuremberg: Forty Five Years Later' (1991) 7 *Connecticut Journal of International Law* 1, 28 (explaining the same).

106 UNTS, available online at <https://treaties.un.org/pages/showDetails.aspx?objid=08000002801572a2> (last accessed 11 October 2024). The states joining were from various regions. They included Australia, Ethiopia, Haiti, Honduras, India, New Zealand, Panama, Paraguay, Uruguay. Ibid.

107 Rome Statute, *supra* note 8, Art. 27(1).

108 Ibid, Art. 126(1) ("*This Statute shall enter into force on the first day of the month after the 60th day following the date of the deposit of the 60th instrument of ratification, acceptance, approval or accession with the Secretary-General of the United Nations.*").

109 There was such regional diversity in the early ratifications of the Rome Statute.

Endorsement by the General Assembly might be another way to *internationalize* the tribunal such that it represents the will of the international community.[110]

A tribunal created by agreement between Ukraine and the Council of Europe would not constitute an 'extraordinary' or 'special' tribunal *within* the Ukrainian system. This should enable it to overcome the Constitutional difficulties under Ukraine's Constitution that would be associated with establishing the tribunal within Ukraine's legal system.[111]

At least one significant question remains with this approach: whether the G7 states are even interested in overcoming immunities, or they will only support a regional tribunal that would *not* overcome immunities. Some states in the core group appear to want an express statement in the tribunal's statute that personal immunities are *not* overcome (i.e., top-level Russian leaders would be immune from prosecution during their term of office). Herein lies something of a Catch-22. These third way proposals either overcome immunities (establishment through a Chapter VI Security Council resolution, or multilateral and/or cross-regional endorsement of a regional approach), or they do not (a regional approach absent multilateral and/or cross-regional endorsement), or an express statement in the tribunal's statute that proceedings against the 'troika' would be suspended during their terms in office). This may be the crux of the difference in views. At heart, one suspects that G7 states (or at least several of them) simply do not wish to overcome immunities due to the precedent it could set for their leaders. Yet, it is critical to other states, including Ukraine, that they *do* overcome immunities – otherwise top Russian leaders cannot be prosecuted (will have personal immunity) for what is a leadership crime. Thus, the same kind of dynamic that previously existed between the option of a General Assembly recommended tribunal (that would overcome personal immunities), or an internationalized Ukrainian chamber (that would not overcome personal immunities) still existed in the core group.[112]

110 It is unclear whether states from other regions would be willing to endorse what might be seen as a primarily European tribunal.

111 *See supra* note 63.

112 Another open issue is whether the internationally accepted definition of the crime of aggression found in Article 8*bis* of the Rome Statute should be utilized. *See* Rome Statute, *supra* note 8, Art. 8*bis*. This was the definition that was adopted by consensus of all Rome Statute States Parties at the 2010 Review Conference in Kampala, Uganda. *See* Review Conference Resolution, *supra* note 11. Other states apparently preferred to use precedent that is from 1945 and use the minimal and circular definition found in the Nuremberg

There is no defensible reason for not overcoming immunities. G7 states should be called out for self-servingly supporting justice that is inherently flawed. In the options they have supported to date, the G7 are essentially protecting the highest-level Russian leaders through their negotiating positions. It is difficult to imagine G7 states having to explain to the public, particularly a Ukrainian public, but also a broader public, why top-level Russian political and military leaders should have immunity from prosecution and thus impunity when it comes to the crime of aggression.

On the other hand, if G7 states cannot be embarrassed in this way – and let us also not forget that they are some of the main suppliers of military assistance, including weapons, to Ukraine[113] – then the alternative may need to be establishing as international a tribunal as possible. It should have as many states as possible joining the endeavor; have internationally appointed judges (or at least ones appointed through the Council of Europe if that is the body that ultimately is involved in the tribunal's establishment); utilize the internationally accepted definition of the crime of aggression found in Article 8*bis* of the Rome Statute, or at least a definition close to it; refrain from holding trials *in absentia* (which are seen as less than fully legitimate by many states);[114] obtain its funding from as broad a group of states as possible; and fully adhere to internationally accepted due process protections. This could represent a partial victory in terms of ensuring the investigation and prosecution of the crime of aggression in a situation where a blatant violation of the UN Charter appears to have occurred.[115] Because the *leadership clause* is broader than simply the troika, there would be persons for such a tribunal to investigate and prosecute even if the troika is immune while in office.[116] Such

---

Charter. *See* London Charter, *supra* note 51, Art. 6(a). Yet, the law on this topic has evolved considerably since 1945.

113 Walter, Jan D., 'Military Hardware for Ukraine: Who Plans to Supply What?' *DW* (3 June 2022) <https://www.dw.com/en/military-hardware-for-ukraine-who-plans-to-supply-what/a-62015239#:~:text=Military%20hardware%20for%20Ukraine%3A%20Who%20plans%20to%20supply,5%20Czech%20Republic%2020> (last accessed 11 October 2024). *See also* Lipovský, Milan, 'Assessing the Legal Boundaries of Military Support to Ukraine from the Perspective of Use of Force', (2025) 50 (1–2) *Review of Central and East European Law* 87.

114 "*Some member states, notably Italy, frequently try defendants in their absence, but the practice is not allowed in other EU member states.*" Brunsden, Jim, 'EU Deal Struck on Trials in Absentia' *Politico* (6 June 2008) <https://www.politico.eu/article/eu-deal-struck-on-trials-in-absentia/> (last accessed 11 October 2024).

115 *See* note 93 *supra* (need to prove the act of aggression).

116 Grzebyk, Patrycja, presentation at Charles University, Prague, Czech Republic, 11 November 2023; *see also* Grzebyk, Patrycja, *Criminal Responsibility for the Crime of Aggression*

a tribunal would, however possess a very significant flaw – entrenching impunity at the top leadership level.

5 Conclusions

The international community stands at an extraordinary historical moment. Will states revive the legacy of the Nuremberg (and Tokyo) tribunals and prosecute the crime of aggression in the face of a flagrant violation of the UN Charter in a meaningful way? Such prosecutions could create massively significant precedent for prosecuting the crime in the future – potentially before the ICC (if the Rome Statute's jurisdiction is fixed to harmonize the court's jurisdiction over the crime with that of its other crimes), or even (to some extent) through domestic prosecutions or future *ad hoc* tribunals.[117]

A clear pathway existed for establishing a fully credible and legitimate tribunal through the United Nations. Either the UN General Assembly could have recommended the establishment of the tribunal or the UN Security Council could have done so through a Chapter VI resolution; in either case, the tribunal would have been established by agreement between the UN and Ukraine. With the Chapter VI approach, Russia, as a party to the dispute, would have needed to abstain from voting on the resolution – as required by the plain language of Article 27(3) of the UN Charter. Because that language has been inconsistently applied in the past, Russia's abstention, however,

---

[Odpowiedzialnos´c´karna za zbrodnie˛ agresji], Konieczna-Purchała, Anna (trans.) (Routledge, 2013), 193–94.

117 Domestic proceedings, however, face various impediments, most significantly, the application of personal immunities, and if Draft Article 7 of the International Law Commission's work on 'Immunity of State Officials from Foreign Criminal Jurisdiction' is not corrected, also, the application of functional immunities. *See* UNGA, A/CN.4/L.969, International Law Commission, Seventy-Third Session, 'Draft Articles on Immunity of State Officials from Foreign Criminal Jurisdiction', Draft Art. 7 (31 May 2022), available online at <https://documents.un.org/doc/undoc/ltd/g22/353/99/pdf/g2235399.pdf?OpenElement> (last accessed 11 October 2024). The application of functional immunities would be even more problematic because, unlike personal immunities, they do not expire when a person's term in office ends but serve as a permanent bar to proceedings before another state's national courts. *See* Van Alebeek, Rosanne, *The Immunity of States and Their Officials in International Criminal Law and International Human Rights Law* (Oxford University Press, 2008), 114 (functional immunity "*is not dependent on an official's term of office*"). As to future prosecution of the crime of aggression before additional *ad hoc* tribunals, that also would be far from ideal in terms of trying to achieve consistent application of the rule of law.

could have been somewhat challenging to achieve. It might have required the General Assembly seeking an Advisory Opinion from the ICJ on whether the Charter's plain language is to be utilized – as it has been numerous times in the past (although admittedly less so more recently).[118] Reaffirming the obligation to utilize such obligatory abstention could even have reaped the additional benefit of revitalizing the Security Council's ability to act more broadly when voting under Chapter VI.[119]

Ukraine may be in a position where it needs to accept a less than ideal tribunal – if there is to be a freestanding aggression-specific tribunal. Even if the tribunal contains significant international elements, the tribunal's establishment, even if implemented by international agreement (without more), risks not being seen to represent the *will* of the international community. The concern is that the tribunal would not constitute an *international tribunal* and would be unable to overcome personal immunities.[120] The establishment of such a non-international tribunal (or any statement in the tribunal's statute that personal immunities apply or that proceedings are suspended during the terms in office of the 'troika') would send a very mixed message for a leadership crime – that top leaders can evade accountability, pinning the blame on those a level below in the hierarchy. The tribunal thus would be hampered in design, and *by design*.

If the tribunal lacks strong, internationalized elements, the downsides increase exponentially, and the detriments of prosecution could even outweigh the benefits, casting doubt on the whole endeavor. Trials done wrong could undermine the validity of crime of aggression proceedings not only in the instant situation but more broadly, bringing into doubt whether such prosecutions should even be pursued in the future. Thus, the stakes of getting this right (or not) are extraordinarily high – not solely related to the situation of Ukraine, but beyond.

118 *See supra* note 97 (inconsistent past application).

119 That is, such mandatory abstention would not only apply in the context of establishing an aggression-specific tribunal, but should apply any time the Security Council is voting on a Chapter VI resolution – a party to the dispute should not be voting.

120 *See supra* notes 36–40 and accompanying text for discussion of immunities.

PART 3

The Crime of Aggression Definition and Immunities from Foreign Criminal Jurisdiction

CHAPTER 5

Personal Scope of Responsibility for the Crime of Aggression: The Case of Russian Aggression against Ukraine

Patrycja Grzebyk

1 Introduction

The Rome Statute (RS) of the International Criminal Court (ICC)[1] became a point of reference for any discussion on responsibility for international crimes, even though the customary status of definitions of the core crimes covered by the jurisdiction of the Court have raised some doubts.[2] Not surprisingly, when debates on possible tracks for the prosecution of persons responsible for Russian aggression started, once again states and international organizations,[3] as well as scholars[4] referred to the RS as the basic template for further negotiations. It seemed to be taken for granted that possible new international or internationalized tribunal should prosecute Russian aggression within the scope of the definition of the crime of aggression included in the Rome Statute.[5]

1 Rome Statute of the International Criminal Court (adopted 17 July 1998, entered into force 1 July 2002) 2187 UNTS 3.

2 Tan, Yudan, *The Rome Statute as Evidence of Customary International Law* (Leiden: Brill, 2021), 180 ff.

3 *See e.g.*, European Union (European Parliament), Resolution 2022/3017(RSP) on the Establishment of a Tribunal on the Crime of Aggression against Ukraine (19 January 2023), Official Journal of the EU 2023/C 214/10; Statement by President von der Leyen on the Establishment of the International Centre for the Prosecution of Crimes of Aggression against Ukraine (4 March 2023), available online at <https://ec.europa.eu/commission/presscorner/detail/es/statement_23_1363> (last accessed 28 May 2024); Ambassador Van Schaack's Remarks on the U.S. Proposal to Prosecute Russian Crimes of Aggression (27 March 2023), available online at <https://www.state.gov/ambassador-van-schaacks-remarks/> (last accessed 28 May 2024).

4 *See e.g.*, Nuremberg Declaration on the Crime of Aggression (8 May 2023), available online at <https://crimeofaggression.info/wp-content/uploads/Nuremberg_Declaration_on_the_Crime_of_Aggression.pdf> (last accessed 28 May 2024).

5 *See e.g.*, Hathaway, Oona A., 'The Case for Creating an International Tribunal to Prosecute the Crime of Aggression Against Ukraine (Part 1)' (blog *JustSecurity.org*, 20 September 2022)

 | DOI:10.1163/9789004740945_007

The definition of the crime of aggression adopted for the purpose of the RS in Kampala includes the leadership clause as its integral and essential part.[6] The clause significantly limits the scope of personal responsibility to only those who exert control over or direct the political and military actions of a state. In consequence, the circle of the potential accused, if constructed based on the Kampala clause, might be narrower in comparison to the list of potential accused based on the Nuremberg law which required a lower level of involvement – ability to shape or influence a state's policy.

This chapter argues that in the case discussed, the leadership clause should be interpreted broadly according to the Nuremberg standard approved by directly interested states (i.e., Ukraine, Russia, Belarus, and other states of the Eastern European region) and implemented in their national laws. Therefore, the standard adopted in the Rome Statute if interpreted narrowly cannot be an obstacle for the inclusion on the list of the accused and convicted. In consequence, a relatively wide circle of persons engaged in all acts of aggression committed by Russia against Ukraine since 2014 (i.e., since the beginning of Russian aggression against Ukraine in the form of occupation and subsequent annexation of Crimea) might be prosecuted for the crime of aggression.

The first part of the chapter explicates the differences between the Kampala and Nuremberg standard. The second part elucidates why the Nuremberg formula should be preferred in case of prosecution of Russian aggressors. The third part indicates the circle of persons who *prima facie* could be prosecuted for the crime of aggression having in mind the different acts of aggression committed by Russia since 2014.

<https://www.justsecurity.org/83117/the-case-for-creating-an-international-tribunal-to-prosecute-the-crime-of-aggression-against-ukraine/> (last accessed 28 May 2024); McDougall, Carrie, 'Why Creating a Special Tribunal for Aggression Against Ukraine is the Best Available Option: A Reply to Kevin Jon Heller and Other Critics' (blog *Opinioiuris.org*, 15 March 2022) <http://opiniojuris.org/2022/03/15/why-creating-a-special-tribunal-for-aggression-against-ukraine-is-the-best-available-option-a-reply-to-kevin-jon-heller-and-other-critics/> (last accessed 28 May 2024).

6 *See more* in Heller, Kevin, 'Retreat from Nuremberg: The Leadership Requirement in the Crime of Aggression' (2007) 18(3) *European Journal of International Law* 477; Hajdin, Nikola, *Individual Responsibility for the Crime of Aggression* (Stockholm: Stockholm University, 2021), 101 ff; McDougall, Carrie, *The Crime of Aggression under the Rome Statute of the International Criminal Court* (Cambridge: Cambridge University Press, 2021), 168 ff; Heinsch, Robert, 'The Crime of Aggression After Kampala: Success or Burden for the Future?' (2010) 2 *Goetingen Journal of International Law* 713, 721 ff.

2 Kampala vs Nuremberg Standard of the Leadership Clause

The Kampala leadership clause – as the definition of the crime of aggression was adopted during the Review Conference in Kampala in 2010[7] – limits the responsibility for the crime of aggression to those who were involved in "*planning, preparation, initiation or execution*" as "*a person in a position effectively to exercise control over or to direct the political or military action of a State*" (Article 8*bis* RS). This limitation is also confirmed in Article 25(3)*bis* RS which states that "[i]*n respect of the crime of aggression, the provisions of this article shall apply only to persons in a position effectively to exercise control over or to direct the political or military action of a State.*" It needs to be stressed that during negotiations of the definition of the crime of aggression, there was a common undeniable agreement that the crime of aggression is a leadership crime, i.e., a crime committed by those who have impact on policy,[8] although the proper wording of the leadership caused controversies.[9] During the negotiations it was noted that the leadership criterion should be applied to all forms of participation in the crime listed in the RS,[10] and that the provision on responsibility of commanders was inapplicable to the crime of aggression.[11]

The Kampala leadership clause does not require the accused to be appointed to an official position. It is sufficient to prove that their factual position enabled them to control or direct military or political action of the state. It does not matter whether the accused is from civil or military circles of power and what their citizenship is. Nevertheless, the Kampala leadership clause has some serious limitations. If there is a need to prove that the accused controls or directs a state's action then the mere influence on a state's policy would not be sufficient. It is also debatable whether the involvement of representatives of the private sector in economic aspects of war (production of essential goods for the conduct of war, securing financial support for the

---

7 ICC, Assembly of States Parties, Review Conference, The Crime of Aggression, Annex I, ICC Doc. RC/Res.6 (11 June 2010).

8 Barriga, Stefan, 'Negotiating the Amendments on the Crime of Aggression' in Barriga, Stefan and Kreß, Claus (ed.), *The Travaux Préparatoires of the Crime of Aggression* (Cambridge: Cambridge University Press, 2011), 10; Politi, Mauro, 'The Debate within the Preparatory Commission for the International Criminal Court' in Politi, Mauro, Nesi, Giuseppe (eds.), *The International Criminal Court and the Crime of Aggression* (Aldershot: Ashgate, 2004), 46; *see also* ICC, Assembly of States Parties, ICC-ASP/5/SWGCA/INF.1, para. 88.

9 Heller, *supra* note 6, 479.

10 *See e.g.*, ICC, Assembly of States Parties, ICC-ASP/6/SWGCA/INF.1, para. 11.

11 *See e.g.*, ICC, Assembly of States Parties, ICC-ASP/3/SWGCA/INF.1, para. 54.

aggressor) could be prosecuted based on Kampala clause, as according to the normal meaning of the word *political*, it should be understood as "*of or relating to government, a government, or the conduct of government.*"[12] However, some dictionaries emphasize that the word *political* refers also to definition of *politics* as activities not only of the government, but also "*of people who try to influence the way a country is governed.*"[13] Even if we agree on broader understanding of *political actions*, still private industrialists do not have power to control over or direct actions of a state.

The Special Working Group on the Crime of Aggression pointed out that the language later adopted in the Kampala clause was sufficiently broad to include persons such as industrialists.[14] Therefore, the crime of aggression is not necessarily limited to high-ranking government officials, but it can include members of the private sector. This opinion is debatable, having in mind a commentary of the International Law Commission (ILC) although made in the context of describing conditions of state responsibility, where the Commission stressed that *control* is more than oversight or influence or concern, and *direct* does not encompass incitement or suggestion "*but rather connotes actual direction of an operative kind.*"[15]

Although the ICC gained the competence to exercise jurisdiction over the crime of aggression in 2018, still there has been no single case of a crime of aggression prosecuted in this court, thus there is no jurisprudence elucidating the scope of leadership clause of the RS. This is an unsurprising fact, keeping in mind that only 49 states ratified the amendments on the crime of aggression so far (as of 18 September 2025) and according to the decision taken in 2017 in New York which clarified the conditions of exercise of the jurisdiction over the crime of aggression by the Court, both states – aggressor and victim of aggression – need to be parties to the RS and its appropriate amendments.[16] This is

12 *See e.g.*, at <https://www.merriam-webster.com/dictionary/political> or <https://www.britannica.com/dictionary/political> (last accessed 28 May 2024).

13 *Cf. with* <https://dictionary.cambridge.org/dictionary/english/political> (last accessed 28 May 2024).

14 *See e.g.*, ICC, Assembly of States Parties, ICC-ASP/7/20/Add/1, para. 25; Clark, Roger S., 'Negotiating Provisions Defining the Crime of Aggression, its Elements and the Conditions for ICC Exercise of Jurisdiction over it' (2010) 20 *European Journal of International Law* 1103, 1105.

15 ILC, Draft Articles on Responsibility of States for Internationally Wrongful Acts with commentaries (2001), YILC, 2001, vol. II, Part Two, 69.

16 ICC, Assembly of States Parties, Activation of the Jurisdiction of the Court over the Crime of Aggression, ICC-ASP/16/Res.5 (14 December 2017), para. 2; *see also* Kreß, Claus, 'On the Activation of ICC Jurisdiction over the Crime of Aggression' (2018) 16 *Journal of International Criminal Justice* 1, 12 ff; Cf. de Souza Dias, Talita, 'The Activation of the Crime of

also the reason why the ICC cannot prosecute Russian aggression as Russia did not ratify the Rome Statute, although Russia signed the Statute[17] and supported the inclusion of the crime of aggression in the Court's jurisdiction.[18] In consequence, without referral of the situation in Ukraine to the ICC by the United Nations Security Council (which is unlikely due to certain veto on behalf of Russia and most probably of China), the Court cannot deal with Russian aggression despite two declarations on recognition of the Court's jurisdiction submitted by Ukraine in 2014 and in 2015.[19]

The Kampala clause seems to depart from the Nuremberg/Tokyo standard. The latter needs to be reconstructed based not only on the scant provisions of the 1945 Charter of the International Military Tribunal (IMT)[20] and of the 1946

Aggression before the International Criminal Court: Some Overlooked Implications Arising for States Parties and Non-States Parties to the Rome Statute' (2019) 24(3) *Journal of Conflict and Security Law* 567.

17 Ukraine signed it on 20 January 2000, and finally became a party on 25 October 2024; Russia signed it on 13 September 2000. However, in a communication received on 30 November 2016, the Government of the Russian Federation informed the Secretary-General about the intention of the Russian Federation not to become a party to the Rome Statute. This communication needs to be treated as an official notification of Russia in accordance with paragraph (a) of Article 18 of the Vienna Convention on the Law of Treaties (Vienna Convention on the Law of Treaties (adopted 22 May 1969, entered into force 27 January 1980) 1155 UNTS 331).

18 United Nations Diplomatic Conference of Plenipotentiaries on the Establishment of an International Criminal Court, Rome, Italy, 15 June–17 July 1998, A/CONF.183/C.1/SR.6, sixth meeting of the Committee of the Whole 176, paras. 95 and 177, para. 106.

19 Ukraine, pursuant to Art. 12(3) RS, lodged the first declaration on 9 April 2014 in which it accepted ICC jurisdiction with respect to alleged crimes committed on Ukrainian territory from 21 November 2013 to 22 February 2014. The second declaration was lodged on 8 September 2015 and extended the time period to encompass ongoing alleged crimes committed throughout the territory of Ukraine from 20 February 2014 onwards. According to the statement made by the Prosecutor Karim Khan on 28 February 2022 "*there is a reasonable basis to believe that both alleged war crimes and crimes against humanity have been committed in Ukraine in relation to the events already assessed during the preliminary examination by the Office. Given the expansion of the conflict in recent days, it is my intention that this investigation will also encompass any new alleged crimes falling within the jurisdiction of my Office that are committed by any party to the conflict on any part of the territory of Ukraine.*" Statement available online at <https://www.icc-cpi.int/news/statement-icc-prosecutor-karim-aa-khan-qc-situation-ukraine-i-have-decided-proceed-opening> (last accessed 28 May 2024).

20 (London) Charter of the International Military Tribunal, Annexed to the Agreement by the Government of the United Kingdom of Great Britain and Northern Ireland, the Government of the United States of America, the Provisional Government of the French Republic and the Government of the Union of Soviet Socialist Republics for the Prosecu-

Charter of International Military Tribunal for the Far East (IMTFE),[21] but also based on the jurisprudence of those tribunals and on the post-Nuremberg judgments of American military tribunals engaged in so-called subsequent Nuremberg trials and of other national courts which were tasked with the prosecution of other than major war criminals and which made attempts to further interpret IMT Charter provisions.

The Charters of the IMT and IMTFE referred to the responsibility of "*major war criminals of European Axis*" or "*in the Far East*" for among others commission of crimes against peace "*namely planning, preparation, initiation or waging a war of aggression, or a war in violation of international treaties, agreements or assurances, or participation in a common plan or conspiracy for the accomplishment of any of the foregoing*" (Article 6(2)(a) and Article 5(2)(a) respectively). Furthermore, both Charters stipulate that leaders, organizers, instigators, and accomplices participating in the formulation or execution of a common plan or conspiracy to commit e.g., crimes against peace are responsible for all acts performed by any persons in execution of such plan (Article 6(3) and Article 5(3) respectively). Accordingly, the chief prosecutor of the Nuremberg Tribunal – Robert Jackson – emphasized that he wished to bring to justice the persons who had planned and designed the crimes: the leaders and the instigators.[22]

Based on the judgments of the Nuremberg and Tokyo tribunals we can derive the following conclusions concerning the personal scope of responsibility for the crime against peace. Firstly, the criminalization of the war of aggression was based on the 1928 Kellogg-Briand Pact (Pact of Paris)[23] which condemned "*recourse to war for the solution of international controversies*" and renounced it "*as an instrument of national policy in their relations with one another.*" In consequence, those who had a significant influence on the policy of the state could be prosecuted for their involvement in the war of aggres-

---

tion and Punishment of the Major War Criminals of the European Axis (adopted and entered into force 8 August 1945) 82 UNTS 279.

21 Charter was proclaimed by the Supreme Commander of the Allied Powers at Tokyo (19 January 1946), available online at <https://www.un.org/en/genocideprevention/documents/atrocity-crimes/Doc.3_1946%20Tokyo%20Charter.pdf≥ (last accessed 28 May 2024).

22 *The Case Against the Nazi War Criminals, Opening Statement for the United States of America by Robert H. Jackson and Other Documents, with Preface by Gordon Dean of Counsel for United States* (New York: Alfred A. Knopf, 1946), 13.

23 General Treaty for Renunciation of War as an Instrument of National Policy (adopted 27 August 1928, entered into force 25 July 1929) 94 LNTS 57.

sion.[24] It was clear that main politicians should be the first suspects in cases of crimes against peace.

Secondly, for the IMT and IMTFE, the essential proof of the guilt in a case of the crime against peace was the fact the person was in the inner circle of power and participated in crucial meetings during which decisions on the initiation of wars of aggression were taken. Therefore, those who left this inner circle too soon, i.e., before decisions on wars were taken, like Franz von Papen[25] or Hjalmar Schacht,[26] or joined it too late, so when wars were already ongoing, like Fritz Sauckel[27] or Albert Speer,[28] were excluded from the scope of responsibility for wars of aggression. Moreover, those, who did not have a sufficient impact on the shaping of the policy, like Hans Fritzsche,[29] did not respond for the crime against peace, although it needs to be stressed that the Tokyo Tribunal recognized the responsibility of Kingoro Hashimoto, who held no high positions during WWII, for instigating a war of aggression, having

24 Lumb, R. D., 'Individual Responsibility for Aggressive War: The Crime Against Peace', (1956–59) 3(4) *University of Queensland Law Journal* 333, 350.

25 *See* IMT, Judgment and Sentences (1 October 1946) in *The Trial of German Major War Criminals. Proceedings of the International Military Tribunal sitting at Nuremberg, Germany, Part 22 (22nd August 1946 to 1st October 1946)*, (IMT Judgment), 519. ("*There is no evidence that he was a party to the plans under which the occupation of Austria was a step in the direction of further aggressive action, or even that he participated in plans to occupy Austria by aggressive war if necessary. It is not established beyond a reasonable doubt that this was the purpose of his activity* [...]").

26 Ibid, 506 ("*He was clearly not one of the inner circle around Hitler which was most closely involved with this Common Plan. He was regarded by this group with undisguised hostility.*").

27 Ibid, 514 ("*The evidence has not satisfied the Tribunal that Sauckel was sufficiently connected with the Common Plan to wage aggressive war or sufficiently involved in the planning or waging of the aggressive wars*").

28 Ibid, 521 ("*He became the head of the armament industry well after all of the wars had been commenced and were under way. His activities in charge of German armament production were in aid of the war effort in the same way that other productive enterprises aid in the waging of war; but the Tribunal is not prepared to find that such activities involve engaging in the Common Plan to wage aggressive war*").

29 Ibid, 526 ("*Never did he achieve sufficient stature to attend the planning conferences which led to aggressive war; indeed, according to his own uncontradicted testimony, he never even had a conversation with Hitler. Nor is there any showing that he was informed of the decisions taken at these conferences.*"). *See also* the dissenting opinion of judge Powers to the judgment in the Ministries case, *Trials of War Criminals before the Nuernberg Military Tribunals under Control Council Law No. 10, Nuernberg October 1946-April 1949* (Washington: United States Government Printing Office), vol. XIV, at 887 ff.

in mind his influence on Japanese commanders.[30] In the case of Hashimoto, the tribunal was persuaded that he indeed shaped the aggressive policy of Japan.

Thirdly, the IMTFE indicated also that holding a specific position could be interpreted as *prima facie* evidence of an involvement in the crime against peace. This position of the Tribunal is particularly visible in the sections pertaining to the defendants Akira Muto and Kenryo Sato, where the IMTFE expressly makes the connection between their participation in a conspiracy to commit a crime against peace with their holding a specific office.[31] However, the jurisprudence of Nuremberg and Tokyo tribunals was not consistent in terms of factoring a defendant's impact on policy into the sentencing. In Schacht's case, despite the fact that he had held a high position (inducing the position of the minister of the economy), it was decided that he remained outside the strict sphere of power, and he had no impact on the shaping of specific political and military plans, but Funk – Schacht's successor – was found responsible. He had held the same positions that Schacht, and yet the Tribunal clearly decided that he had sufficient policy impact. The inconsistency of the rulings could result from the fact that the judges in Nuremberg attempted to distinguish between the grounds for responsibility for the participation in a conspiracy (holding a relevant office and having impact on policy) and the grounds for responsibility for the crime against peace, where the Nuremberg Tribunal at least appeared to be of the opinion that proof of significant involvement is sufficient.[32]

The provisions of the IMT and IMTFE Charters referred to responsibility for crimes against peace as pertaining to not only those engaged in planning, preparation, and initiation of a war of aggression, but also to those who engaged in waging such a war (Article VI(2)(a) and Article 5(a) respectively). The notion of *waging a war* is broad enough to cover not only the top representatives of a state, i.e., those who make the decisions to engage in military operations, but also the lower-grade soldiers who participate in these operations. Theoretically, any person who in any manner contributed to the military operations on the side of the aggressor could be charged with the crime

30 IMTFE Judgment, 4/12 November 1948, published in Pritchard, John and Zaide, Sonia M. (eds.), *The Tokyo War Crimes Trial*, vol. 22, at 49, 780; *see also* Kittichaisaree, Kriangsak, *International Criminal Law* (Oxford: Oxford University Press, 2001), 223.

31 Kittichaisaree, *supra* note 30, 223. *See also* United Nations War Crimes Commission, *Law Reports of Trials of War Criminals* (London: His Majesty's Stationery Office, 1947–1949), vol. 15, at 147.

32 Brownlie, Ian, *International Law and the Use of Force by States* (Oxford: Oxford University Press, 1968), 205.

against peace.[33] This interpretation – although favored in the former occupied states – has proved unacceptable.[34] Otherwise, the entire population of the aggressor state could be charged with the crime against peace, leading to the absurd situation with low-ranking soldiers, farmers supplying the army with produce, and even housewives manufacturing the most basic goods used by the military industry placed on the defendants' bench.[35] The absurdity of this approach was emphasized by the American military tribunal in the 1948 judgment in the *IG Farben* Case:

> If we lower the standard of participation to include them, it is difficult to find a logical place to draw the line between the guilty and the innocent among the great mass of German people. It is, of course, unthinkable that the majority of Germans should be condemned as guilty of committing crimes against peace. This would amount to a determination of collective guilt to which the corollary of mass punishment is the logical result for which there is no precedent in international law and no justification in human relations. We cannot say that a private citizen shall be placed in the position of being compelled to determine in the heat of war whether his government is right or wrong, or, if it starts right, when it turns wrong. We would not require the citizen, at the risk of becoming a criminal under the rules of international justice, to decide that his country has become an aggressor and that he must lay aside his patriotism, the loyalty to his homeland, and the defense of his own fireside at the risk of being adjudged guilty of crimes against peace on the one hand, or of becoming a traitor to his country on the other, if he makes an erroneous decision based upon facts of which he has but vague knowledge. To require this of him would be to assign to him a task of decision which the leading statesmen of the world and the learned men of international law have been unable to perform in their search for a precise definition of aggression.[36]

33 Dinstein, Yoram, *War, Aggression and Self-Defence* (4 edn., Cambridge: Cambridge University Press, 2005), 133.

34 Maugham, Viscount, *U.N.O. and War Crimes* (London: Johny Murray Albebarle Stree, 1951), 19, where author claims that this approach would be a tool of "systematic holocaust".

35 *Trials of War Criminals*, vol. VIII, at 1124–1125.

36 Ibid, 1126.

Nobody, for example, made an effort to focus on the Japanese pilots who carried out the attack on Pearl Harbor, or their immediate superiors: all the attention went to those who had made the political decision to attack.[37] It is therefore unsurprising that the option of significantly extending the circle of those potentially responsible for the war of aggression was generally rejected in subsequent documents and trials.

The Control Council Law No. 10 specified that the charge of the crime against peace could be made only against persons who "*held a high political, civil or military (including General Staff) position in Germany or in one of its Allies, co-belligerents or satellites or held high position in the financial, industrial or economic life of any such country*" (Article II (2) (f)).[38]

Therefore, the CC Law no. 10 required the prosecutors to prove that the accused had a high position and the question appeared: what should we mean by *high position* in all kinds of administration and private sector. The American military tribunals in the High Command case clarified that:

> [i]nternational law condemns those who, due to their actual power to shape and influence the policy of their nation, prepare for, or lead their country into or in an aggressive war. But we do not find that, at the present stage of development, international law declares as criminals those below that level who, in the execution of this war policy, act as the instruments of the policy makers. Anybody who is on the policy level and participates in the war policy is liable to punishment. But those under them cannot be punished for the crimes of others. The misdeed of the policy makers is all the greater in as much as they use the great mass of the soldiers and officers to carry out an international crime; however, the individual soldier or officer below the policy level is but the policy makers' instrument, finding himself, as he does, under the rigid discipline which is necessary for and peculiar to military organization.[39]

American tribunals adopted *shape and influence* standard as they stressed in that responsibility for the crime against peace is limited to persons:

37 Fletcher, George P., *Romantics at War. Glory and Guilt in the age of Terrorism* (Princeton-Oxford: Princeton University Press, 2002), 5.

38 CCL no. 10, available online at <https://www.legal-tools.org/doc/ffda62/pdf/> (last accessed 28 May 2024).

39 *Trials of War Criminals,* vol. XI, at 489.

> in a position to shape or influence the policy that brings about its initiation or its continuance after initiation, either by furthering, or by hindering or preventing it. If he then does the former, he becomes criminally responsible; if he does the latter to the extent of his ability, then his action shows the lack of criminal intent with respect to such policy.[40]

Tribunals stressed then that the distinction needed to be made between leaders and followers.[41] It is true that if the question is asked whose participation is necessary to accomplish a crime against peace, it becomes evident that a low-ranking soldier is easily replaceable, whereas a visionary politician is not.[42] Thus, somebody's potential influence on policy is not necessarily crucial in determining the circle of those potentially guilty, but it must be considered in determining the cause-and-effect relationship between the actions of a given person and the commission of the crime of aggression.[43]

In the case of the High Command, American military tribunal argued that Hitler, even if his absolute power is presumed, could not possibly have formulated and implemented the policy of aggressive war on his own: he needed the support of many others at the stage of the preparing, planning and waging such a war.[44] As the tribunal stressed:

> He had to have the cooperation of statesmen, military leaders, diplomats, and business men. When they, with knowledge of his aims, gave him their co-operation, they made themselves parties to the plan he had initiated. They are not to be deemed innocent because Hitler made use of them, if they knew what they were doing. That they were assigned to their tasks by a dictator does not absolve them from responsibility for their acts.[45]

However, only those who held positions giving them actual influence on the state's policy could bear criminal responsibility for the crime against peace.[46]

---

40 Ibid, 488.

41 Ibid, vol. VIII, at 1126.

42 May, Larry, *Aggression and Crimes against Peace* (Cambridge: Cambridge University Press, 2008), 238.

43 May, Larry, 'Act and Circumstance in the Crime of Aggression, Symposium: War & Responsibility' (2007) 15 *Journal of Political Philosophy* 169, 180.

44 *Trials of War Criminals,* vol. XI, at 486.

45 IMT Judgment, 448.

46 *Trials of War Criminals,* vol. XI, at 486–489.

It is worth noting that American military tribunals did not exclude the possibility to identify those responsible for shaping or influencing aggressive policy in all kinds of circles – political, military, or industrial ones, and they made an attempt to identify those who were in charge of "*formulation and execution of policies.*"[47] The charges of the crime against peace were filed in in 4 out of the 12 Nuremberg trials, among which two – the *IG Farben* Trial (*USA v Carl Krauch et al.*, 30 July 1948) and the *Krupp* Trial (*USA v Alfried Krupp et al.*, 31 July 1948) – were focused on those responsible for the war economy, and the other two dealt with responsibility of those engaged at the Ministry level (*USA v Ernst von Weizsäcker et al.*, 11 April 1949) or in the High Command Trial (*USA v Wilhelm von Leeb et al.*, 27 October 1948). Even if the accused in the *IG Farben* and the *Krupp* case were not found guilty of the crime against peace, the American tribunals did not exclude responsibility of the members of the industry sector. It should be also emphasized that we cannot attach too much importance to the list of those who were not charged with the crime against peace by American prosecutors, as other factors (as e.g., the need to finish quickly trial) also played some role, which case of Erhard Milch proved.[48]

Neither the Charters of the International Military Tribunals nor the Control Council Law No. 10 differentiate between state representatives and private persons. Based on Nuremberg law it is therefore allowed to charge individuals from both of these categories with the crime against peace. It is then possible to charge a person with aggression who is not a cabinet member, but has relevant impact on public issues or on the economy of a state.[49]

The greatest controversy pertains to the responsibility of the military commanders. The Nuremberg Tribunal convicted Erich Raeder and Wilhelm Keitel, despite the finding that they were not leaders, had no policy impact, had no decision-making powers, and had no special influence among the top-ranking officials.[50] Apparently, their role in implementation of decisions on initiation and waging wars of aggression was too important to ignore. The Nuremberg Tribunal decided at the same time that Alfred Jodl and Karl Dönitz

47 *Trials of War Criminals,* vol. VIII, at 1124.

48 Final Report to the Secretary of the Army on the Nuernberg War Crimes Trials Under Control Council Law No. 10 by Telford Taylor, Brigadier General, U.S.A. Chief of Counsel for War Crimes, Washington, D. C. (15 August 1949), 67; *see also* Grzebyk, Patrycja, *Criminal Responsibility for the Crime of Aggression* (London-New York: Routledge, 2013), 168.

49 Dinstein, *supra* note 33, 134.

50 *See* UN, Preparatory Commission for the International Criminal Court, PCNICC/2002/WGCA/L.1/Add.1, 32 and subs.

had influence on Hitler's decisions as to the scale of the military operations, and therefore were found guilty of the crime against peace. Dönitz, it was noted, was a military man who eventually became a state leader.[51]

A few years later, the American military tribunal in the High Command Trial decided that Georg-Hans Reinhardt, Walter Warlimont, and Hans von Salmuth, with whom Hitler consulted his decisions and who advised him to escalate the military operations, were not responsible for the war of aggression.[52] All defendants were found to have had no impact on policy, and to have been ordinary military personnel simply doing their job.

The Dutch Judge in the IMTFE – Bernard Röling argued that the army was only an instrument in the hands of politicians, and military personnel may only be responsible for the crime against peace if they make decisions of political significance.[53] This principle however is not consistently reflected in the judgments of the IMT and IMTFE.

As it was mentioned, the IMT and IMTFE were supposed to deal only with major war criminals. This does not mean that the Charters of those tribunals precluded bringing other, less prominent individuals responsible for the war of aggression to justice before other courts. Nevertheless, American military tribunals referred to the mentioned limitation of the IMT's jurisdiction in their judgments while drawing contours of responsibility for the crime against peace.[54] However, it needs to be recalled that the IMT's judgment was supposed to be one of the whole series of judgments concerning major war criminals and only because of political constraints (beginning of the Cold War, high costs and legal difficulties related with organization of trials together with representatives of four powers i.e., France, UK, USA, USSR), the IMT works were brought to an end and replaced by proceedings before occupational courts, including American military tribunals. American tribunals judged cases based on the 1945 Control Council Law no. 10, intended as a uniform basis for bringing to justice Nazi criminals in all occupation zones, and consequently to follow up on the provisions of the Moscow Declaration of

51 Harris, Whitney R., *Tyranny on Trial. The Evidence at Nuremberg* (Dallas: Southern Methodist University Press, 1954), 532–533.

52 Lumb, *supra* note 24, 350.

53 Röling, Bernard V. A. and Rüter, Christiaan F., *The Tokyo Judgment, The International Military Tribunal for the Far East (I.M.T.F.E.) 29 April 1946 – 12 November 1948* (Amsterdam, University Press Amsterdam, 1977), vol. 2, at 1061–1062.

54 *Trials of War Criminals*, vol. VIII, at 1124. More about the crime against peace in subsequent Nuremberg trials *see* Heller, Kevin, *The Nuremberg Military Tribunals and the Origins of International Criminal Law* (Oxford: Oxford University Press, 2011), 180 ff.

1943 and the London Agreement of 1945.[55] Therefore, occupational tribunals took over the task of the prosecution of major war criminals and that is why they referred only to this category, but this does not impact the jurisdiction of national courts over other than major war criminals who could also be charged with the crime against peace. Polish Supreme National Tribunal found several persons guilty of the crime against peace and whose involvement in this crime consisted in the exercise of occupational powers and in facilitation of annexation, like it was in a case of Arthur Greiser (Gauleiter of the Warthegau), Albert Forster (Gauleiter and Head of State of Danzig), Ludwig Fischer (Governor of the Warsaw District), or Josef Bühler (State Secretary of the General Government of Occupied Poland).[56] Therefore, those whose work was essential for waging a war of aggression in the form of the occupation of territories and their legal or factual annexation were also prosecuted based on the law derived from the IMT Charter. It is also noticeable that the judgment in the case of Greiser was issued even before the Nuremberg Tribunal announced its verdict. This proves (together with the Nuremberg judgment in the case of Frick, and the judgment of the American military tribunal in the Ministries Trial) that responsibility for the crime against peace can also be assigned to individuals who had no impact on the shaping of the general state's policy, but who played a significant role in the implementation of that policy.[57]

---

55 Control Council Law No. 10, Punishment of Persons Guilty of War Crimes, Crimes against Peace and Against Humanity, 20 December 1945, Official Gazette of the Control Council for Germany, No. 3, 31 January 1946, 50–55.

56 Grzebyk, *supra* note 48, 182 ff; *see also* Grzebyk, Patrycja, 'The Role of the Polish Supreme National Tribunal in the Development of Principles of International Criminal Law' in Bergsmo, Morten, Ling, Cheah Wui and Ping, Yi (eds.), *Historical Origins of International Criminal Law*, vol. 2 (Torkel Opsahl Academic EPublisher, 2014), 603 ff.; Finder, Gabriel and Prusin, Alexander, *Justice Behind the Iron Curtain: Nazis on Trial in Communist Poland* (Toronto: University of Toronto Press, 2018), 6; Epstein, Catherine, *Model Nazi: Arthur Greiser and the Occupation of Western Poland* (Oxford: Oxford University Press, 2010), 305 ff.; Prusin, Alexander, 'Poland's Nuremberg: The Seven Court Cases of the Supreme National Tribunal, 1946–1948' (2010) 24 *Holocaust and Genocide Studies* 1. The judgment of the Polish Supreme National Tribunal in case of Arthur Greiser is described in: United Nations War Crimes Commission, *Law Reports of Trials of War Criminals* (London: His Majesty's Stationery Office, 1949), vol. 13, at 70. *See also* Drumbl, Mark, 'Germans are the Lords and Poles are the Servants': The Trial of Arthur Greiser in Poland, 1946, in Heller, Kevin and Simpson, Gerry (eds.), *The Hidden Histories of War Crimes Trials* (Oxford: Oxford University Press, 2013), 411.

57 Pompe, C. A., *Aggressive War. An International Crime* (The Hague: Martinus Nijhoff, 1953), 233.

3 In the Search for the Ideal Formula for the Leadership Clause in the Context of Russian Aggression

It is undisputed that states consider the leadership clause as a requirement for the responsibility for the crime of aggression. The Code of Crimes against the Peace and Security of Mankind adopted by the International Law Commission in 1996[58] stipulates clearly that only an individual who, as a leader or an organizer, actively participates in or orders the planning, preparation, initiation, or waging of aggression committed by a state shall be responsible for a crime of aggression (Article 16). However, the comments to the draft argue that the notion of a leader or of an organizer should be interpreted broadly, so as to encompass not only government members, but also individuals holding high positions in the military, diplomacy, political parties, and the industry.[59]

Leaders need to be then found responsible for the crime of aggression. The problem is whether we should be guided by the broad Nuremberg and post-Nuremberg understanding of the leadership clause or by – in theory – narrower standard of the RS. Whether the Nuremberg standard is so different from the one adopted in the Rome Statute? The answer is not so obvious, as on the one hand, the RS imposes higher standard to be proven i.e., "*to exercise control over or to direct the political or military action of a state*" in comparison to the mere "*shape or influence*" standard of Nuremberg law. On the other hand, the broad understanding of the RS provisions is possible, as everything depends on the interpretation of the notion of "*direct*" and "*control over*" in particular cases.

Article 8*bis* of the Rome Statute starts with the words "*For the purpose of this Statute*" which suggests that not necessarily the definition of the crime of aggression included in the Statute should be applied in other than this Court's proceedings. However, it needs to be stressed that other definitions of international crimes adopted in the RS begin with exactly the same way and the customary status of definition of genocide or of majority of war crimes does not raise any doubts on behalf of any state.

To make the proper (just and fair) decision in the case of the framework of responsibility for Russian aggression we need to refer to statements of par-

58 ILC, Draft Code of Crimes against the Peace and Security of Mankind (1996), YILC, 1996, vol. II, Part II. More on the work of the ILC on the crime of aggression *see* Šturma, Pavel, 'Back to the ILC's Legislative History: Code of Crimes against the Peace and Security of Mankind' (2015) 6 *Czech Yearbook of Public & Private International Law* 37.

59 Text of the commentary available at <https://legal.un.org/ilc/texts/instruments/english/commentaries/7_4_1996.pdf> (last accessed 28 May.2024); *see* comments at 43.

ticularly interested and affected states. Interestingly, both states – aggressor and its victim – supported delegalization and criminalization of aggression at international law level[60] and they criminalize the crime of aggression in their criminal codes, but appropriate provisions are shaped in Nuremberg law style. Russia, in Article 353 of its Criminal Code of 1996 stipulates that: "*1. Planning, preparing, or unleashing an aggressive war shall be punishable by deprivation of liberty for a term of seven to fifteen years. 2. Waging an aggressive war shall be punishable by deprivation of liberty for a term of 10 to 20 years.*"[61] At the same time, the Ukrainian Criminal Code of 2001 in Article 427 criminalizes: "*1. Planning, preparation or waging of an aggressive war or armed conflict, or conspiring for any such purposes*" as well as "*Conducting an aggressive war or aggressive military operations*".[62] The similar wording is used in Article 122 of the Belarussian Criminal Code of 1999,[63] which is of particular importance as Belarus should also be considered as an aggressor state as it has placed its territory at the disposal of Russia, to be used by Russia for perpetrating an act of aggression against Ukraine.[64] In fact, the overwhelming majority of Eastern European states have norms concerning the criminalization of aggression mostly shaped according to the letter of the IMT Charter.[65]

The above facts indicate that in case of hesitance whether a narrow or broad reading of the leadership clause should be taken into account by the court prosecuting Russian aggression, the latter solution should be favored due to regional standards. This is of particular importance as war in Ukraine, which started in 2014 with the annexation of Crimea and the beginning of hostilities in Eastern Ukraine,[66] went into another decade. Different persons were engaged at its different stages and the exclusion of those who joined the war of aggression at the stage of waging it and not at its initiation would be unjustified. Especially if we keep in mind that with each year, knowledge

60 *See more* in Grzebyk, Patrycja, 'Crime of Aggression against Ukraine: The Role of Regional Customary Law' (2023) 21(3) *Journal of International Criminal* Justice 435, 442 ff.

61 Text available at <https://wipolex-res.wipo.int/edocs/lexdocs/laws/en/ru/ru080en.html> (last accessed 28 May 2024).

62 Text available at <https://sherloc.unodc.org/cld/uploads/res/document/ukr/2001/criminal-code-of-the-republic-of-ukraine-en_html/Ukraine_Criminal_Code_as_of_2010_EN.pdf> (last accessed 28 May 2024).

63 Text available at <https://www.wipo.int/wipolex/en/legislation/details/20145> (last accessed 28 May 2024).

64 *See* UNGA Res 3314 (XXIX), Definition of Aggression (14 December 1974), Art. 3(f).

65 *See* Grzebyk, *supra* note 60, 453 ff.

66 Bílková, Veronika, 'The Use of Force by the Russian Federation in Crimea' (2015) 75 *Heidelberg Journal of International Law* 27; Grant, Thomas D., *Aggression Against Ukraine. Territory, Responsibility, and International Law* (New York: Palgrave, 2015); Grze-

about the aggressive character of Russian policy is more and more obvious and confirmed by e.g., the UN General Assembly resolutions.[67]

The consistent application of the Nuremberg standard would also mean that prosecution should focus on the war of aggression and not on all acts of aggression which did not achieve the level of a war of aggression. Therefore, the court dealing with Russian aggressors would have to answer if war started in 2022 or already in 2014, despite a lack of direct hostilities between Russian and Ukrainian army during the process of occupation and annexation of Crimea and during the subsequent years of hostilities in Eastern Europe in which Russia was not officially engaged, although it did exercise some kind of control over Ukrainian separatists.[68] This has consequences for eventual responsibility for such acts of aggression like: the annexation of Crimea; Kerch Strait Incident; blockade of the ports before 2022; or the involvement in the conflict in Eastern Ukraine 2014–2022. In my opinion, it needs to be recalled that although the Nuremberg tribunal did not consider the annexation of Austria and of Czechoslovakia as examples of a war of aggression for which responsibility for the crime against peace can be claimed, in the subsequent Nuremberg trials based on altered wording of the crime against peace included in CC Law no.10 this line of reasoning of the tribunal was rectified.

4 Candidates to Be Put in the Dock

The first propositions of the list of the potential accused were already made.[69] In this part of the chapter, I would like to indicate certain categories of persons from different circles which could be considered by prosecutors.

The most obvious candidates for the dock are the President of Russian Federation – Vladimir Putin and the President of Republic of Belarus – Alexander Lukashenka – as those people rule within authoritarian regimes which they helped to create, and no decision on policy of their states can be taken without

---

byk, Patrycja, 'Classification of the Conflict between Ukraine and Russia in International Law (Ius ad Bellum and Ius in Bello)' (2014) 34 *Polish Yearbook of International Law* 39.

67 *See e.g.*, UNGA Res ES-11/1, Aggression against Ukraine (2 March 2022).

68 *See e.g.*, ECtHR, *Ukraine and the Netherlands v Russia*, app. nos. 8019/16, 43800/14 and 28525/20, Grand Chamber's Decision of 25 January 2023 "*The Court found that areas in eastern Ukraine in separatist hands were from May 11, 2014, and up to at least January 26, 2022, under the jurisdiction of the Russian Federation.*" ECHR 026 (2023).

69 *See more* in Bogush, Gleb, "'Committed by Men': Individual Criminal Responsibility for Aggression against Ukraine" (2023) 12(2) *Polish Review of International and European Law* 93.

their knowledge. Similarly, with the involvement of North Korea in hostilities against Ukraine, Kim Jong Un became a potential accused in proceedings concerning aggression against Ukraine.[70]

From the political circles, the highest members of the Russian Presidential Executive office like Anton Vaino (Chief of Staff), Alexei Gromov (First Deputy of Chief of Staff), Sergei Kiriyenko (First Deputy of Chief of Staff), and other Deputies like Dmitry Kozak, Magomedov Magomedsalam, Vladimir Ostrovenko, and Dmitry Peskov need to be considered for prosecution as they were and are – having in mind the positions they held – direct influence on the Russian policy.

Keeping in mind the extensive legal staffage which was used to justify acts of aggression in 2014 and in 2022, the involvement of Larisa Brychova – the Head of the Presidential State-Legal Directorate, could be examined. In the context of Russian policy, it is not without meaning that the two main Russian leaders – Putin and Dmitry Medvedev (deputy chairman of the Security Council of Russia) – are lawyers who extensively referred in their statements to international law,[71] how important of a role the formal legitimization for foreign policy plays in Russian culture.[72]

The political circle of power could be reconstructed also based on the membership in Russian Security Council where, apart from the mentioned Putin, Medvedev, Vaino there were: Mikhail Mishustin (Prime Minister), Valentina Matviyenko (Chairwoman of the Council of Federation), Sergein Naryshkin (Director of the Foreign Intelligence Service), Vyacheslav Volodin (State Duma Speaker), Ivanov Sergei (Special Presidential Representative for Environmental Protection, Ecology and Transport), Nikolai Patrushev (Secretary) and his deputy – Rashid Nurgaliyev, Sergei Shoigu (Defense Minister), Sergei

70 *See* Milanovic, Marko, 'North Korea's Troop Deployment in the Russian War of Aggression against Ukraine: The DPRK as a Principal or as an Accomplice?' (blog *Ejiltalk.org*, 4 November 2024) <https://www.ejiltalk.org/north-koreas-troop-deployment-in-the-russian-war-of-aggression-against-ukraine-the-dprk-as-a-principal-or-as-an-accomplice/> (last accessed 23 May 2025), who argues that North Korea became principal in Russia's aggression against Ukraine.

71 *See e.g.*, Address by President of the Russian Federation (18 March 2014), available online at <http://en.kremlin.ru/events/president/news/20603> (last accessed 28 May 2024); Address by the President of the Russian Federation (24 February 2022), available online at <http://en.kremlin.ru/events/president/news/67843> (last accessed 28 May 2024); *see also* Letter dated 24 February 2022 from the Permanent Representative of the Russian Federation to the United Nations addressed to the Secretary-General, S/2022/154 (5 March 2022).

72 *See more* in Mälksoo, Lauri, *Russian Approaches to International Law* (Oxford: Oxford University Press, 2015) passim.

Lavrov (Minister of Foreign Affairs), Vladimir Kolokoltsev (Minister of Interior), Alexander Bortnikov (Director of the Federal Security Service), Anton Siluanov (Minister of Finance), and Viktor Zolotov (Director of the Federal Service of National Guard) as well as presidential plenipotentiary envoys who were responsible for the mobilization. Some indicators could be the fact of who was included in the membership of Special Coordination Council headed by Prime Minister Mikhail Mishustin, whose task was "*to meet any needs that arise during the course of the special military operation*" and which includes apart from vice-premiers and representatives of law enforcement agencies and of the Presidential Administration and State Council, also heads of the main social and economic departments of the government.[73]

Gleb Bogush also indicates the role of Putin's advisers like Yuri Kovalchuk or the president of the Russian Constitutional Court Valery Zorkin – responsible for strengthening the formal legitimization of the aggressive war and for legal facilitation of engagement in the aggressive war for millions of people.

In case of the civil administration, in my opinion the leaders of the occupying authorities in Crimea, Luhansk, and Donetsk districts could be considered for eventual prosecution of the crime of aggression (like e.g., Vladimir Konstantinov, Siergiej Aksionow, Leonid Pasechnik, and Denis Pushilin), as well as other high representatives of occupying power in other regions like Vitaly Ganchev – head of the Kharkiv Oblast, or Vladimir Saldo, Oleksandr Kobets or Andrey Alekseyenko who were responsible for occupation administration in Kherson Oblast, and Halyna Danylchenko and Yevhen Balytskyi in Zaporizhzhia Oblast, as well as Sergey Kiryenko who was generally responsible for Russian-occupied territories. As the majority of the mentioned people from occupational authorities have Ukrainian nationality, in case of their prosecution in Ukrainian courts, they will be accused rather of collaboration crime.[74] However, all Russian high officials responsible for the occupation and preparation of annexation like Kiryenko might be accused of the crime against peace.

From military circles, already mentioned Shoigu (MoD) and Bortnikov (FSB), Valery Gerasimov (Chief of General Staff), and commanders of different

73 Tass, 'Putin Orders Creation of Special Council for Military Operation Needs' *Tass* (19 October 2022) <https://tass.com/politics/1524957> (last accessed 28 May 2024).

74 *See Ukraine: New Laws Criminalize Collaboration with an Aggressor State, available online at* <https://www.loc.gov/item/global-legal-monitor/2022-04-04/ukraine-new-laws-criminalize-collaboration-with-an-aggressor-state/> (last accessed 28 May 2024)*; see also Matuszak, Sławomir and Żochowski, Piotr,* 'Ukraine: New Wartime Legislation' (*OSW Analyses*, 17 March 2022) <https://www.osw.waw.pl/en/publikacje/analyses/2022-03-17/ukraine-new-wartime-legislation> (last accessed 28 May 2024).

forces like Igor Kostyukov (GRU), Oleg Salyukov (Ground Forces), Mikhail Mizintsev (Logistical Support), Sergey Surovikin (Aerospace Forces), Andrey Serdyukov and Mikhail Teplinsky (Airborne Forces), Nikolai Yevmenov (Navy) as well as other crucial commanders responsible for the conduct of hostilities like Andrei Aleksandr Dvornikov or Gennady Zhidko.

Apart from governmental and military circles, the role of the private sector which might have been engaged in the preparation for war needs to be examined, including the role of leading Russian oligarchs engaged in particular crucial – from military point of view – industries (oil, gas, or weapons) and who are beneficiaries of the war and allegedly closely cooperated with Putin's administration.[75]

Most of the above mentioned names are already on the European Union or US sanction list, but of course this kind of listing is not a final proof of involvement in aggression.[76] The fact of holding a particular position in the government and in an army should not be treated as a final proof of the guilt as e.g., the Russian Army has its specificity – it is centralized and interpersonal relations play a greater role than official position.[77] What needs to be checked is the fact who participated not only in public or media related gatherings during which crucial decisions were announced but also in closed meetings where decisions were forged and who in reality executed the occupational and annexation policy.

In the context of prosecution of the crime of aggression, it is worth considering the responsibility of those accountable for incitement of this crime i.e., those who publicly encouraged the start of the war of aggression. Eastern European states were among the first ones which introduced a prohibition of war propaganda[78] and appropriate provisions are also included in the Russian criminal code – Article 354

75 *See e.g.*, Grynszpan, Emmanuel, 'Russian Oligarchs Get Richer from the war in Ukraine' *Le Monde* (3 August 2023) <https://www.lemonde.fr/en/international/article/2023/08/03/russian-oligarchs-get-richer-from-the-war-in-ukraine_6077914_4.html> (last accessed 28 May 2024).

76 European Council / Council of the EU Webpage <https://www.consilium.europa.eu/en/policies/sanctions/restrictive-measures-against-russia-over-ukraine/> (last accessed 28 May 2024).

77 Blanc, Alexis A. et al.,*'The Russian General Staff. Understanding the Military's Decision-making Role in a "Besieged Fortress"*, (Rand Corporation, 2023).

78 Art. 113 § 2 of the Polish Criminal Code of 1932 and Art. 229 of Romanian Criminal Code of 1936; *see also* Article 20 of International Covenant on Civil and Political Rights

> [Public Appeals to Unleash an Aggressive War 1. Public appeals to unleash an aggressive war shall be punishable (…) 2. The same deeds, committed with the use of the mass media or by a person who holds a state post of the Russian Federation or a state post of a subject of the Russian Federation, shall be punishable (…).];

as well as in the Ukrainian Criminal Code – Article 435 ["*Public calls to an aggressive war or an armed conflict, and also making of materials with calls to any such actions for distribution purposes or distribution of such materials, shall be punishable* (…)"]. A similar provision is also in Article 123 of the Belarusian Criminal Code and in Codes of other states in the region.[79] The role of war propaganda is enormous in the current conflict and analyses clearly indicate names of persons who encouraged the start of the war against Ukraine and to expand it also to other states.[80]

5 Conclusions

This chapter has proven that the leadership clause of the Rome Statute ("*to exercise control over or to direct*") if understood narrowly, i.e., excluding some civilian officials or representatives of industry, would be against the standard derived from the Nuremberg Charter ("*to shape and influence*") – the standard which was also adopted in the criminal codes of states involved in the current conflict. Thus, this Nuremberg-like standard needs to be considered in the eventual prosecution of the Russian, Belarussian, and Ukrainian perpetrators acting on Russian orders who were responsible for the war of aggression.

The Nuremberg tribunal decided that in a totalitarian state, Hitler could not unleash an aggressive war without other people who supported him. In con-

---

(adopted 16 December 1966, entered into force 23 March 1976) 999 UNTS 171; cf. e.g., ECOSOC Res 306 B (XI) (A/1397 and A/C.3/L.ll2), Interference with Radio Signals (17 November 1950); Kearney, Michael, *Prohibition of Propaganda for War in International Law* (Oxford: Oxford University Press, 2007).

79 *See e.g.,* Art. 117 § 3 of 1997 Polish Criminal Code (Polish Journal of Laws of 2022, item 1138). Polish Criminal Code goes even further than Russian or Ukrainian criminal codes' provisions as it criminalizes not only incitement to initiate a war of aggression, but also public praising of the initiation and waging of war of aggression. Unfortunately, available English versions are not reflecting in full the mentioned provision.

80 Chawryło, Katarzyna, 'Weapons of Mass Deception. Russian Television Propaganda in Wartime' (*OSW Commentary*, 6 May 2022) <https://www.osw.waw.pl/en/publikacje/osw-commentary/2022-05-06/weapons-mass-deception-russian-television-propaganda-wartime> (last accessed 28 May 2024).

sequence, also in the case of Russia – responsibility for the crime of aggression cannot be limited only to Putin – the head of an authoritarian regime. Putin would not be able to engage in different acts of aggression that turned into the full-fledged war of aggression without a number of civilian and military associates who influenced him, supported his decisions, and eagerly implemented them. That is why responsibility for the crime of aggression is borne by dozens of various persons from various circles of power. Not all of those who could be potentially accused with the crime of aggression benefit – based on international law – from personal immunities as members of the Troika or as diplomatic envoys. In addition, the works of the International Law Commission indicate that there is growing support for the opinion according to which involvement in the crime of aggression should not be encompassed by the functional immunity.[81] In consequence, at least some of the potential accused (if not all) can be prosecuted not only in an international court but also in national courts which have jurisdiction over the crime of aggression (which is the case of the majority of Eastern European states).

Responsibility for the crime of aggression should also encompass those who incite to the commission of the crime of aggression, having in mind the well-established norm of international law on prohibition of war propaganda and provisions of national criminal codes.

Responsibility for the crime of aggression should be applied to all distinct stages of Russian aggression thus to those involved in annexation of Crimea, to those who unleashed hostilities in Eastern Ukraine, as well as to those who prepared, initiated, and waged the so-called special operation against Ukraine in 2022 – which should be properly named with a notion of the aggressive war against Ukraine, and to those who prepared the whole process of occupation of the territories in Eastern Ukraine.

---

81 ILC, Report of the ILC, Seventy-seventh Session, Supplement No. 10, UN Doc. A/77/10, 239.

CHAPTER 6

Relevance of Personal Immunities before Treaty-Based International Criminal Courts

Kristýna Urbanová

1 Introduction

While it has been argued that the crucial difference between international and hybrid tribunals lies in the alleged authority of the former to set aside the personal immunities of members of the troika,[1] it is submitted here, that under the current rules of customary international law, a treaty-based international criminal tribunal is equally unable to set aside the personal immunity of an official of a state not party to the treaty constituting such an international tribunal.

It is undisputed that under international law states cannot set aside the personal immunity of officials of other states unless they receive a waiver from such state. It is suggested here that a treaty-based international criminal tribunal derives its powers from constituting states that may waive the personal immunity of *their* officials. Considering that in compliance with rule *pacta tertiis*,[2] the State Party to such an international tribunal cannot waive personal immunity on behalf of the non-participating State and against its will, it is unclear how the participating States could delegate a power that none of them possess on the international tribunal they are creating.

It is submitted here that the only *truly international* tribunal capable of setting aside personal immunities of officials of non-participating states is (i) the tribunal created by the Security Council acting under Chapter 7, alter-

1 Trahan, Jennifer, 'Why a 'Hybrid' Ukrainian Tribunal on the Crime of Aggression is not the Answer' (blog *Justsecurity.org*, 6 February 2023) <https://www.justsecurity.org/85019/why-hybrid-ukrainian-tribunal-on-crime-of-aggression-is-not-the-answer/> (last accessed 30 November 2023); Lipovský, Milan, 'What is a 'certain international criminal court' and Does the Choice of a Fully International or Internationalized (Hybrid) Court/Chambers Matter for the Crime of Aggression Committed against Ukraine?' (2023) *Polish Yearbook of International Law* 213.

2 Art. 34 of the Vienna Convention on the Law of Treaties (adopted 22 May 1969, entered into force 27 January 1980) 1155 UNTS 331.

 | DOI:10.1163/9789004740945_008

natively (ii) other tribunals when their authorization to set aside the immunities results from the Security Council resolution adopted under Chapter 7.

Since the recent debate on the capability of setting aside personal immunities is closely connected to the ICJ judgment in the *Arrest Warrant* Case,[3] the Special Court for Sierra Leone Decision on Immunity of Charles Taylor (*Taylor* Decision),[4] and the ICC Appeals Chamber's judgment on Jordan's Appeal (*Jordan Appeal* Judgment),[5] all these decisions are going to be subject to detailed analysis below. It is submitted here that these decisions are significantly less unequivocal than it is sometimes claimed and their conclusions are often misinterpreted and exaggerated.

For the avoidance of any doubts, it is stated that this piece is concerned solely with personal immunities and not with the immunities *ratione materiae*.

2 ICJ and *Arrest Warrant* Case

Both the Special Court for Sierra Leone (SCSL) in the *Taylor* Decision and the International Criminal Court (ICC) in the *Jordan Appeal* Judgment relied on the International Court of Justice's (ICJ) decision in the *Arrest Warrant* Case. For this reason, it seems necessary at the outset to look at what the ICJ said in that decision, and perhaps even more significantly what the ICJ did not say.

The ICJ first stated that:

> The Court would observe at the outset that in international law it is *firmly established* that, as also diplomatic and consular agents, certain holders of high-ranking office in a State, such as the Head of State, Head of Government and Minister for Foreign Affairs, *enjoy immunities from jurisdiction in other States, both civil and criminal.*[6]

Therefore, it can be safely deduced that for the ICJ the customary law to provide for personal immunities from jurisdiction in other states was uncontro-

3 ICJ, *Arrest Warrant of 11 April 2000* (Democratic Republic of the Congo v Belgium), Judgment of 4 February 2002, ICJ Reports 2002 (*Arrest Warrant*).

4 SCSL, *Prosecutor v Taylor* (Decision on Immunity from Jurisdiction) SCSL-2003-01- I, ACh (31 May 2004).

5 ICC, *Prosecutor v Omar Hassan Ahmad Al-Bashir* (Judgment in the Jordan Referral Re Al-Bashir Appeal) ICC-02/05-01/09-397-Corr, ACh (6 May 2019).

6 ICJ, *Arrest Warrant, supra* note 3, para. 51 (emphasis added).

versial. The chosen wording "*firmly established*" shows the absence of any doubts on the ICJ side.

Subsequently, the ICJ dealt with the arguments of Belgium, which sought to assert that personal immunities cannot provide protection in cases involving suspected war crimes or crimes against humanity. In this regard, Belgium referred to statutes establishing international criminal tribunals, examples from national legislation, and decisions of national and international courts.[7]

However, the ICJ dismissed the argument, holding that it was unable to deduce "*that there exists under customary international law any form of exception to the rule according immunity from criminal jurisdiction and inviolability to incumbent Minister of Foreign Affairs.*"[8] Clearly according to the ICJ, the seriousness or nature of the underpinning act, i.e., war crime or crime against humanity, was insufficient to establish an exception to the rule providing for immunities.

After these conclusions, the ICJ explained that immunities from jurisdiction do not automatically amount to impunity. In this context the ICJ made the following notoriously famous *obiter dicta* statement:

> [...] an *incumbent* or former Minister for Foreign Affairs may be subject to criminal proceedings before *certain* international criminal courts, where they have jurisdiction. Examples include the International Criminal Tribunal for the former Yugoslavia, and the International Criminal Tribunal for Rwanda, established pursuant to Security Council resolutions under Chapter 7 of the United Nations Charter, and the future International Criminal Court created by the 1998 Rome Convention. The latter's Statute expressly provides, in Article 27, paragraph 2, [...][9]

It can be said that according to the ICJ, personal immunities may be set aside by *certain* international criminal courts. However, there is more missing in this famous paragraph than it is said by it.

First, it is unclear what exactly qualifies as a *certain* international criminal court. Second, the ICJ failed to explain 'why'; why states cannot disregard the immunities but certain international criminal tribunals can? The lack of this explanation makes it rather difficult to interpret this statement. Third, it does not determine *to what extent* or concerning whom, in the meaning of state nationality, the international criminal tribunals may disregard personal

7 Ibid, para. 56.
8 Ibid, para. 58.
9 Ibid, para. 60 (emphasis added).

immunities. In other words, even if a hypothetical international criminal court qualifies as the *certain* court that may set aside the personal immunities of *some* officials, does it mean it can disregard the personal immunities of officials of non-participating states? Or is there a difference based on the different legal foundations of such *certain* international criminal courts? The answer to the third question is crucial in assessing whether a treaty-based international criminal court is or is not entitled to set aside the personal immunities of a member of the troika of the state not party to the relevant treaty-based court.

The ICJ provided the following examples as the *certain* criminal tribunals that are authorized to disregard personal immunities (without saying concerning whom): the International Criminal Tribunal for the former Yugoslavia (ICTY) and the International Criminal Tribunal for Rwanda (ICTR) established under Security Council resolutions under Chapter 7 of the United Nations Charter[10]. The ICJ also referred to the International Criminal Court, established by the Rome Statute[11], i.e., an international treaty. Therefore, according to the ICJ, the treaty-based international criminal court may qualify as a *certain* court that may disregard personal immunities. However, the more compelling question is whether this *obiter* remark may serve as a legal basis for setting aside immunities by a treaty-based tribunal concerning a national of a state not party to such an international tribunal. And the ICJ remained silent on this topic.

The ICJ merely referred to the existence of Article 27(2) RS, but it held neither that (i) Article 27(2) reflects customary law, nor (ii) that the ICC is entitled to exercise jurisdiction over a troika member of a state not party to the Rome Statute.

Is it possible that the ICJ meant that there was no impunity because States Parties to the Rome Statute waived their officials' immunities through Article 27(2) RS and that the ICC may set aside personal immunities of officials of the member states? Is it possible that ICJ meant that the ICC may disregard immunities of a national of non-State Party when the Security Council is involved? Is it possible that the ICJ meant that the ICC may set aside the personal immunities of anyone irrespective of the states' membership status? The *Arrest Warrant* judgment does not provide an answer to these questions. Since this statement of the ICJ was made just *obiter dicta*, it is not that surprising that

10 Charter of the United Nations (adopted 26 June 1945, entered into force 24 October 1945) 892 UNTS 119 (UN Charter).

11 Rome Statute of the International Criminal Court (adopted 17 July 1998, entered into force 1 July 2002) 2187 UNTS 3 (Rome Statute or RS).

the ICJ did not provide further explanation. But under these circumstances, it is highly questionable to use such an unclear and *obiter dictum* remark as a legal basis for setting aside personal immunities by a treaty-based international criminal court concerning a high state representative of the non-State Party. The *Arrest Warrant* judgment itself neither negates nor supports such a conclusion.

Nevertheless, this unclear and mere *obiter dictum* remark in the *Arrest Warrant* judgment eventually served as a basis for setting aside the immunities for both, SCSL in *Taylor* Decision and the ICC in the *Jordan Appeal* Judgment.[12]

3 The SCSL and *Taylor* Decision on Immunities

The first relevant court that built its decision on the *Arrest Warrant* judgment was the SCSL. In the *Taylor* Decision, the Appeals Chamber dealt with an application of Charles Taylor, who had been the president of Liberia at the time of the indictment (though not at the time of the process itself).[13] The indictment included crimes against humanity and war crimes and the SCSL also issued a related arrest warrant. Both these documents were issued in June 2003 at a moment when Taylor undertook an official visit to Ghana for peace negotiations. However, the Ghana authorities had failed to execute the arrest. Taylor himself resigned a few months later in August 2003.[14] Charles Taylor challenged the indictment and while referring to the *Arrest Warrant* Case, he stated that as incumbent Head of State at the time of his indictment, he enjoyed absolute immunity from criminal prosecution.[15]

The Appeals Chamber concluded that the official position of Mr. Taylor as an incumbent Head of State at the time when the criminal proceedings were initiated against him did not constitute a bar to his prosecution by the SCSL.[16] In this context, the Appeals Chamber held that

---

12 Nouwen, Sarah, 'Return to Sender: Let the International Court of Justice Justify or Qualify International-Criminal-Court Exceptionalism Regarding Personal Immunities' (2019) 78(3) *Cambridge Law Journal*, 597.

13 For a more detailed analysis of facts, *see* Uhlířová, Kateřina, *Head of State Immunity in International Law – The Charles Taylor Case before the Special Court for Sierra Leone* (Acta Universitatis Brunensis Iuridica, 2013), 38.

14 Nouwen, Sarah, 'The Special Court for Sierra Leone and the Immunity of Taylor: The Arrest Warrant Case Continued' (2005) 18 *Leiden Journal of International Law*, 647.

15 Uhlířová, *supra* note 13, 42.

16 SCSL, *Taylor* Decision, *supra* note 4, para. 53.

> [t]he principle seems now established that the sovereign equality of states does not prevent a Head of State from being prosecuted before an international criminal tribunal or court.[17]

The SCSL reached the cited conclusion on the following basis. First, the Special Court analyzed the legal nature of the SCSL with the result of classifying itself as an international criminal tribunal. Second, it analyzed its own statute and other statutes of different international criminal tribunals or courts and the *Arrest Warrant* judgment, and on this basis, it concluded that as an international criminal tribunal, it may disregard Charles Taylor's immunities. Both these levels of argumentation are analyzed in detail below.

3.1 *The Nature of the Tribunal*

Unlike the ICTY and ICTR, the SCSL was not established by a resolution adopted by the Security Council acting under Chapter 7 of the UN Charter. On 14 August 2000, the Security Council reacting to the serious crimes committed within the territory of Sierra Leone against the people of Sierra Leone and the United Nations and associated personnel and at the prevailing situation of impunity, adopted Resolution 1315.[18] Within the resolution, the Security Council "*reiterated that the situation in Sierra Leone continues to constitute a threat to international peace and security in the region*" and requested the Secretary-General of the United Nations "*to negotiate an agreement with the Government of Sierra Leone to create an independent special court consistent with this resolution.*"[19] But the SCSL was constituted by the Agreement[20] concluded between the United Nations and the government of Sierra Leone while Liberia was not a party to the Agreement.

Therefore, although there was some involvement of the Security Council in the establishment of the SCSL, the involvement was far more indirect than in the case of the ICTY and ICTR, and it is usually accepted that the SCSL was a so-called hybrid tribunal or internationalized tribunal which was not endowed with the coercive powers associated with the Security Council's

17 Ibid, para. 52.

18 UNSC Res 1315 (2000) (14 August 2000).

19 Ibid.

20 Agreement between the United Nations and the Government of Sierra Leone on the Establishment of a Special Court for Sierra Leone (adopted 16 January 2002, entered into force 12 April 2002) 2178 UNTS 137.

resolutions adopted under Chapter 7.[21] Given the nature of the SCSL, the *Taylor* Decision is considered by proponents of the theory of *ius puniendi* as a proof that within the international community, "*have crystallized an exception to the CIL rule on personal immunity through a general practice of States accepted as law.*"[22] This view is not supported here. First, it is questionable whether a judicial decision constitutes 'a general practice of States' and whether the decision was as accepted as assumed there, and second, a closer analysis of the *Taylor* Decision does not seem to provide a solid basis for such a conclusion.

It is worth noting that within the analysis of its 'international nature', the SCSL devoted a significant part of its decision demonstrating an allegedly close link between its existence and the Security Council involvement in its constitution. Thus, the SCSL commenced its analysis with a statement that the founding Agreement was entered into pursuant to Resolution 1315 (2000) and mentioned that subsequent to that resolution, the Security Council sent a mission to Sierra Leone. Then the SCSL continued explaining that

> [a]lthough the Special Court was established by treaty, unlike the ICTY and the ICTR which were each established by resolution of the Security Council in its exercise of powers by virtue of Chapter 7 of the UN Charter, *it was clear that the power of the Security Council to enter into an agreement for the establishment of the court was derived from the Charter of the United Nations both in regard to the general* purposes of the United Nations as expressed in Article 1 of the *Charter and the specific powers of the Security Council in Articles 39 and 41. These powers are wide enough to empower the Security Council to initiate, as it did by Resolution 1315, the establishment of the Special Court by Agreement* with Sierra Leone. Article 39 empowers the Security Council to determine the existence of any threat to the peace. *In Resolution 1315, the Security Council reiterated that the situation in Sierra Leone continued to constitute a threat to international peace and security in the region.*[23]

---

21 Deen-Racsmány, Zsuzsanna, '*Prosecutor v. Taylor*: The Status of the Special Court for Sierra Leone and its Implications for Immunity' (2005) 18 *Leiden Journal of International Law*, 309.

22 Kreß, Claus, 'Article 98' in Ambos, Kai (ed.), *Rome Statute of the International Criminal Court: Article-by-Article Commentary* (München-Oxford-Baden-Baden: Beck-Hart-Nomos, 2022), 2644–2645.

23 SCSL, *Taylor* Decision, *supra* note 4, para. 37 (emphasis added).

The reference to specific powers and Articles 39 and 41 clearly echoes Chapter 7. Correspondingly, the Special Court also referred to the "*high involvement of the Security Council in the establishment of the Court.*"[24] Then, the SCSL remarked that "*the absence of the so-called Chapter VII powers does not by itself define the legal status of the Special Court.*"[25] This does not seem to be a controversial conclusion, because the SCSL was constituted by the Agreement between the UN and Sierra Leone, therefore its international legal status was defined by its international founding act.[26] This on its own should be sufficient to deduce the international (or hybrid) character of the SCSL. However, from the Special Court's own reasoning, it is obvious that it was insufficient for the SCSL itself.

As was shown above, the SCSL felt compelled to strongly emphasize the involvement of the Security Council in its establishment and importantly the related Security Council's powers under Chapter 7. Though such emphasis seems to be unnecessary, it is hard not to notice that this emphasis on the Security Council involvement (and powers under Chapter 7) played an important role for the SCSL itself. The SCSL further deepened this dependence on the alleged Security Council involvement in its key statement, which provided the following:

> It is to be observed that *in carrying out its duties under its responsibility for the maintenance of international peace and security,* ***the Security Council acts on behalf of the members of the United Nations.*** The Agreement between the United Nations and Sierra Leone is *thus an agreement between* ***all*** *members of the United Nations and Sierra Leone.* This fact makes the Agreement an *expression of the will of the international community.* The Special Court established in such circumstances is truly international.[27]

While it is agreed here that due to its constituent instrument, the SCSL was an international court, the arguments provided for this conclusion by the Special Court are highly questionable.

First, the conclusion that the Agreement was an agreement between *all* members of the United Nations is disputable considering that the United Nations as an international organization is endowed with a separate legal

24 Ibid, para. 36.

25 Ibid, para. 38.

26 Nouwen, *supra* note 14, 650.

27 SCSL, *Taylor* Decision, *supra* note 4, para. 38 (emphasis added).

personality distinctive of its member states.[28] However, the possible legal consequences of the said SCSL's statement appear to be even more questionable. Does it mean that this legal construction would represent a waiver of personal immunities of *all* possible officials of *all* UN Member States, including Liberia? Would it mean that an international criminal tribunal founded by a treaty between the United Nations and one state could set aside personal immunities of any official of any member state and that all member states would be under obligation to cooperate with such tribunal? Despite of the absence of coercive powers associated with the Security Council's resolutions adopted under chapter 7?

The wording of the SCSL's Statute suggest contrary to such extensive interpretation in case of the Special Court for Sierra Leone. According to Article 17 of the Statute "*the Government shall cooperate with all organs of the Special Court at all stages of the proceedings.*"[29] The word "Government" refers only to the government of the Sierra Leone.[30] Accordingly, the legal doctrine has also supported the view that the Agreement between the United Nations and Sierra Leone was binding only on the United Nations and Sierra Leone. In this context, Antonio Cassese argued that the Agreement "*is only binding upon the United Nations and Sierra Leone. It is not binding upon third countries, in particular, neighbouring countries.*"[31] Similarly, Fox claimed that "[s]*ince the Special Court was set up by treaty between Sierra Leone and the United Nations; no other state is party to this treaty and hence is not bound by it.*"[32] This interpretation would result in the effect that other States, Ghana included, would not be bound by the Agreement.[33]

Considering that the Agreement and the Statute of the SCSL did not anyhow provide for obligations of other states than Sierra Leone, the above-cited conclusions of the legal doctrine sound convincing. That seemed to also be the position of Liberia which filed for a proceedings before the ICJ claiming that

---

28 ICJ, *Reparation for Injuries Suffered in the Service of the United Nations*, Advisory Opinion, ICJ Reports 1949, 174 – 180.

29 Annex to the Agreement between the United Nations and the Government of Sierra Leone, *supra* note 20, Art. 17.

30 Ibid, Preamble.

31 Cassese, Antonio, 'The Role of Internationalized Courts and Tribunals in the Fight Against International Criminality' in Romano, Cesare P. R., Nollkaemper, André, Kleffner, Jaan K. (eds.), *Internationalized Criminal Courts: Sierra Leone, East Timor, Kosovo and Cambodia* (Oxford University Press, 2004), 9.

32 Fox, Hazel, *The Law of State Immunity* (Oxford University Press, 2004), 23.

33 Uhlířová, *supra* note 13, 66.

the SCSL's indictment and arrest warrant failed to respect the personal immunity.[34]

In this context it is fundamentally important to notice the reason why the SCSL considered the Agreement as being concluded between all UN member states and thus expressing the will of international community. Most importantly that it was not merely for the reason that one party of the Agreement were the United Nations. The decisive element for the SCSL was the repeatedly highlighted involvement of the Security Council in the establishment of the Special Court.

This is most visibly clear from the wording of the above-cited paragraph 38 of the *Taylor* Decision. The SCSL declared that "*in carrying out its duties under its* responsibility for the maintenance of international peace and security" which clearly echoes the Chapter 7 powers, "the Security Council acts on behalf of the members *of the United Nations."* On this basis the Special Court concluded that "[t]*he Agreement between the United Nations and Sierra Leone* is thus *an agreement between* all members *of the United Nations and Sierra Leone. This fact makes the Agreement an* expression of the will of the international community." Therefore, according to the SCSL the Agreement was concluded between *all* members of the UN because Security Council, when acting under Chapter 7, acts on behalf of all members of the UN.

While this legal construction does not seem to be persuasive because the involvement of the Security Council in the establishment of the SCSL was too indirect, and it is also subject to doubts whether Resolution 1315 (2000) was adopted under Chapter 7,[35] it represented an important corner stone in the SCSL's conclusion of being truly international.

After establishing that the SCSL was the *truly international court*, the SCSL determined that it is the different nature of the tribunals which is relevant for the question if there is an exception from rule on immunity.[36] Then the SCSL referred to Article 6(2) of its Statute which provides that "[t]*he official position of any accused persons, whether as Head of State or Government or as a responsible government official, shall not relieve such person of criminal responsibility nor mitigate punishment.*" The SCSL also compared this Article with the similar provisions in the ICTY Statute, ICTR Statute, Rome Statute, Nuremberg Charter, and Nuremberg Principle III.[37] This line of arguments also caries certain weak points, but since a similar line of arguments was later also pre-

34 Ibid, 65.

35 Nouwen, *supra* note 14, 651; Deen-Racsmány, *supra* note 21, 310–313.

36 SCSL, *Taylor* Decision, *supra* note 4, para. 49.

37 Ibid, paras. 45–46.

sented in the *Jordan Appeal* Judgment, it will be critically addressed below within the analysis of the *Jordan Appeal* Judgment.

What is more important is that the SCSL was probably itself highly aware that its alleged powers to set aside Charles Taylor's personal immunities were rather fragile. It follows from its reliance on the alleged role of the Security Council and its powers under Chapter 7 in establishing the SCSL in order to identify its truly international nature. This reliance thus helped the SCSL to bypass the problematic issue. As it was shown above, the reasoning is rather unconvincing. However, regardless of the highly questionable persuasiveness, it is even more important to see that this alleged and repeatedly highlighted involvement of the Security Council and its powers under Chapter 7 in the establishment of the Special Court was the crucial element for the Special Court itself and the key point which enabled the SCSL to disregard Taylor's immunities.

The reasoning of the SCSL thus strongly undermines the proposition that the *Taylor* Decision provides support for the conclusion that personal immunities of an official of non-State Party are inapplicable before the international criminal tribunal which is not backed by these coercive powers of the Security Council.[38]

4 ICC and *Omar Al Bashir* Case

Personal immunities became highly topical issue after the ICC issued two warrants of arrest for at that time Sudanese president Omar al Bashir. Since the ICC was a treaty-based international court and Sudan was not a party to the Rome Statute, it was clear that Sudan did not waive personal immunities of its officials via ratifying the Rome Statute. However, Sudan has been a member state of the United Nations and the related situation in Darfur was referred to the ICC by the Security Council acting under Chapter 7, in accordance with Article 13(b) of the Rome Statute. The Security Council triggered the exercise of the ICC's jurisdiction by Resolution 1593.[39]

In Resolution 1593 (2005) the Security Council explicitly stated that the Security Council: (i) is acting under Chapter 7, (ii) is referring the situation in Darfur since 1 July 2002 to the Prosecutor of the ICC, (iii) decides that the Government of Sudan and all other parties to the conflict in Darfur, shall

38 Heller, Kevin J., 'Options for Prosecuting Russian Aggression against Ukraine: A Critical Analysis' (2022) *Journal of Genocide Research* 26.

39 UNSC Res 1593 (2005) (31 March 2005).

cooperate fully with and provide any necessary assistance to the Court and the Prosecutor pursuant to this resolution, and (iv), while recognizing that states not party to the Rome Statute have no obligation under the Statute, urges all states and concerned regional and other international organizations to cooperate fully.

The central issue was whether the ICC was authorized to request the States Parties to the Statute for the arrest and surrender of Omar al Bashir and whether the States Parties were obliged to execute such request when Omar al Bashir was located in their territory due to an official visit.

The key provisions of the Rome Statute are Articles 27(2) and 98(1). Article 27(2) provides that "[i]mmunities *or special procedural rules* which may attach to the official capacity of a person, *whether under national or international law,* shall not bar the Court from exercising its jurisdiction over such a person (emphasis added)."

Article 98(1) (Cooperation with respect to waiver of immunity and consent to surrender) stipulates the following:

> The Court may not proceed with a request for surrender or assistance which would require the requested State to act inconsistently with its obligations under international law with respect to the State or diplomatic immunity *of a person or property of a third State*, unless the Court can first obtain the cooperation of that third State for the waiver *of the immunity.*
>
> (emphasis added)

In this context, several States Parties refused to arrest al Bashir when he visited their territory arguing that Article 98(1) of the Rome Statute prohibits the Court from proceeding with the request for arrest if such request would create a conflict of obligations on behalf of the States Parties. In their view the States Parties were obliged to respect President al Bashir Head of State's immunities and such obligation did not vanish by effect of Article 27(2) of the Rome Statute, because this article represents a waiver of the personal immunities of the States Parties, among which Sudan did not belong. In addition, a number of resolutions issued by the African Union urged its member states not to execute the arrest warrant concerning President al Bashir referring to Article 98(1) of the Rome Statute.[40]

40 African Union (Assembly) 'Decision on the Meeting of African States Parties to the Rome Statute of the International Criminal Court (ICC) Doc. Assembly/AU/13(XIII)' (3 July 2009), Assembly/AU/Dec.245(XIII) Rev. 1 (3 July 2009 AU Decision), para. 10; African

Dealing with the non-cooperative attitude of a number of States Parties, different Pre-Trial Chambers took different views. In summary, these diverse reasonings can be categorized as: (i) there is an exception from the immunities before an international criminal court, (ii) the waiver of the immunities was effectively provided by the Security Council Resolution 1593, (iii) the Security Council Resolution 1593 put Sudan in a position analogous with the States Parties to the Rome Statute and the States Parties waived the immunities via ratifying the Rome Statute Article 27 included.[41]

The first Pre-Trial Chamber that addressed the issue was the Pre-Trial Chamber I (PTChI) in a decision concerning the failure of Malawi to execute the warrant of arrest. The PTChI referred to *Arrest Warrant* judgment, *Taylor* Decision, *Milosevic* trial and concluded that "*customary international law creates an exception to Head of State immunity when international court seeks a Head of State's arrest for commission of international crimes.*"[42] Regarding Article 98(1) of the Rome Statute, the Pre-Trial Chamber I took a view that as a result of the stated exception, Article 98(1) does not apply because there are no conflicting obligations of the requested state.[43] The PTChI opined that "*when cooperating with this Court and therefore acting on its behalf, States Parties are instruments for the enforcement of the jus puniendi of the international community whose exercise has been entrusted to this Court when States have failed to prosecute those responsible for the crimes within its jurisdiction.*"[44]

This line of 'surrogacy' argumentation placing States Parties into a position of a mere instrument of the ICC was also invoked later in a general discussion of the Appeals Chamber in the *Jordan Appeal* Judgment and therefore will be subject to critical analysis below. However, it is submitted here that the

Union (Assembly) 'Decision on the Progress Report of the Commission on the Implementation of Decision Assembly/AU/Dec.270(XIV) on the Second Ministerial Meeting on the Rome Statute of the International Criminal Court (ICC) Doc. Assembly/AU/10 (XV)' (27 July 2010), Assembly/AU/Dec.296(XV), paras. 5–6; African Union (Assembly) 'Decision on the Implementation of the Decisions on the International Criminal Court (ICC) Doc. EX.CL/639(XVIII)' (30–31 January 2011), Assembly/AU/Dec.334(XVI), para. 5; African Union (Assembly) 'Decision on the Implementation of the Assembly Decisions on the International Criminal Court – Doc. EX.CL/670(XIX)' (30 June–1 July 2011), Assembly/AU/Dec.366(XVII) (30 June–1 July 2011 AU Decision).

41 Nouwen, *supra* note 12, 600–603.

42 ICC, *Prosecutor v Omar Hassan Ahmad Al Bashir* (Decision Pursuant to Article 87(7) of the Rome Statute on the Failure by the Republic of Malawi to Comply with the Cooperation Requests Issued by the Court with Respect to the Arrest and Surrender of Omar Hassan Ahmad Al Bashir) ICC-02/05-01/09-139, PTChI (12 December 2011), para. 43.

43 Ibid, para. 43.

44 Ibid, para. 46.

PTChI failed to preserve any possible meaning of Article 98(1) and effectively deprived this Article of any meaning (in detail, see below the analysis concerned with the *Jordan Appeal* Judgment). The PTChI referred to *Malawi* decision and adopted the same lines of reasons also in the decision concerning the failure to cooperate of the Republic of Chad.[45]

However, a considerably different view was taken by the Pre-Trial Chamber II (PTChII) in its *Democratic Republic of Congo* (DRC) non-cooperation decision. The PTChII considered Article 27(2) of the Rome Statute to be an explicit treaty exception to the rule of personal immunities which in accordance with rules governing international treaties should be confined to the States Parties which have accepted it and could not impose obligations on third states without their consent.[46]

According to the PTChII, in the situation when the ICC seeks prosecution of a head of a non-party state, the question of immunities may validly arise. Therefore, Article 98(1) of the Rome Statute directed the Court to secure the cooperation of the third State for the waiver or lifting of the immunity of its Head of State.[47] However, in the case of Sudan, the PTChII opined that the waiver of the immunities required by Article 98(1) was ensured by Security Council Resolution 1593. Since according to this resolution, Sudan was obliged to *"cooperate fully"* and to *"provide any necessary assistance to the Court"*, the Security Council thus waived the immunities granted to President al Bashir. Therefore, there were no conflicting obligations for the DRC, since the immunities in question were lifted by the Security Council acting under Chapter 7.[48]

The PTChII clearly did not embrace the PTChI's argument based on the international law exception from immunities before international courts and associated inapplicability of Article 98. It can be criticized that the Security Council remained silent on issue of immunities and since the Council referred to the ICC the 'situation' of Sudan which is far broader concept then the 'case' concerning Omar al Bashir, the Security Council did not necessarily have to foresee that a situation of Darfur would develop into a case concerning the president. Nevertheless, it is fundamental to note that for the PTChII the

---

45 ICC, *Prosecutor v Omar Hassan Ahmad Al Bashir* (Decision Pursuant to Article 87(7) of the Rome Statute on the Refusal of the Republic of Chad to Comply with the Cooperation Requests Issued by the Court with Respect to the Arrest and Surrender of Omar Hassan Ahmad Al Bashir) ICC-02/05-01/09-140, PTChI (13 December 2011), para. 13.

46 ICC, *Prosecutor v Omar Hassan Ahmad Al Bashir* (Decision on the Cooperation of the Democratic Republic of the Congo Regarding Omar Al Bashir's Arrest and Surrender to the Court) ICC-02/05-01/09-195, PTChII (9 April 2014), para. 26.

47 Ibid, paras. 26–27.

48 Ibid, para. 29.

decisive element for the obligation of the State Party to cooperate with the Court was the existence and wording of the Security Council resolution adopted under Chapter 7.

A few years later in the decision concerned with a non-cooperation of South Africa, the PTChII developed an alternative approach. It stated that "[t]*he Chamber is unable to identify a rule in customary international law that would exclude immunity for Heads of State when their arrest is sought for international crimes by another State, even when the arrest is sought on behalf of an international court, including, specifically, this Court.*"[49] It also explained that the States Parties cannot invoke their own immunities and cannot refuse to comply with a request by the Court for the arrest of a person of another State Party "*as any possible immunity vis-à-vis the Court has been rendered inapplicable with the ratification of the Rome Statute.*"[50] The ICC did not leave any space for doubts and explicitly added that "[i]*t is evident that this applies* only to States *that have consented to such a regime, which are in the first instance States Parties to the Statute and States which accept the jurisdiction of the Court.*"[51]

This statement represented an obvious rejection of the reasoning put forward in the *Malawi* decision, however the PTChII found its own reasons for finding South Africa obliged to cooperate with the Court. Once again it relied on effect of Resolution 1593 but it considered that effect from a different angle than within the *DRC* decision. The PTChII interpreted the Security Council's referral and the imposition of the obligation on Sudan to cooperate fully with the Court as putting Sudan, for the limited purpose of the situation in Darfur, into a position analogous to those of States Parties. The first consequence thus was that Article 27(2) of the Rome Statute was also applicable to Sudan, and second, that al Bashir's immunities were inapplicable to the States Parties complying with the request of the ICC (concerning solely the situation in Darfur).[52]

The Pre-Trial Chambers' practice shows that while all of them reached the same conclusion, it happened for fundamentally different reasons. While in *Malawi* the PTChI identified the exception from the customary international

49 ICC, *Prosecutor v Omar Hassan Ahmad Al Bashir* (Decision under Article 87(7) of the Rome Statute on the Non-compliance by South Africa with the Request by the Court for the Arrest and Surrender of Omar Al-Bashir) ICC-02/05-01/09-302, PTChII (6 July 2017), para. 68.

50 Ibid, para. 80.

51 Ibid, para. 82.

52 Ibid, paras. 87–93.

law of immunities before international criminal courts and pronounced on inapplicability of Article 98(1) of the Rome Statute, the essential element for the PTChII was the Security Council resolution adopted under Chapter 7.

In the decision on non-cooperation concerning *Jordan*, the PTChII chose the same approach as it had done in the *South Africa* decision, and relied on Resolution 1593 and its alleged effect of putting Sudan into a position analogous with a State Party to the Rome Statute.[53]

5 The *Jordan Appeal* Judgment

When Jordan filed its appeal against the Pre-Trial Chamber II's decision, the Appeals Chamber eventually got the chance to unify the diverse opinions produced by the Pre-Trial Chambers and to put some clarity on the ICC's position regarding the personal immunities of an official of a non-State Party member (though under modified circumstances due to Resolution 1593).

The Appeals Chamber confirmed the obligation of Jordan to comply with the Court's request for the arrest and surrender of Omar al Bashir. However, it failed to be sufficiently unequivocal on the underlying reasons, and some conclusions are not persuasively argued.[54]

In addition, a careful reading of the judgment reveals that there is a significant difference between the reasons provided by the Appeals Chamber in a general discussion and the reasoning presented in the individual findings (see below). Moreover, the Appeals Chamber chose a rather vague and ambiguous narrative. This ambiguity is further deepened by the Joint Concurring Opinion which was signed by 4 of 5 Appeals Chamber judges. It will be shown below that all these documents suffer from vagueness and may lead to contradictory conclusions.

53 ICC, *Prosecutor v Omar Hassan Ahmad Al Bashir* (Decision under Article 87(7) of the Rome Statute on the Non-compliance by Jordan with the Request by the Court for the Arrest and Surrender of Omar Al-Bashir) ICC-02/05-01/09-309, PTChII (11 December 2017), paras. 33–39.

54 Nouwen, *supra* note 12, 604; Galand, Alexandre S., 'A Hidden Reading of the ICC Appeals Chamber's Judgment in the Jordan Referral Re Al-Bashir' (blog *Ejiltalk.org*, 6 June 2019) <https://www.ejiltalk.org/a-hidden-reading-of-the-icc-appeals-chambers-judgment-in-the-jordan-referral-re-al-bashir/> (last accessed 9 November 2023).

5.1 The Jordan Appeal *Judgment* Eventually Supports the 'Security Council Route'

Certain authors use the Appeals Chamber's (ACh's) decision on Jordan's obligation to cooperate to support the view that there is not a customary international rule of personal immunity before sufficiently representative treaty-based international criminal tribunal (of even the officials of a state not party to such treaty).[55] However, it is submitted here that even if the judgment were to be accepted without any criticism, rather the *Jordan Appeal* Judgment eventually provides for the Security Council route. The careful reading of the judgment and the Joint Concurring Opinion reveals that the initial 'progressive' part is eventually seriously undermined by the latter parts and individual findings made in the judgment.

It is true that the Appeals Chamber started its analysis by stating that "[t]*he most direct effect of Article 27(2) of the Statute is that a Head of State cannot claim Head of State immunity when he or she appears before the ICC for prosecution in accordance with the provisions on the exercise of jurisdiction*" and added that Article 27(2) of the Statute "*reflects the status of customary international law.*"[56] After referring to several international instruments (see below in detail), the *Taylor* Decision, and the *Malawi* decision, the ACh found that these decisions confirmed the "*the absence of a rule of customary international law recognising Head of State immunity before international courts in the exercise of jurisdiction.*"[57] The ACh did not seem to be occupied with the fact that both, *Taylor* and *Malawi* decisions did not recognize the absence of such a rule of customary international law, but were of the opinion that customary law creates an *exception* to Head of State immunity,[58] which is a significantly different test than the one provided by the Appeals Chamber.

According to the Appeals Chamber, the alleged absence of a rule of customary international law recognizing Head of State immunity *vis-à-vis* international courts is relevant also for the horizontal relationship when a state is requested by an international court to arrest the Head of State of another State.[59] In the section dealing with the horizontal effect of Article 27(2) of the Rome Statute, the Appeals Chamber initially seems to adopt the *Malawi* 'sur-

---

55 Kreß, Claus, 'Article 98' in Ambos, Kai (ed.), *Rome Statute of the International Criminal Court: Article-by-Article Commentary* (München-Oxford-Baden-Baden: Beck-Hart -Nomos, 2022), 2639; Trahan, *supra* note 1.

56 ICC, *Jordan Appeal* Judgment, *supra* note 5, paras. 102 -103.

57 Ibid, para. 114.

58 SCSL, *Taylor* Decision, *supra* note 4, para. 49; ICC, Malawi decision *supra* note 42, para. 43.

59 ICC, *Jordan Appeal* Judgment, *supra* note 5, paras. 114, 127.

rogacy' argument by stating that following the international court's requests, the requested state is only lending assistance to the Court.[60] This would suggest that the requested state does not exercise its own jurisdiction, and therefore is not obliged to respect personal immunities.[61]

However, the further analysis and conclusions reached by the Appeals Chamber distinctively differ from the previous statement. Thus, in its conclusion, the Appeals Chamber stated:

> In sum, the Appeals Chamber finds that, by *ratifying or acceding to the Statute, States Parties have consented to the inapplicability of Head of State immunity* for the purpose of proceedings before the Court. As a result, both in the ***State Parties'*** *vertical relationship with the Court and in the horizontal relationship between* ***States Parties*** *there is no Head of State immunity* if the Court is asking for the arrest and surrender of a person. Therefore, the Pre-Trial Chamber correctly found that a *State Party cannot refuse to arrest and surrender the Head of State of* ***another State Party*** on the ground of Head of State immunity.[62]

The ACh thus found that at vertical and horizontal levels, there is no Head of State immunity in the States Parties' relationship with the ICC and between States Parties.

This is a significantly narrower standard than the suggestions made in the previous part of the judgment. It seems that according to the Appeals Chamber, the argument based on lending mere assistance to the Court is applicable *only* in the relationships of States Parties to the Statute. Moreover, the ACh also found the absence of Head of State immunity in the relationship between States Parties and the ICC. But notably, the ACh was silent on the possible inapplicability of the immunities of officials of states not party to the statute.

This narrower interpretation of the judgment is further supported by the subsequent analysis conducted by the Appeals Chamber. After the cited conclusion, the Court analyzed the effect of Resolution 1593 arguing that this Resolution modified the legal obligations of concerned states and brought Sudan under the Rome Statute cooperation regime, which prevented Sudan

60 Ibid, para. 127.

61 Kreß, Claus, 'The International Criminal Court and Immunities under International Law for States Not Party to the Court's Statute' in Bergsmo, Morten, Ling, Yan (ed.), *State Sovereignty and International Criminal Law* (FICH Publication Series No. 15, 2012), 246–250.

62 ICC, *Jordan Appeal* Judgment, *supra* note 5, para. 132 (emphasis added).

from invoking personal immunities. It stated that the legal obligations under Resolution 1593 prevailed as *lex specialis* over any immunity that would otherwise exist between Sudan and Jordan.[63] This part of the *Jordan Appeal* Judgment thus supports the view that the customary law argument was not an independent route for the ACh and reminds the PTChII's reasoning in the *South Africa* decision based on Security Council action under chapter 7.[64]

The reliance on Resolution 1593 is also visible in the Joint Concurring Opinion.[65] The judges started their dispositive consideration stating that

> [...] this case immediately concerns the application of Security Council resolution 1593 (2005) and the Rome Statute [...] But that primary focus must also take customary international law into account, in the sense of considering whether there is any extent to which it obstructs the operation of resolution 1593 (2005) and the Rome Statute.[66]

Furthermore, the judges also completed their analysis of the 'surrogacy' argument with the following statement:

> It is important to stress, in this connection, that this conclusion, as it specifically concerns Security Council resolution 1593 (2005), depends on the unique circumstances of that resolution as a Chapter 7 measure, which all UN Member States are obligated (or expected) to implement.[67]

The judges thus pointed out that at the heart of this case stood Resolution 1593 which created a unique situation. Moreover, customary law was taken into account in a very limited way – that is only in connection with whether it obstructs the operation of the resolution or the Rome Statute.

The view that the ACh eventually relied on Resolution 1593 is further supported by another part of the Joint Concurring Opinion. In para. 450 of the JCO, the judges explained their view on the principle of effectiveness stating that a rule of customary law operating at the horizontal level cannot operate reasonably to frustrate the jurisdiction of an international criminal tribunal.

---

63 Ibid, paras. 144–146.

64 Nouwen, *supra* note 12, 606; Galand, *supra* note 54, 1.

65 ICC, Joint Concurring Opinion of Judges Eboe-Osuji, Morrison, Hofmański and Bossa to Judgment in the Jordan Referral Re Al-Bashir Appeal, ICC-02/05-01/09-397-Anx1 (6 May 2019) (Joint Concurring Opinion or JCO).

66 Ibid, para. 269.

67 Ibid, para. 445.

Then the judges analyzed in what situations therefore states cannot successfully invoke immunities and explained that "*in the circumstances of Article 98(1) of the Rome Statute the difficulty presented to the assertion of immunity at the horizontal plane involves three scenarios*":

- the first scenario covered the situation when the State Party was requested to execute a request concerning an official of another State Party (i.e., the State Party–State Party situation),
- the second scenario addressed the situation of the UN Member State (not party to the Statute) and State Party, when the Security Council adopted a resolution under Chapter 7 specifically requiring the third state to cooperate fully with the ICC, and
- the third scenario was concerned with a situation of two UN Member States not parties to the Rome Statute, when the Security Council made referral under article 13(b) of the Rome Statute and merely urged the States to cooperate with the ICC. Here, the result depended on the text of the resolution and it could create just expectations, not obligations to cooperate.

While the analysis may be subject to some criticism, it is evident that the judges were typologically considering only two situations when states may disregard personal immunities following the request of the ICC: (i) when both concerned States were States Parties to the Statute, or (ii) the Security Council adopted the appropriate resolution under Chapter 7. On the other hand, one possible scenario is notably missing in the Joint Concurring Opinion – the scenario of a State Party requested by the ICC to cooperate concerning an official of a non-State Party in a situation where the Security Council resolution was not adopted.[68] The judges refrained from claiming that a State Party would be obliged to comply with a request concerning a non-State Party when the Security Council resolution under Chapter 7 is not present.

The foregoing analysis showed that the judges did not adopt the 'surrogacy' argument universally but limited its effect to situations of State Party – State Party relationship, or when there is a Security Council resolution adopted under Chapter 7.[69] Both, the *Jordan Appeal* Judgment and the JCO eventually heavily relied on this Resolution 1593 to establish Jordan's obligation to comply with the request of the ICC. It is therefore submitted that even if the judgment is embraced uncritically, it does not provide for obligations to comply with the request of a treaty-based tribunal unless (i) the request is concerned with the State Party – State Party relationship, or (ii) in the situation when the

68 Galand, *supra* note 54, 3.

69 Nouwen, *supra* note 12, 607.

Security Council adopted a resolution under Chapter 7 modifying the underlying obligations of the States.

5.2 *A Critical Analysis of the Appeals Chamber's Finding that There Is No Rule of Customary Law Recognizing Personal Immunities before International Courts*

It was already shown that the Appeals Chamber referred to *Taylor* and *Malawi* decisions stating that in both cases the courts "*have adequately and correctly confirmed the absence of a rule of customary international law recognising Head of State immunity before international courts in the exercise of jurisdiction.*"[70]

However, despite of this Appeals Chamber's proclamation, the SCSL in the *Taylor* Decision and PTChI in the *Malawi* decision had taken a significantly different approach and were of the opinion that there was an *exception* to a rule of personal immunity before international criminal courts. The Appeals Chamber on the other hand claimed that "*there is neither State practice nor opinio juris that would support the existence of Head of State immunity under customary international law vis-à-vis an international court.*"[71] The Appeals Chamber therefore reversed the test, and as a result of this reversion, the burden of proof was on Jordan to prove that there had been a sufficient practice and *opinio iuris* supporting the existence of a rule of personal immunities before international criminal courts.

5.2.1 The Alleged Different Nature of the International Criminal Court

In its analysis the Appeals Chamber relied (as well as the SCSL) on the alleged difference between the character of national and international courts.

The ACh was of the opinion that while national courts "*are essentially an expression of a State's sovereign power, which is necessarily limited by the sovereign power of the other States*", the international courts

> do not act on behalf of a particular State or States. Rather, international courts act on behalf of the international community as a whole. Accordingly, the principle of par in parem non habet imperium, which is based on the sovereign equality of States finds no application in relation to an international court such as the International Criminal Court.[72]

---

70 ICC, *Jordan Appeal* Judgment, *supra* note 5, paras. 113–114.

71 Ibid, para. 113.

72 Ibid, para. 115.

While the SCSL referred to an exception to the rule on immunity, it was also similarly of the view that "*the* nature *of the Tribunals has always been a relevant consideration in the question whether there is an exception to the principle of immunity.*"[73]

First, it is submitted here that the Appeals Chamber as well as the SCSL put too much emphasis on the principle of equality of states in connection to personal immunities. Both these courts failed to take into account that the rationale behind personal immunities is not limited to the principle *par in parem non habet imperium*.[74] It is true that, one of the reasons behind personal immunities is to preclude any intervention of a state into internal matters of another state, which is associated with the principle of equality of states.[75] The ICJ explained that the rationale behind the personal immunities is also to secure the possibility of troika members to exercise their functions without any concerns. As the ICJ put it,

> even the mere risk that, by traveling to or transiting another State a Minister of Foreign Affairs might be exposing himself or herself to legal proceedings could deter Minister from traveling internationally when required to do so for the purposes of the performance of his or her official functions.[76]

The unconcerned exercise of the functions is not to be jeopardized only by potential national prosecution, but as well by prosecution of an international court. The risk of exposure to arrest as described by the ICJ would be present in both cases, in the latter at the request of the international court. But the effect of the national/international prosecution on the exercise of the troika's functions would be identical. The recent cancelation of the Russian president's official visit of South Africa to avoid the possible execution of the arrest warrant issued by the ICC provides obvious support for such a conclusion.[77] Therefore, the potentially destabilizing effect is connected to both inter-

73 SCSL, *Taylor* Decision, *supra* note 4, para. 49 (emphasis added).

74 ICJ, *Arrest Warrant, supra* note 3, para. 54.

75 Akande, Dapo and Shah, Sangeeta, 'Immunities of State Officials, International Crimes and Foreign Domestic Courts: A Rejoinder to Alexander Orakhelashvili' (2011) 22 *European Journal of International Law* 3, 824.

76 ICJ, *Arrest Warrant, supra* note 3, para. 54.

77 *See e.g.*, McKenzie, David, 'Putin Will Not Attend BRICS Summit in South Africa, as ICC Arrest Warrant Overshadows Key Talks' *CNN* (20 July 2023) <https://edition.cnn.com/2023/07/19/world/putin-brics-summit-south-africa-intl/index.html> (last accessed 30 November 2023).

national and national prosecution. It does not seem that international prosecution is able to provide any more safeguards to protect these reasons behind personal immunities than the national prosecution.

Second, the states create both, the national courts and the international courts as well. The latter ones are created (in the case of treaty-based tribunals) by an international treaty. The capability to conclude or enter into international treaties is nothing else than a manifestation of a state's sovereign power. Therefore, international courts do derive their powers from their creators in equal manners to national courts. States merely exercise their sovereign power in a manner that they delegate the judicial powers to an international institution. Such an international institution thus also derives its powers from the sovereign powers of the states. There is no other source of its powers than the powers delegated by its creators, i.e., states. Then, it is hard to see, how such an institution created by the states can exceed the powers of its creators.[78]

Although both the SCSL and the ICC referred to the *Arrest Warrant* judgment, it was shown above that the ICJ neither stated that the alleged differences would have been in the 'international community mandate', nor provided the basis for the alleged safeguard against the destabilizing effect. The *Arrest Warrant* judgment was also silent on a possibility of a treaty-based tribunal powers to disregard immunities of official of state not party to such treaty.

Both the SCSL and the ICC failed to answer the question of how is it possible that two or even 150 states together are allowed to create an entity which is authorized to do something that none, not a single one, of its founders, is under "*firmly established*" law authorized to do. The so-called 'international community mandate' represents a strong clash with the principle that no one can transfer more rights (to another) than themselves have (*Nemo plus iuris ad alium transferre potest quam ipse habet*).

The explanation of such a clash cannot be validly provided by referring to the example of the Security Council establishing the ad hoc tribunals by its resolutions adopted under Chapter 7.[79] The Security Council acting under Chapter 7 is endowed with *coercive* powers and the resolutions adopted

---

78 Heller, *supra* note 38; Akande, Dapo, 'International Law Immunities and the International Criminal Court' (2004) 98 *American Journal of International Law* 3, 417; Nouwen, *supra* note 12.

79 Schabas, William, *The International Criminal Court, A Commentary on the Rome Statute* (Oxford University Press, 2010), 450.

under Chapter 7 are binding on all member states. Moreover, in accordance with Article 103 of the UN Charter, the obligations under the Charter prevail over other international obligations of the member states. By accepting the UN Charter, the member states of the United Nations expressed their consent to such coercive power and binding effect of these resolutions.

However, in the case of a treaty-based tribunal that was not established by the Security Council acting under Chapter 7, the coercive powers are not present, and neither is the equivalent consent of the third state that is not party to that treaty. Therefore, it is submitted here that typologically only those international criminal tribunals established by the Security Council resolution adopted under Chapter 7 are entitled to set aside the personal immunities of an official of any UN Member State due to the coercive powers vested in the Security Council within the Chapter 7. The treaty-based international tribunals could (if their constitutive instrument provides accordingly) disregard the personal immunities of the officials of the states providing consent to such treaty or if the Security Council adopts an appropriate resolution under Chapter 7 in that regard.

5.2.2 What Practice and *Opinio Iuris* Could Hypothetically Satisfy the ACh Test?

The Appeals Chamber itself confirmed that in inter-state relations a rule providing for personal immunities is firmly established in international law and that immunity prevents one state from exercising jurisdiction over the head of another state.[80] However on the international level, the Appeals Chamber took the view that "*there is neither State practice nor opinio juris that would support the existence of Head of State immunity under customary international law vis-à-vis an international court.*"[81] The crucial question is what could possibly constitute a hypothetical practice and *opinio iuris* supporting the existence of a rule of personal immunities before international criminal courts.

Concerning state practice and *opinio iuris* both, the SCSL and the ICC supported their conclusions by comparing various international legal instruments. Therefore, it is necessary to carefully read these international instruments and compare them with the Rome Statute. Moreover, it is necessary to focus on their wording and analyze in what article of the Rome Statute these instruments are reflected, and in what Article of the Rome Statute they are not.

The text of the relevant international instruments is as follows:

80 Ibid, para. 101.
81 Ibid, para. 113.

- **IMT in Nuremberg, Charter Article 7**: "*The official position of defendants, whether as Heads of State or responsible officials in Government Departments, shall* not be considered as freeing them from ***responsibility*** or mitigating punishment."
- **Nuremberg Principle III**: "*The fact that a person who committed an act which constituted a crime under international law acted as Head of State or responsible official* does not relieve him from ***responsibility*** under international law."
- **ICTY, Article 7(2) of the Statute**: "*The official position of any accused person, whether as Head of State or Government or as a responsible Government official, shall* not relieve such person of criminal ***responsibility*** nor mitigate punishment."
- **ICTR, Article 6(2) of the Statute**: "*The official position of any accused person, whether as Head of state or government or as a responsible government official, shall* not relieve such person of criminal ***responsibility*** nor mitigate punishment."
- **SCSL, Article 6 of the Statute**: "*The official position of any accused persons, whether as Head of State or Government or as responsible Government Official, shall* not relieve such a person of criminal ***responsibility*** nor migrate punishment."

The text of the Rome Statute is as follows:

- **Article 27(1)**: "*This Statute shall apply equally to all persons without any distinction based on official capacity. In particular, official capacity as a Head of State or Government, a member of a Government or parliament, an elected representative or a government official shall in no case* exempt a person from criminal ***responsibility*** under this Statute, nor shall it, in and of itself, constitute a ground for reduction of sentence."
- **Article 27(2)**: "Immunities *or special procedural rules* which may attach to the official capacity of a person, *whether under national or international law,* shall not bar the Court from exercising its jurisdiction over such a person."

A closer look at these international instruments shows that all of them were concerned with *substantive* responsibility and mitigation of punishment which are reflected in Article 27(1) of the Rome Statute. However, personal immunities are addressed in Article 27(2) of the Rome Statute. This view was also adopted by the Joint Concurring Opinion, where the judges expressed the view that "*Article 27(1) negates the idea of immunity ratione materiae* […] *Article 27(2) of the Rome Statute specifically negates immunity ratione personae.*"[82]

82 ICC, JCO, *supra* note 65, paras. 250–251.

Therefore, the overview of the instruments shows no more than that the ability to disregard the personal immunities by the international court was for the first time addressed no earlier than in Article 27(2) of the Rome Statute. From this reason, it could be conceivable to assume that all those instruments may support a possible customary law character of removal of *ratione materiae* immunities, but not of *ratione personae* immunities.

One could ask, how is it possible to use the absence of a positive rule providing for authority to set aside the immunity as proof of a customary law providing for a power of the international tribunals to disregard the immunities? The answer lies in the nature of the reversed test developed by the Appeals Chamber. It was shown that the ACh concluded that "*there is neither State practice nor opinio juris that would support the existence of Head of State immunity under customary international law vis-à-vis an international court.*"[83] It seems that the Appeals Chamber would require a proof of existence of a positive state practice (and *opinio iuris*) prohibiting the international courts to exercise jurisdiction over troika members. Only such positive state practice (and *opinio iuris*) directly connected to the international tribunals, could lead to establishment of a custom on immunity before international tribunals.

From the above cited international instruments, it follows that according to this reversed test a consistent silence on a matter of personal immunity in the international treaties establishing the tribunals would not qualify as a practice satisfying the creation of a custom on existence of the immunity. It seems that the reversed test could be satisfied only if those international instruments would consistently incorporate an explicit and positive prohibition to exercise jurisdiction by the corresponding tribunal over a member of the troika. Otherwise, not addressing the matter of personal immunities in the statutes inevitably leads to insufficient practice or *opinio iuris.*

It is submitted here that such approach is flawed and potentially dangerous. The adoption of the Appeals Chamber's test would eventually result in a situation in which international organizations would be by default authorized to do something its creators are not allowed to do according to law; unless the creators explicitly prohibit that in the founding instrument of such tribunal. Because if states do not include the explicit prohibition in the founding document of an international tribunal, there cannot ever be identified a sufficient practice or *opinio iuris* that there is a rule of customary law preventing the international organization from doing something their creators had been pre-

83 Ibid, para. 113.

vented to do by law. Such an outcome does not seem to be acceptable, and it supports the view that the test developed by the Appeals Chamber is flawed.

Regarding the other practice, the Appeals Chamber also referred to the fact that the ICTY issued an indictment against Slobodan Milošević, while he was still president of Serbia.[84] Claus Kreß correctly points out that at the time the arrest warrant was issued, Milošević was still Head of State, and importantly that the FRY was not a member of the UN. He concludes that this "*set the first judicial precedent for the exercise of jurisdiction by an international criminal tribunal over an incumbent Head of State*"[85] and, together with the decision in the *Taylor* case, he considers these two cases to be crucial for the crystallization of the alleged rule regarding the exception to personal immunities before international courts.[86]

The fragile foundations of the *Taylor* Decision have been discussed above. With regard to the arrest warrant for Milošević it is necessary to take into account, among other things, that by signing the Dayton Accords, the Federal Republic of Yugoslavia, as a non-member state, undertook obligation to cooperate with the ICTY and comply with the issued orders and arrest warrants,[87] such obligations were also referred to in 1998 by the President of the ICTY.[88]

During the trial, Milošević was no more a president, accordingly the ICTY did not address the issue of personal immunities. In addition, the ICTY was not a treaty-based tribunal but had a fundamentally different legal basis backed by the coercive powers of the Security Council acting under Chapter 7.[89] Considering the fundamentally different legal nature of the ICTY and the FRY's Treaty commitments, this case also cannot provide support for the possibility of a treaty-based tribunal disregarding the personal immunities of an official of a state not party to a statute.

It is also worthy to note that there is a type of state practice and *opinio iuris* not taken into account at all by the Appeals Chamber. And it is the practice of Ghana failing to arrest Charles Taylor and of numerous (not only) African

84 ICC, *Jordan Appeal* Judgment, *supra* note 5, para. 107.

85 Kreß, *supra* note 22, 2645.

86 Ibid.

87 Dayton Peace Agreement, General Framework Agreement for Peace in Bosnia and Herzegovina, 21 November 1995, S/1995/999.

88 ICTY President McDonald addresses the Security Council (2 October 1998), available online at <https://www.icty.org/en/press/icty-president-mcdonald-addresses-security-council> (last accessed 30 April 2025).

89 Kolb, Robert, *International Law on the Maintenance of Peace* (Edward Elgar, 2018), Chapter 5: Chapter 7 of the Charter: Coercive Powers of the Security Council.

states not executing the request of the ICC concerning the arrest of President al Bashir.[90] It is also the consistently negative position of the African Union towards the cooperation with the ICC in the context of the personal immunities.[91] While it may be argued that this is a mere treaty practice, it can also be argued that such subsequent practice of States Parties could serve as an interpretation method as provided in Article 31(3)(b) of the Vienna Convention on the Law of the Treaties and it may be "*objective evidence of the understanding of the parties as to the meaning of the treaty*" and "*may also contribute to the clarification of the meaning of a treaty.*"[92]

This practice and views expressed by the states, and ignored by the ICC, could support the interpretation of Article 27(2) of the Rome Statute as a form of waiver of immunities given by the States Parties with respect to their officials. That would mean that the States Parties to the Statutes waived their right of their own officials to object the personal immunity before the ICC. However, it would leave untouched the possible immunity objection of the officials of states not parties to the Rome Statute, because these non-participating states did not waive such immunity *vis-à-vis* the ICC.[93]

The above presented interpretation of Article 27(2) of the Rome Statute seems to also correspond with Article 98(1) RS which prohibits the Court to

> proceed with a request for surrender or assistance which would require the requested State to act inconsistently *with its obligations under international law with respect to the State or diplomatic immunity of a person* or property of a third State, unless the Court can first obtain the cooperation of that third State for the waiver of the immunity.

While it is true that Article 98(1) of the RS does not itself provide for any immunity, it is hardly deniable that the drafters were aware of certain 'immunities of a person' which could collide with the obligations of the States

---

90 Van Alebeek Rosanne, van den Herik, Larissa and Ryngaert, Cedric, 'Prosecuting Russian Officials for the Crime of Aggression: What About Immunities?' (2023) *European Convention on Human Rights Law Review* 4, 125.

91 Heller, Kevin J., 'The AU's Position on Personal Immunity: A Response to Coracini & Trahan' (blog *Opinioiuris.org*, 9 November 2022) <https://opiniojuris.org/2022/11/09/the-aus-position-on-personal-immunity-a-response-to-trahan/> (last accessed 30 November 2023).

92 ILC, Draft Conclusions on Subsequent Agreements and Subsequent Practice in Relation to the Interpretation of Treaties (2018), YILC, vol. II, Part Two, Conclusions 3 and 7.

93 Schabas, *supra* note 79, 450.

Parties to cooperate. The ICJ confirmed that under firmly established customary law, the troika members enjoy immunities from jurisdiction in other states, without an exception with respect to the nature of the possible criminal act.[94] The preferable reading is that the Court is not allowed to proceed with a request for the arrest of a troika member of a non-State Party unless it can first obtain the cooperation of that state for the waiver of the immunity. If the Court were to proceed with a request absent receiving the waiver of state not party to the Statute, it would exceed its powers based on the Rome Statute and the requested state would not be obliged to cooperate.[95]

The wording of Article 98(1) RS represents another reason for a rejection of the so-called 'surrogacy' argument. That argument is based on the notion that the requested state is only lending assistance to the ICC and does not exercise its own jurisdiction.[96] It was shown above that the surrogacy argument was not eventually unequivocally adopted by the Appeals Chamber (unless there is the resolution adopted under Chapter 7). However, it should be rejected also because the surrogacy would effectively deprive Article 98(1) of the Rome Statute of any meaning.[97] If the states would have been seen as not exercising its own jurisdiction in cooperation with the Court, they could never hypothetically "*act inconsistently with its obligations under international law*" as envisaged by Article 98(1) RS. There would be no possible explanation how and if ever Article 98(1) could operate.

It seems more reasonable to choose the method of interpretation which gives full meaning to both Articles, rather than the one depriving one treaty provision of any possible meaning. Moreover, the surrogacy argument would enable states to easily circumvent their legal obligations. It would lead to situations when states obliged to refrain from doing something by law, could create an international entity, and then following requests of such entity (created by them) they could suddenly ignore their obligations provided by law. Such operation of law would go directly to the statement of the ACh that "[t]*he law*

94 ICJ, *Arrest Warrant*, *supra* note 3, paras. 51 and 58.

95 ICC, Request by Professor Roger O'Keefe for Leave to Submit Observations on the Merits of the Legal Questions Presented in 'The Hashemite Kingdom of Jordan's appeal against the "Decision under Article 87(7) of the Rome Statute on the non-compliance by Jordan with the request by the Court for the arrest and surrender [of] Omar Al-Bashir" of 12 March 2018 (ICC-02/05-01/09-326), ICC-02/05-01/09-334 (19 April 2018).

96 Ibid, para. 127.

97 ICC, Observations by Professor Roger O'Keefe, pursuant to Rule 103 of the Rules of Procedure and Evidence, ICC-02/05-01/09-360 (18 June 2018).

does not readily condone to be done through the back door something it forbids to be done through the front door"[98] and should thus be rejected.

6 Conclusions

While one can easily understand the desire to prosecute those who are seen as the most responsible for horrendous crimes under international law, this prosecution should happen within the parameters set up by the (international) law. The above reflections lead to the conclusion that under the current state of customary international law personal immunities of officials of non-participating states remain applicable before a treaty-based international tribunal. That applies unless the respective state waives the immunities of its officials or unless the Security Council adopts a respective resolution under Chapter 7. It does not mean that states are obliged to resign on the prosecution of those responsible for the crimes under international law in Ukraine. First, personal immunities protect only a very limited number of officials, and not even the entire leadership of a state. Second, they last only for the time the troika members are in the office.

It seems important to stress that the customary law is not made by judicial activism. It is necessary to follow the state practice and *opinio iuris* rather than the opinions of a very limited number of international judges.

Moreover, it was shown that the findings of the *Arrest Warrant* judgment, *Taylor* Decision, and the *Jordan Appeal* Judgment tend to be exaggerated and not to be read in its entirety.

The ICJ in the *Arrest Warrant* judgment determined that the customary law provides for personal immunities from jurisdiction in other states. While the ICJ reflected that members of the troika may be subject to criminal proceedings before certain international criminal courts, and it referred also to the ICC, nowhere did the ICJ make a finding that the ICC could also set aside an immunity of an official on a non-participating state. The ICJ remained silent on that particular issue. This famous, but rather brief *obiter dicta* remark, does not provide a solid basis for a conclusion that treaty-based international tribunals may set aside personal immunities of officials of states not parties to such tribunals.[99]

The detailed analysis of the *Taylor* Decision revealed that it was the involvement of the Security Council and its powers under Chapter 7 in the establish-

98 ICC, *Jordan Appeal* Judgment, *supra* note 5, para. 127.

99 Nouwen, *supra* note 12, 598, 610–611.

ment of the court, that made the SCSL in its eyes *truly international.* While the link to the Security Council does not seem to be persuasively argued by the SCSL, it was vital for the SCSL's identification as the 'certain international criminal court' that may disregard Taylor's immunities.

The Appeals Chamber in the *Jordan Appeal* Judgment put forward certain strong determinations claiming that Article 27(2) of the Rome Statute is a clear provision of customary international law. However, the analysis of findings and later parts of the judgment and the JCO has revealed that the Appeals Chamber eventually relied not on the alleged state of customary law, but on the Security Council's Resolution 1593. In both cases, the ultimate decisive element was the (alleged) involvement of the Security Council's coercive powers.

It was also analyzed why the alleged different nature of the international tribunal does not provide for sufficient guarantees for safeguarding the interests protected by personal immunities. The personal immunities protect both, the equality of states, and the undisturbed exercise of function by the highest states' representatives. The latter interest is not anyhow secured by the mere fact that the prosecution would appear before the international institution. The effect of national and international prosecution seems to be identical in this regard, which seems to be ignored by both SCSL and the ICC.

Further, the Appeals Chamber's development of the reversed test on the non-existence of custom providing for personal immunities *vis-à-vis* an international court was put under scrutiny. First, the references to past international instruments such as IMT, ICTY, ICTR, etc. showed that the issue of personal immunities was for the first time explicitly addressed in the Rome Statute. The previous instruments dealt with *substantive* responsibility and mitigation of punishment which are reflected in Article 27(1) of the Rome Statute, but not in Article 27(2) RS.

Second, the analysis showed why the reversed test proposed by the Appeals Chamber is flawed. The approbation of the test would eventually result in a situation in which international organizations would by default be authorized to do something the states (their creators) are not allowed to do according to law; unless the creators explicitly prohibit that in the founding instruments of such tribunals. Similarly, a potential adoption of the 'surrogacy' argument would enable the states to circumnavigate their obligations from international law. It was also shown that neither the SCSL, nor the ICC have provided any satisfactory answer to the question of how it would be possible for states to be allowed to create an entity that is in respect of a non-participating state authorized to do something that none of its founders are authorized to do. This cannot be bridged by a reference to the example of the Security Council establishing the ad hoc tribunals by adopting the resolutions under Chapter 7. The states endowed the Security Council acting under Chapter 7 with coercive powers and the states accepted that the obligations under the Charter shall prevail. However, in a case of a state not party to a treaty (establishing a tribunal) a similar acceptance or a waiver is not present. From this reason, it does not seem sufficient if the international tribunal was created by a treaty with the UN or with the approval of the UN General Assembly. Regardless of how many states would approve the tribunal voting in the General Assembly, they cannot escape the missing coercive powers, which the states vested only in the Security Council, but not in other organs of the United Nations.

However, the law is a dynamic instrument, and the customary law may develop. The states remain the creators of the international customs and they may put the preference on international justice over the institute of personal immunities if they wish. If there was significant support among the states for the removal of personal immunities before a treaty-based international tribunal also concerning officials of non-participating states, the states may attempt to create a custom, or an instant custom in this regard. However, it would not seem to be satisfactory to merely adopt even a multilateral treaty providing for the power of a tribunal to set aside such immunity concerning a non-participating state. The states would be also required to declare that it is their view that such a rule reflects customary international law.[100]

100 ILC, Identification of Customary International Law, Third Report by Sir Michael Wood, Special Rapporteur, A/CN.4/682, 27 March 2015, para. 39.

PART 4

Trial Issues

CHAPTER 7

The Shortest Trial of the Century?

How Judicial Notice of Facts of Common Knowledge Might Be Used in Criminal Prosecutions of Senior Leaders for the Crime of Aggression

Simon De Smet

1 Introduction

If there will ever be a prosecution of the senior leadership of the Russian Federation for the alleged crime of aggression against Ukraine before an international(ized) tribunal,[1] one of the key challenges will be evidentiary. In particular, will prosecutors be able to collect and present enough evidence to prove complex factual allegations involving the use of force over time and space beyond reasonable doubt? How long will this process take, and will the tribunal be able to process so much information in a reasonable amount of time and at a reasonable cost? This chapter explores the possibility and extent to which a future tribunal could take judicial notice of some of the relevant facts and sidestep the regular judicial fact-finding process in relation to certain factual propositions. To do so, the chapter will first briefly introduce the concept of judicial notice of facts of common knowledge from a theoretical point of view. Following this, the chapter will review a few examples of how judicial notice of facts of common knowledge has been used in relation to the prosecution of the crime of aggression and other international crimes. The purpose is not to provide an exhaustive overview, but rather to illustrate some of the issues and obstacles that courts have encountered when considering using judicial notice in high profile cases. The chapter concludes by making a few recommendations as to how a future tribunal might approach the taking of judicial notice of relevant facts in a possible criminal trial for aggression.

1 This chapter assumes that the ICC does not have jurisdiction over any alleged crime of aggression involving nationals of non-State Parties, including the Russian Federation.

 | DOI:10.1163/9789004740945_009

2 Judicial Notice as a Fact-Finding Method

Judicial notice is a procedural mechanism whereby the adjudicator accepts a particular legal or factual proposition as a given without hearing formal evidence on it.[2] It can be used in relation to the content of the law, the existence and authenticity of documents, general background information that is used in evidentiary reasoning, and factual propositions that are considered to be of common knowledge. It is with the latter category that this paper is concerned.

Although judicial notice as a technique for establishing facts may be relatively unfamiliar to non-specialists, it is an essential and well-established tool for adjudicators.[3] Without having the ability to take judicial notice, courts would have to hear evidence on every factual proposition that is relevant in a trial, including the most trivial ones. This would obviously not be workable. It would also be quite pointless to hear evidence in relation to issues that are not subject to serious dispute. Accordingly, adjudicators do not expect or allow parties to present evidence about whether 24 February 2003 fell on a Monday or a Tuesday or whether Donald Trump was the 44th or the 45th president of the United States. There are literally hundreds of such facts that are judicially noticed in the course of a trial, usually without anyone noticing it. Similarly, reasoning about facts and evidence is impossible without relying on generalizations that serve as warrants for inferential reasoning.[4] For example, when a witness testifies that they saw one person running followed by another running person in a particular uniform, the adjudicator will probably infer that the former was being chased by a law enforcer. This inference would be based on three generalizations, namely (i) that persons wearing a particular uniform generally belong to a particular law enforcement force; (ii) that law enforcement officers in uniform are usually on duty; and (iii) that law enforcement officers generally do not engage in running contests with random members of the public when they are on duty. In most instances, adjudicators rely on such generalizations without being briefed, let alone receiving evidence, on them.

2 Munday, Roderick, *Cross and Tapper on Evidence* (13th edn, Oxford University Press, 2018), 78.

3 McNaughton, John, 'Judicial Notice–Excerpts Relating to the Morgan-Wigmore Controversy' (1961) 14 *Vanderbilt Law Review* 779, 783, who claims the practice in common law courts dates back six centuries.

4 Anderson, Terence, Schum, David and Twining, William, *Analysis of Evidence* (Cambridge University Press, 2005), 262–280.

This same principle – that it is pointless to hear evidence in relation to factual propositions that are obviously true – also underlies the adjudicator's authority to exclude certain facts from litigation or at least relieve the party with the burden of proof from the burden of producing evidence in relation to such facts. This is the adjudicator's power to take judicial notice of facts of common knowledge. For example, when a witness testifies that the person being chased by the police officer on 24 February 2003 was Beatles' lead singer John Lennon, the adjudicator will usually not require evidence on who John Lennon was or indeed on the fact that he died long before the alleged chase.

Facts of common knowledge come in two flavors: *notorious facts*, so called because of their general notoriety among the general population; and *verifiable facts*,[5] which, although not necessarily known to the population at large, are nevertheless undisputable because their content and indisputability can be ascertained by anyone with access to reliable sources. An example of a notorious fact might be that on 11 September 2001, the Twin Towers in New York City were attacked and destroyed by two hijacked commercial planes. An example of a verifiable fact is that at an altitude of 1,000 meters above sea level water boils at 96 degrees Celsius.

As these two examples show, the epistemic warrant for the taking of judicial notice of notorious facts is different from that of judicially noticing verifiable facts. In the case of notorious facts, the adjudicator may take judicial notice on the basis of the fact that an average member of the relevant community would readily acknowledge the veracity of the factual proposition in question. In other words, because the fact is part of the cognitive consensus of society,[6] there is no need for and no point in litigating it.

A verifiable fact, on the other hand, may be judicially noticed because the reliability of its source is generally accepted by the relevant epistemic community.[7] A typical example would be for the adjudicator to consult leading scien-

5 This form of judicial notice is sometimes referred to as 'judicial notice after inquiry' (*see* Keane, Adrian and McKeown, Paul, *The Modern Law of Evidence* (14th edn, Oxford University Press, 2022, 117) or 'judicial notice after reference' (*see* Glover, Richard, *Murphy on Evidence* (15th edn, Oxford University Press, 2017), 149.

6 Anderson, Schum and Twining, *supra* note 4, 380 define cognitive consensus as "[t]*he idea that there is a generally shared 'stock of knowledge' in a given society, commonly reflected by common sense generalizations or generally known facts of which a tribunal will take judicial notice or the like.*" They attribute the notion to Cohen (Cohen, L. Jonathan, *The Probable and the Provable* (Oxford University Press, 1977), 274–276).

7 Haas (Haas, Peter, 'Introduction: Epistemic Communities and International Policy Coordination' (1992) 46 *International Organization* 1, 3) defines an epistemic community as "*a network of professionals with recognized expertise and competence in a particular domain and an authoritative claim to* [...] *relevant knowledge within that domain or issue-area.*"

tific publications on a particular topic. However, verifiable facts are not limited to scientific propositions. Any factual proposition which the adjudicator believes can be accurately and reliably garnered from one or more authoritative sources may be judicially noticed. For example, the price of a particular stock traded on the NASDAQ on a particular day can be ascertained via the NASDAQ's website.[8] Although there are no formal standards for determining what qualifies as a verifiable fact, Bellin and Ferguson[9] propose the following criteria: the source's expertise of the subject matter; the absence of relevant biases and/or prejudice of the source; and the source's incentive to ensure accuracy. One might add an additional criterion, namely that adjudicators should refrain from taking judicial notice if there are members of the relevant epistemic community who hold methodologically sound alternative views.

Crucially, judicial notice of facts of common knowledge is not limited to factual propositions that are universal and eternal truths.[10] What matters is that the proposition is uncontroversial among the vast majority of the relevant community, be that society at large or a particular epistemic community, at the time it is being noticed. There is no requirement of unanimous acceptance.[11] One will find deniers or agnostics for almost any factual proposition. Whether or not they undermine the cognitive consensus depends on their relative number as well as the validity of their arguments against the proposition. As will be discussed below, the fact that there are Holocaust deniers does not mean that there is no cognitive consensus that the Holocaust happened.

There is also no requirement of certainty. Communities sometimes collectively believe factual propositions that turn out to be wrong.[12] This possibility does not prevent adjudicators from taking judicial notice of factual proposi-

8 NASDAQ Webpage, available online at <https://www.nasdaq.com/market-activity/quotes/historical> (last accessed 10 October 2024).

9 Bellin, Jeffrey and Ferguson, Andrew G., 'Trial by Google: Judicial Notice in the Information Age' (2014) 108 *Northwestern University Law Review* 1137, 1167.

10 SCSL, *Prosecutor v Norman et al., Fofana* (Decision on Appeal against 'Decision on Prosecution's Motion for Judicial Notice and Admission of Evidence') – Separate Opinion of Justice Ayoola, SCSL-2004-14-AR73, ACh (16 May 2005), para. 24.

11 ICTR, *Prosecutor v Laurent Semanza* (Decision on the Prosecutor's Motion for Judicial Notice and Presumptions of Facts Pursuant to Rules 94 and 54) ICTR-97-20-I, TChIII (3 November 2000), para. 31.

12 For example, in USA, *City Bank Farmers Trust Co. v. United States*, 74 F.2d 692 (2d Cir. 1935), the US Court of Appeals for the Second Circuit overturned a legal presumption that women could bear children at any age, by pointing out that statistics for the years 1923 to 1932 recorded that on a total of 20,389,873 of births during that period not a single child had been born to a woman of 55 years or over.

tions that are, at the relevant time, generally accepted as true by the relevant community.

3 Judicial Notice before International Courts and Tribunals

Given that the warrant for taking judicial notice lies in the epistemic authority of the cognitive consensus of a particular society or epistemic community, it becomes relevant to decide how the relevant societies/epistemic communities whose shared beliefs adjudicators may draw upon can be defined and identified. This question is particularly poignant for international courts and tribunals, as their jurisdictional remit is generally broader in geographical terms than most domestic courts. It is instructive to consider a few examples from practice in this regard.

In Nuremberg, the International Military Tribunal was at some point confronted with the suggestion, made by a French prosecutor, that what had happened to General Henri Giraud's family under German occupation was a fact of common knowledge. General Giraud was a well-known personality in France. Nevertheless, the Tribunal declined to take judicial notice of these events on the grounds that the

> Tribunal [was] of the opinion that the facts with reference to General Giraud's deportation and the deportation of his family, although they are matters of common knowledge or of public knowledge within France, cannot be said to be of common knowledge or of public knowledge within the meaning of Article 21, which applies generally to the world.[13]

By contrast, the United Nations International Criminal Tribunal for Rwanda, based in Tanzania, held that it could take judicial notice of "*facts that are notorious within the territories of Rwanda, Burundi and other neighbouring states.*"[14] Similarly, the Special Court for Sierra Leone, a hybrid tribunal based in Freetown, Sierra Leone, stated that

13 Nuremberg Trial Proceedings, Volume 6, Forty-Third Day, Friday, 25 January 1946, Morning Session.

14 ICTR, *Prosecutor v Laurent Semanza* (Decision on the Prosecutor's Motion for Judicial Notice and Presumptions of Facts Pursuant to Rules 94 and 54) ICTR-97-20-I, TChIII (3 November 2000), para. 30.

> [a] judge may rely on his own local knowledge, which is the case here, especially, as the SCSL is located in Sierra Leone. The fact that there was an armed conflict in Sierra Leone is a notorious fact of history. Furthermore, in the context of Sierra Leone these facts cannot be subject to reasonable dispute taking into consideration the general knowledge of the population.[15]

In other words, whereas the IMT limited judicial notice to facts that were part of the global cognitive consensus, modern international tribunals have relied on the shared knowledge of the communities that are most directly concerned by the events falling within the tribunal's geographic jurisdiction. This is a significant difference in approach, which allowed the tribunals to take judicial notice of facts that may not have been familiar beyond the affected region. By focusing on the cognitive consensus of the directly affected population, the adjudicator can draw upon the experiences of the people who lived through the events and who will have a much more vivid and detailed understanding of recent history. But it may also give rise to situations where particular groups within the affected population have significantly different understandings of what happened. It suffices to think of how differently fans of Real Madrid and FC Barcelona interpret the referee's decisions in almost every El Clásico. Even though both sides watch the same game and have the same information, they still have very differing views about what happened. Adjudicators should obviously not take sides by choosing to accept one version of events at the expense of the cognitive consensus of the other group. On the other hand, adjudicators should not be prevented from taking judicial notice of facts which they consider incontrovertible, merely because they are denied or twisted as part of propaganda among a certain group in society. Understanding the true content of the cognitive consensus of one or more groups may take time and effort. And in some cases, the events may be too recent for a true cognitive consensus to have developed, as will be illustrated below in the context of the Rwandan genocide.

15 SCSL, *Prosecutor v Norman et al., Fofana* (Decision on Appeal against 'Decision on Prosecution's Motion for Judicial Notice and Admission of Evidence) SCSL-2004-14-AR73, ACh (16 May 2005), para. 36.

4 The Purpose and Effects of Judicial Notice of Facts of Common Knowledge

As noted in the introduction, judicial notice can be used for different purposes.[16] However, when it comes to judicially noticing facts of common knowledge, there is a long-standing controversy about what the purpose and effects of judicial notice are. On one hand, there is the view that judicial notice of facts of common knowledge is limited to factual propositions that are so obvious and uncontroversial that it would undermine the credibility and reputation of the judicial process if the adjudicator allowed them to be questioned, let alone enter contrary findings. This view was famously articulated by Morgan:

> [J]ust as the court cannot function unless the judge knows the law and unless the judge and jury have the fund of information common to all intelligent men in the community as well as the capacity to use the ordinary processes of reasoning, so it cannot adjust legal relations among members of society and thus fulfil the sole purpose of its creation if it permits the parties to take issue on, and thus secure results contrary to, what is so notoriously true as not to be the subject of reasonable dispute, or what is capable of immediate and accurate demonstration by resort to sources of indisputable accuracy easily accessible to men in the situation of members of the court.[17]

Factual propositions that are judicially noticed in this manner are considered incontrovertible. They are not subject to further discussion and the adjudicator will refuse to hear evidence in relation to them. This approach to judicial notice of facts of common knowledge will henceforth be referred to as *conclusive judicial notice*.

On the other hand, there is a view that judicial notice of facts of common knowledge is (also) a tool for adjudicators to streamline and expedite the fact-finding process. Under this view, adjudicators are allowed to take judicial notice of factual propositions which they consider to be highly probable. Factual propositions that are judicially noticed in this manner are merely presumed to be true.[18] This means that the parties are allowed to present evidence to dispute the veracity of factual propositions that were judicially

---

16 McNaughton, *supra* note 3, 783–4.

17 Morgan, Edmund, 'Judicial Notice' (1944) 57 *Harvard Law Review* 269, 273.

18 Thayer, James B., *A Preliminary Treatise on Evidence at the Common Law* (1898), 308–309.

noticed.[19] This approach to judicial notice of facts of common knowledge will henceforth be referred to as *presumptive judicial notice*.

It stands to reason that adjudicators who conclusively notice factual propositions will have to exercise great restraint, given that, if they judicially notice an incorrect factual proposition, there will be no recourse for the parties to challenge it.[20] This also makes it all the more important for the adjudicator to hear the parties before taking judicial notice. Indeed, as Morgan conceded: "*Whether or not the truth of a given proposition is disputable may itself be the subject of dispute among reasonable men.*"[21] This means that, in principle, the parties must be given notice of the fact that the adjudicator is considering whether or not certain factual propositions qualify as facts of common knowledge.[22] They may then bring arguments for or against this, without being bound by the regular rules of evidence.

As noted, however, in most cases, adjudicators tacitly notice dozens, if not hundreds, of factual propositions without hearing the parties on all or even most of them. To require adjudicators to hear extensive argument in relation to all judicially noticed facts would undermine the very idea behind judicial notice of facts of common knowledge: that it is pointless to spend time discussing them because they are not subject to reasonable dispute. It would also take up a lot of procedural time and energy, thereby defeating one of the advantages of taking judicial notice. Davis has proposed three factors to be considered to determine whether or not notification and discussion is required: (i) the nature of the factual proposition to be noticed; (ii) whether and to what extent the factual proposition is central to the controversy between the parties; and (iii) how certain the adjudicator is about the accuracy of the factual proposition.[23]

When judicially noticed facts are only considered presumptively established, the parties have an additional opportunity to rebut the finding. They may do so by submitting arguments showing that the factual proposition is in fact disputed or by submitting evidence to prove that the factual proposition is wrong or at least subject to genuine doubt. Just as with the requirement to offer parties an opportunity to make submissions before judicial notice is taken, there can equally be no unlimited right to allow parties to challenge

19 Wigmore, John H., *9 Evidence § 2567* (3rd ed. 1940).

20 The only recourse they have would be to challenge the propriety of the judicial notice on appeal.

21 Morgan, *supra* note 17, 275.

22 McCormick, Charles, 'Judicial Notice' (1952) 5 *Vanderbilt Law Review* 296, 319.

23 Davis, Kenneth C., 'Judicial Notice' (1955) 55 *Columbia Law Review* 945, 977.

factual propositions once they have been judicially noticed. Davis suggests that parties should be entitled to challenge judicially noticed facts under the same conditions that they would be allowed to ask for reconsideration of other decisions.[24] This is a sound suggestion, as it would take into consideration arguments that had already been aired in submissions before judicial notice was taken. Accordingly, if an adjudicator wanted to move more rapidly at the beginning of the trial by limiting the scope of the litigation by taking judicial notice of certain factual propositions without giving the parties a genuine opportunity to be heard, this might result in more time being spent on dealing with motions to reconsider and the presentation of rebuttal evidence. Conversely, if the adjudicator heard extensive argument about whether a particular factual proposition was genuinely undisputable before judicially noticing it, this would limit the scope for challenges afterwards. In other words, if judicial notice is considered to only establish the noticed facts presumptively, the adjudicator retains a measure of flexibility and discretion in terms of how and when to give the parties an opportunity to challenge the indisputability and/or accuracy of the factual proposition.

It is interesting to note that the *ad hoc* tribunals have taken the view that facts of common knowledge that have been judicially noticed are established conclusively, whereas adjudicated facts that are judicially noticed are only accepted presumptively.[25] Accordingly, although in both instances the prosecutor is relieved of their burden to produce evidence, defendants are only allowed to introduce rebuttal evidence in relation to adjudicated facts that are judicially noticed. The *ad hoc* international tribunals have further held that judicial notice should not be taken of factual propositions relating to the acts, conduct, mental state, or the specific position of the accused.[26] Justice Robertson explained this position thus:

> The defendant, by pleading *not guilty*, puts in issue his *mens rea* or guilty mind which cannot in consequence be the subject of judicial notice. He also puts in issue the *actus reus* [...] In practice, any fact which is within the knowledge of the defendant, but which he denies, cannot be made the subject of judicial notice: his denial must be accepted by the court as

24 Ibid, 978–979.

25 ICTR, *Prosecutor v Karemera et al.* (Decision on Prosecutor's Interlocutory Appeal of Decision on Judicial Notice) ICTR-98-44-AR73(C), ACh (16 June 2006), para. 42.

26 Ibid, para. 50; SCSL, *Prosecutor v Norman et al.*, *Fofana* (Decision on Appeal against 'Decision on Prosecution's Motion for Judicial Notice and Admission of Evidence) SCSL-2004-14-AR73, ACh (16 May 2005), para. 43.

> indicative that the alleged fact is reasonably disputable if only because the defendant himself disputes it and intends to do so on oath or affirmation or to call witnesses to dispute it.[27]

In principle, there is no reason why judicial notice should be limited in this manner. If a factual proposition is genuinely deemed indisputable and the parties, including the accused, have had a genuine opportunity to be heard on the matter, it is difficult to see why adjudicators should not be allowed to take judicial notice of such a proposition. To be sure, there will not be many cases where the acts and conduct of an accused or their position will be genuine facts of common knowledge. But the possibility cannot be excluded. For example, the fact that Donald J. Trump was the 45th President of the United States of America and that he met with North Korean leader Kim Jong Un could safely be judicially noticed, even if the defendant denied them.[28]

Nevertheless, one readily appreciates the uneasiness such an approach engenders, especially in the context of an adversarial trial. Allowing adjudicators to take judicial notice of factual propositions that go to the heart of the charges against an accused seems antithetical to the notion of a fair trial, in which the accused is presumed innocent, the prosecutor bears the burden of proof and the defendant is entitled to challenge and confront all incriminating evidence.[29] For example, if an adjudicator were to take judicial notice of the acts and conduct of the accused, which they deny, this would seem to rob the trial of much of its meaning.

5 Reluctance to Use Judicial Notice

This reluctance to use judicial notice for factual propositions that, although essentially beyond dispute, went to the heart of the charges was also on dis-

---

27 SCSL, *Prosecutor v Norman et al., Fofana* (Decision on Appeal against 'Decision on Prosecution's Motion for Judicial Notice and Admission of Evidence') – Separate Opinion of Justice Robertson, SCSL-2004-14-AR73, ACh (16 May 2005), para. 16.

28 If Mr. Trump were to deny either proposition, it would take little effort for a prosecutor to prove it. However, this confirms the status of the factual proposition as essentially not open to serious discussion, which is precisely the reason why it can be appropriately judicially noticed.

29 In an inquisitorial context, such objections, while still formally valid, lose some of their force. Indeed, in an inquisitorial trial, it is the presiding judge who decides which witnesses to call. If the presiding judge deems a particular factual proposition to be beyond dispute, they have no obligation to call any evidence on this during the trial.

play in Nuremberg, during the first trials on the crime of aggression. For example, Major Frank B. Wallis, Assistant Trial Counsel for the United States, presenting the case in relation to Count I – The Common Plan or Conspiracy – to the International Military Tribunal, started his presentation as follows:

> It will be my purpose to establish most of the material allegations of the Indictment running from Paragraph IV on Page 3, to Subparagraph E on Page 6. The subjects involved are: The aims of the Nazi Party, their doctrinal techniques, their rise to power, and the consolidation of control over Germany between 1933 and 1939 in preparation for aggressive war. This story has already been sketched by the American Chief Prosecutor. Moreover, *it is history, beyond challenge by the defendants*. For the most part, we rely upon the Tribunal to take judicial notice of it. What we offer is *merely illustrative material*-including statements by the defendants and other Nazi leaders – laws, decrees, and the like. We *do not need to rest upon captured documents or other special sources*, although some have been used.
>
> [...]
>
> The main objectives of the [Nazi] Party, which are fastened upon the defendants and their co-conspirators by reason of their membership in, or knowing adherence to the Party, were openly and notoriously avowed. They were set out in the Party program of 1920, were publicized in Mein Kampf and in Nazi literature generally, and were obvious from the continuous pattern of public action of the Party from the date of its founding. Now, two consequences of importance in the Trial of this case derive from the fact that the major objectives of the Party were publicly and repeatedly proclaimed: First, the Court may take judicial notice of them. Second, the defendants and their co-conspirators cannot be heard to deny them or to assert that they were ignorant of them.
>
> The Prosecution offers proof of the major objectives of the Party-and hence of the objectives of the conspiracy only to *refresh or implement judicial recollection*.[30]

The next day, Mr. Alderman, another counsel for the United States, addressed the case in relation to the planning, preparation, initiation, and waging of illegal and aggressive war, as well as the conspiracy to commit that crime:

30 Nuremberg Trial Proceedings, Volume 2, Third Day, Thursday, 22 November 1945, Afternoon Session (emphasis added).

My introduction to the presentation of evidence in this matter would be faulty if I did not invite the Tribunal to consider with me the relationship between history and the evidence in this case. Neither counsel nor Tribunal can orient themselves to the problem at hand – neither counsel nor Tribunal can present or consider the evidence in this case in its proper context, neither can argue or evaluate the staggering implications of the evidence to be presented without reading that history, reading that evidence against the background of recorded history. And by recorded history, I mean the history merely of the last 12 years. [quotes Oliver Wendell Holmes] I submit that in the present case *a page of history is worth a hundred tons of evidence*. As lawyers and judges we cannot blind ourselves to what we know as men. *The history of the past 12 years is a burning, living thing in our immediate memory*. The facts of history crowd themselves upon us and demand our attention.

[discusses Article 21 of the Charter of the Tribunal and gives examples of historical facts of common knowledge]

If I may be allowed to interpolate, an old law professor of mine used to present the curiosity of the law: that a judge is held to responsibility for no knowledge of the law whatsoever, that a lawyer is held to a reasonable knowledge of the law, and a layman is held to an absolute knowledge of all the laws. It works inversely as to facts, or facts of common knowledge. There, the judge is imputed to know all of those facts, however many of them he may have forgotten as an individual man. So one of the purposes of this presentation will be *to implement the judicial knowledge which by hypothesis exists, and which probably actually exists*. It is not our purpose however, to convert the record of these proceedings into a history book. The evidence which we offer in this case is evidence which for the moment has been concealed from historians. It will fill in recorded history, but it must be read against the background which common knowledge provides. The evidence in this case consists primarily of captured documents. These documents fill in the inside story underlying the historical record which we already knew. This evidence which we will offer *constitutes an illustrative spot check* on history – on the history of the recent times as the world knows it. The evidence to be offered *is not a substitute for history*. We hope the Tribunal will find it to be an *authentication of history*. The evidence which we have drawn from captured documents *establishes the validity of the recent history of the past 12 years* – a history of many aggressions by the Nazi conspirators accused in this case.

> As I offer to the Tribunal document after document, I ask the Court to see in those documents definite additions to history, the addition of new elements long suspected and now proved.[31]

These two passages clearly illustrate the heart of the problem international courts and tribunals face when they are called upon to sit in judgment of events that are part of or constitute recent geopolitical history. On the one hand, the events will be so fresh on the minds of everyone that it may seem pointless to hold a trial and ask evidence to be presented in relation to them. On the other hand, because the events are so recent, historians and other researchers will not have had time to go through the historical evidence and establish a clear record of what really happened. This probably explains why the Nuremberg prosecutors quoted above adopted such an ambivalent position. On the one hand, they claimed that many of the charged facts were common knowledge and therefore qualified for judicial notice. At the same time, they still introduced relatively large amounts of documents in relation to these same facts. From a formal point of view, there would have been no need to present any evidence in relation to facts that were claimed to be of common knowledge. It is worth pointing out that these documents were not relied upon to show that the factual propositions were part of a global cognitive consensus, nor were they professed to be authoritative sources. So why did these prosecutors still go through the trouble of presenting evidence? A few possible reasons come to mind. First, in some cases, the documents were meant to prove additional details that might not be so widely known as to qualify as notorious facts. Second, documents and other evidence were submitted to circumscribe the precise content of the facts of common knowledge. Third, the evidence may have been submitted as a safeguard to convince the judges that the historical facts were really beyond dispute and that the prosecutors could fully prove them with evidence, if necessary. Finally, it is possible that the prosecutors recoiled somewhat from the consequence of what they were arguing. Indeed, by proclaiming that the charges were essentially based on recent history, which was fundamentally beyond dispute, the prosecutors were effectively saying that there was no need for a trial on the facts. This would have put in doubt the need for the creation of a brand-new international tribunal and undermined the claim that the victors were prepared to offer the vanquished a fair hearing. The prosecutors may therefore have been keen to keep up an appearance of regular litigation by presenting a selection

31 Nuremberg Trial Proceedings, Volume 2, Fourth Day, Friday, 23 November 1945 (emphasis added).

of evidence to show that they could meet their burden of proof if called upon to do so. It also gave the defendants an opportunity to challenge the evidence, even if this would have been futile if the facts were really considered to be common knowledge and the Tribunal had formally judicially noticed them. Moreover, the UK prosecutor, Sir Hartley Shawcross, had declared that the tribunal would provide "*a contemporary touchstone and an authoritative and impartial record to which future historians may turn for the truth*".[32] Taking judicial notice of some of the most consequential events would have short-circuited this objective. Indeed, prosecutors often use evidence to *tell a story* and in some cases the public presentation of evidence may have a didactic effect. In this sense, a single well-chosen item of evidence may well say more than a thousand words.[33]

Unfortunately, the record does not show how the Tribunal dealt with this situation. The IMT judgment does not contain the litany of detailed references to evidence which we have become accustomed to from modern international criminal courts and tribunals. The IMT also did not clearly state which facts it judicially noticed, if any,[34] even though the succinctness and affirmative tone of some of the findings may give rise to the impression that it probably did.[35]

---

32 'Twelfth Day, Tuesday, 4 December 1945: Morning Session', Trial of the Major War Criminals before the International Military Tribunal, Nuremberg, 14 November 1945–1 October 1946: Volume III: Proceedings 1 December 1945–14 December 1945 (Nuremberg IMT 1947) 91, 92.

33 For example, at Nuremberg, Prosecutors famously showed a documentary (Document 2430-PS, Exhibit USA-79) containing graphic images from a number of concentration camps as they were liberated. Nuremberg Trial Proceedings Volume 2, Eighth Day, Thursday, 29 November 1945, Morning Session. Although the showing of the documentary made a profound impression on many inside and outside the courtroom, Telford Taylor later reflected that although "*the public showing of the film certainly hardened sentiment against the defendants generally,* [...] *it contributed little to the determination of their individual guilt.*" Taylor, Telford, *The Anatomy of the Nuremberg Trials* (Back Bay, 1992), 187.

34 The only instance where the Tribunal used language suggesting it had judicially noticed a fact is in relation to Funk. After finding that Funk had participated in his official capacity in a number of programmes that involved crimes, the Tribunal held that "*Funk was never a dominant figure in the various programmes in which he participated. This is a mitigating fact of which the Tribunal takes notice.*" IMT, *USA, France, UK, and USSR v Hermann Wilhelm Goring, et al.*, Judgment, Trial of the Major War Criminals (1 October 1946), 504.

35 *See e.g.*, the part of the judgment dealing with the invasion of the Benelux countries, which occupies less than a page. IMT, *USA, France, UK, and USSR v Hermann Wilhelm Goring, et al.*, Judgment, Trial of the Major War Criminals (1 October 1946), 437.

A similarly ambivalent attitude can be detected in the ICTR's Appeals Chamber's (in)famous decision to take judicial notice of the fact that genocide was committed in Rwanda in 1994 as a fact of common knowledge. Here again, it is worth considering the Appeals Chamber's own words *in extenso:*

> There is no reasonable basis for anyone to dispute that, during 1994, there was a campaign of mass killing intended to destroy, in whole or at least in very large part, Rwanda's Tutsi population, which (as judicially noticed by the Trial Chamber) was a protected group. That campaign was, to a terrible degree, successful; although exact numbers may never be known, the great majority of Tutsi were murdered and many others were raped or otherwise harmed. These *basic facts were broadly known even at the time of the Tribunal's establishment*; indeed, reports indicating that genocide occurred in Rwanda were a key impetus for its establishment, as reflected, in the Security Council resolution establishing it and even the name of the Tribunal. *During its early history, it was valuable for the purpose of the historical record for Trial Chambers to gather evidence documenting the overall course of the genocide and to enter findings of fact on the basis of that evidence.* Trial and Appeal Judgements thereby produced (while varying as to the responsibility of particular accused) have unanimously and decisively confirmed the occurrence of genocide in Rwanda, which has also been documented in countless books, scholarly articles, media reports, U.N. reports and resolutions, national court decision, and government and NGO reports. *At this stage,* the Tribunal need not demand *further documentation.* The fact of the Rwandan genocide is a part of world history, a fact as certain as any other, a classic instance of a "fact of common knowledge".[36]

Leaving aside the question as to whether it would have been more appropriate for the Appeals Chamber to take judicial notice of the genocide as an adjudicated fact (rather than a fact of common knowledge),[37] it is interesting to pause and take the Judges' reasoning at face value. As the quote seems to

36 ICTR, *Prosecutor v Karemera et al.* (Decision on Prosecutor's Interlocutory Appeal of Decision on Judicial Notice) ICTR-98-44-AR73(c), ACh (16 June 2006), para. 36 (emphasis added).

37 Heller, Kevin J., 'Prosecutor v. Karemera, Ngirumpatse, & Nzirorera' (2007) 101 *American Journal of International Law* 157; Mamiya, Ralph, 'Taking Judicial Notice of Genocide – The Problematic Law and Policy of the Karemera Decision' (2007) 25 *Wisconsin International Law Journal* 1.

suggest, the fact that a genocide took place in Rwanda was considered a fact of common knowledge from the start of the Tribunal's operations in 1995. Yet, it took more than ten years – and perhaps the admonition of the UN Security Council to adopt a completion strategy[38] – for the Judges to finally take judicial notice of it. Tellingly, the Appeals Chamber did not say that there had been a need for more evidence in order to establish the indisputable nature of the genocide. Nevertheless, the court suggested that it had been useful to let the ordinary evidentiary process take its course a number of times and to wait until historians and others had had a chance to study and write about the events in Rwanda before finally declaring that the Rwandan genocide had become part of world history.

This approach reflects the tension between relying on what everyone knows from personal experience or following the news and the need for a methodologically sound epistemological warrant for this knowledge. Trials about contemporary geopolitical events place adjudicators in a fundamentally different position compared to regular cases. Normally, adjudicators will have no idea about what may have happened, and the purpose of the trial is to reconstruct a very specific part of the past, usually in great detail. The adjudicators learn about these events from witnesses and other sources of evidence. When trials are about the type of geopolitical events such as the full-scale invasion by one state into another, adjudicators will usually be well aware of at least the broad contours of what has happened from media reporting and public pronouncements of national and international entities. In this sense, they are themselves (indirect) witnesses of the events they sit in judgment over. In principle, judicial notice is designed exactly for situations like this. As Judge Robinson declared in *Norman et al*,

> [t]hat a prolonged armed conflict took place in Sierra Leone is a truly *notorious* matter of historical record and indeed is obvious to anyone living in or visiting this country, and to all the judges of this court. [In a footnote, the Judge added that the judges 'may use the evidence of their own eyes, and rely upon local knowledge'][39]

Yet, judges are not historians. Their beliefs about contemporary geopolitical events are based on a layman's understanding of news reports, etc., which they

38 UNSC Res 1503 (2003) (28 August 2003).

39 SCSL, *Prosecutor v Norman et al., Fofana* (Decision on Appeal against 'Decision on Prosecution's Motion for Judicial Notice and Admission of Evidence') – Separate Opinion of Justice Robertson, SCSL-2004-14-AR73, ACh (16 May 2005), para. 18.

have not independently verified. This raises the question as to whether international courts and tribunals should contribute to the writing of contemporary history by consolidating certain historical narratives through judicially noticing them or whether they should see the trial as an opportunity to create an evidentiary record about a specific part of history.[40] There is no categorical answer to this question. In some cases, failing to take judicial notice may be perceived as an insult to the suffering, if not the intelligence, of the affected population. For example, in the context of the conflict in Sierra Leone, the Appeals Chamber held that

> [t]he fact that there was an armed conflict in Sierra Leone is a "notorious fact of history". Furthermore, in the context of Sierra Leone these facts cannot be subject to reasonable dispute taking into consideration the general knowledge of the population. A multitude of victims with mutilations which cannot stem from anything other than an armed conflict allows for an accurate and ready determination of this fact by immediately obtainable evidence. To contest the fact that there was an armed conflict is frivolous.[41]

In some cases, taking judicial notice may also be used as a tool to quell conspiracy theories, such as Holocaust denial. However, as the Ernst Zündel trial in Canada shows, courts may be reluctant to judicially notice even the Holocaust. Ernst Zündel was tried under Canada's criminal statute against spreading false news[42] for publishing a pamphlet entitled 'Did Six Million Really

---

40 For a more general discussion of the role of international courts and tribunals in writing history, *see, e.g.*, Arendt, Hannah, *Eichmann in Jerusalem: A Report on the Banality of Evil* (Penguin Classics, 1963); Wilson, Richard A., 'Humanity's Histories Evaluating the Historical Accounts of International Tribunals and Truth Commissions' (2007) 4 *Politix* 31; Wilson, Richard A., *Writing History in International Criminal Trials* (Cambridge University Press, 2011); Douzinas, Costas, 'History Trials: Can Law Decide History?' (2012) 8 *Annual Review of Law and Social Science* 273; Borda, Aldo Z., 'History in International Criminal Trials – The "Crime-Driven Lens" and Its Blind Spots' (2020) 18 *Journal of International Criminal Justice* 543; Kosso, Peter, 'Historical Evidence and Epistemic Justification: Thucydides as a Case Study' (1993) 32 *History and Theory* 1; Sander, Barrie, 'Unveiling the Historical Function of International Criminal Courts: Between Adjudicative and Sociopolitical Justice' (2018) 12 *International Journal of Transitional Justice* 334.

41 SCSL, *Prosecutor v Norman et al., Fofana* (Decision on Appeal against 'Decision on Prosecution's Motion for Judicial Notice and Admission of Evidence) SCSL-2004-14-AR73, ACh (16 May 2005), para. 36.

42 Zündel was charged under Section 177 of the Canadian Criminal Code, which provided that "[e]*very one who wilfully publishes a statement, tale or news that he knows is false and*

Die?' by Richard Harwood. In a first trial, the court refused to take judicial notice and obliged the prosecution to prove the Holocaust. Although Zündel was convicted, his conviction was quashed on appeal because the trial court had allowed into evidence a documentary film produced by the US Army in violation of the hearsay rules.[43]

It is interesting to consider the first trial judge's reasons for denying the prosecution's motion to take judicial notice. As reported by the Court of Appeal, the judge felt that taking judicial notice of the reality of the Holocaust would have the effect, in the eyes of the public, as well as perhaps in the eyes of the jury and the accused, of not providing the accused with an opportunity to defend himself.[44] The Court of Appeal approved the trial court's refusal to take judicial notice in large part on the grounds that judicial notice would have forced the jury to accept that the Holocaust was real and not subject to reasonable dispute. Since the burden was on the prosecution to demonstrate that Zündel knowingly published falsehoods, taking judicial notice would tell the jury that the reality of the Holocaust was indisputable and would implicitly cast Mr Zündel's denial as unreasonable.[45] Tellingly, the appellate judges referred to the doctrinal dispute adumbrated above on the conclusive or presumptive nature of judicially noticed facts and accepted Morgan's position in this regard.[46]

On remand, the new trial court had fewer qualms and did take judicial notice of the fact that "*the mass murder and extermination of Jews in Europe by the Nazis during the Second World War is so notorious as not to be subject of dispute.*"[47] After Zündel was convicted for a second time, the defendant challenged the decision to take judicial notice on appeal. The Court of Appeal upheld the trial judge's decision on the basis of the following reasoning:

> We think the trial judge took judicial notice of *noncontentious historical facts which were background* and declined to take judicial notice of historical facts which the Crown had to demonstrate in proving that specific statements or allegations in the pamphlet were false and that the

causes or is likely to cause injury or mischief to a public interest is guilty of an indictable offence and liable to imprisonment […]." This section was later in the case found to be unconstitutional by Canada's Supreme Court in Canada, *R. v. Zundel*, [1992] 2 S.C.R. 731.

43 Canada, *R. v. Zundel*, 1987 CanLII 121 (ON CA), available online at <https://canlii.ca/t/1npn1> (last accessed 4 December 2023).

44 Canada, *R. v. Zundel*, 1987 CanLII 121, para. 162.

45 Kahn, Robert A., *Holocaust Denial and the Law* (Palgrave, 2004), 37–43.

46 Canada, *R. v. Zundel*, 1987 CanLII 121, paras. 165–6.

47 Quoted in Canada, *R. v. Zundel*, Ontario Court of Appeal, 1990 CarswellOnt 1075, para. 21.

> accused knew them to be false when he published them. These latter were issues of fact for the jury and the trial judge had no intention of resolving their proof by judicial notice or of diminishing the accused's right to make full answer and defence with respect to these facts. He did not take judicial notice of any policy of the National Socialist government and/or Adolf Hitler, he did not take judicial notice of the specific numbers of persons who died and he did not take judicial notice of the use of gas chambers.[48]

In other words, the trial court, with the approval of the appellate court, took judicial notice of the Holocaust as an abstract notion. It did not judicially notice the more specific constituent elements of the Holocaust, which the prosecution still had to prove and which the defence could still contest.[49] The factual proposition that was judicially noticed – by design – did not settle any contested issue in the trial. The court's approach may thus be regarded as a symbolic but largely empty gesture. Indeed, the Holocaust is a compound factual proposition. Without its essential composing parts (e.g., that the mass killings were committed pursuant to a genocidal policy decided at the highest level, the methods used, or the number of victims), *the Holocaust* is little more than an empty shell. It is no different than if the court had judicially noticed that the Beatles performed at Shea Stadium in New York City on 15 August 1965, but decided that this did not settle the question whether either John Lennon, Paul McCartney, Ringo Starr, or George Harrison were present there that day. As Douglas remarks, the *Zündel* case serves as an example of how "*the formal evidentiary agnosticism of adversarial jurisprudence may have the ironic effect of contributing to the erosion of the very boundary between truth and fiction that the law attempts to police.*"[50]

The *Zündel* case also shows that the willingness to make use of the power to take judicial notice in a meaningful way is heavily influenced by the conception of judicial notice as conclusively determining the factual propositions at issue. It is impossible to know whether the judges would have been more willing to take judicial notice of the Holocaust if they had conceptualized it

48 Canada, *R. v. Zundel*, Ontario Court of Appeal, 1990 CarswellOnt 1075, para. 24 (emphasis added).

49 Ibid, para. 27.

50 Douglas, Lawrence, 'The Memory of Judgment: The Law, the Holocaust, and Denial' (1995) 7 *History and Memory* 100, 113. The case also illustrates the challenge of proving complex historical events without falling foul of the hearsay rules. Kahn, *supra* note 45, 45–63.

as creating a presumption, but it would certainly be easier to criticize them for refusing to do so. This is not to say that using judicial notice to create a rebuttable presumption raises no fair trial concerns. Indeed, although presumptive judicial notice allows the defendant to challenge the noticed factual propositions, this might seem to put the onus on the accused, who bears no burden of proof.[51] However, if judicial notice is to play a meaningful role in contentious historical cases, this objection has to be overcome.

It is worth remembering, in this regard, that presumptive judicial notice does not shift the burden of persuasion, only the prosecution's burden of evidence.[52] Moreover, the defendant does not have to prove that the judicially noticed factual proposition is wrong. It suffices for them to produce enough evidence to create a reasonable doubt. Whilst this prevents the defendant from adopting a purely reactive strategy, whereby the defense limits itself to trying to discredit the prosecution's evidence, this may not always be unreasonable. As the *Zündel* case and other Holocaust denial cases show, there is a real risk that the judicial system's structural limitations for dealing with complex historical events may be weaponized for propagandistic purposes or to frustrate the course of justice.[53] As Koskenniemi points out, "[t]*he more you try to prove such facts in court, the more fragile they become.*"[54]

Moreover, such trials come at a tremendous cost. Not only in terms of enormous amounts of resources, but also in terms of putting large numbers of witnesses through stressful and sometimes traumatizing experiences in the witness box and witness protection programs. If the main purpose of this is to create an evidentiary record for something that is otherwise already obvious, such costs may be hard to defend. They may also be difficult to justify purely on the basis of appeals to the need to give the accused a normal fair trial. There is little normal about aggression and mass atrocity trials of senior political and military leaders. So, what constitutes a fair trial in such cases may look different from the standard adversarial trial. Indeed, if the purpose of

51 *See*, McDermott, Yvonne, *Proving International Crimes*, Chapter 4 (forthcoming).

52 ICTR, *Prosecutor v Karemera et al.* (Decision on Prosecutor's Interlocutory Appeal of Decision on Judicial Notice) ICTR-98-44-AR73(c), ACh (16 June 2006), paras. 37, 42.

53 Kahn, *supra* note 45; *see also* Vergès, Jacques M., *De la stratégie judiciaire* (Les Editions de Minuit, 1968), who describes how he used a "strategy of rupture" when defending former Nazi Klaus Barbie and others.

54 Koskenniemi, Marti, 'Between Impunity and Show Trials' (2002) 6 *Max Planck Yearbook of United Nations Law* 1, 33. It suffices to read Nancy Coombs' work to understand some of the problems that are involved. Combs, Nancy, *Fact-Finding Without Facts* (Cambridge University Press, 2011); Combs, Nancy, 'Deconstructing the Epistemic Challenges to Mass Atrocity Prosecutions' (2018) 75 *Washington and Lee Law Review* 223.

international prosecutions is to hold senior leaders to account, the trials should be about more than poking holes in the prosecution's evidence. Putting the accused in a position where it is in their interest to present their side of the historical story and to challenge the cognitive consensus of the *international community* may go some way to ensuring that the adjudicator will be able to make nuanced and balanced findings. The defendant suffers no fundamental unfairness if they have an opportunity to challenge the indisputable nature of the factual proposition before it is judicially noticed as well as a genuine chance to submit evidence to rebut it once it has been noticed.

6 Judicial Notice in a Future Prosecution for Aggression?

It is important not to overstate the case. Many international prosecutions will not involve events that can genuinely be considered to be common knowledge. However, a potential prosecution by a future tribunal of senior leaders of the Russian Federation for the crime of aggression might present a different picture.

If such a case were brought on the basis of the definition of aggression that is contained in the Rome Statute,[55] the prosecution would have to establish the following elements: (1) the accused planned, prepared, initiated, or executed an act of aggression; (2) the accused was a person in a position effectively to exercise control over or to direct the political or military action of the state which committed the act of aggression; (3) an act of aggression – the use of armed force by a state against the sovereignty, territorial integrity, or political independence of another state, or in any other manner inconsistent with the Charter of the United Nations – was committed; (4) the accused was aware of the factual circumstances that established that such a use of armed force was inconsistent with the Charter of the United Nations, even though there is no requirement to prove that the perpetrator made a legal evaluation as to whether the use of armed force was inconsistent with the Charter of the United Nations; (5) the act of aggression, by its character, gravity, and scale, constituted a manifest violation of the Charter of the United Nations; and (6) the accused was aware of the factual circumstances that established such a manifest violation of the Charter of the United Nations; again without any

55 Rome Statute of the International Criminal Court (adopted 17 July 1998, entered into force 1 July 2002) 2187 UNTS 3.

requirement to prove that the perpetrator made a legal evaluation as to the manifest nature of the violation of the Charter of the United Nations.[56]

It will be interesting to see whether or not a future tribunal would consider any of the underlying events to be facts of common knowledge. In relation to some of the elements mentioned above, there are a number of publicly available sources that might be considered sufficiently reliable to allow a tribunal to treat the status of Vladimir Putin as president of the Russian Federation as verifiable facts of common knowledge. For example, the proposition that Mr. Putin was the President of the Russian Federation in 2022 might be considered a verifiable fact on the basis of reliable sources, such as the Kremlin's own website or the Organization for Security and Co-operation in Europe's Final Report of 6 June 2018 on the Presidential elections in the Russian Federation, held on 18 March 2018, which found that Vladimir Vladimirovich Putin won 76.69 % of votes.[57]

The fact that Russian armed forces entered Ukrainian territory and used kinetic force was relayed almost in real-time by hundreds of news outlets. This might well lead a future tribunal to consider the proposition that Russian forces used force against Ukraine as a notorious fact of common knowledge. It will also be interesting to see what a future tribunal would do with the fact that the President of the Russian Federation publicly declared that:

> [I]n accordance with Article 51 (Chapter 7) of the UN Charter, with permission of Russia's Federation Council, and in execution of the treaties of friendship and mutual assistance with the Donetsk People's Republic and the Lugansk People's Republic, ratified by the Federal Assembly on February 22, *I made a decision* to carry out a special military operation.[58]

A future international court or tribunal might well wish to streamline the proceedings by taking judicial notice of certain facts. Whether or not this would be appropriate or would violate the defendants' rights depends, in my view, on three factors. First, the accused should be heard on the question of whether the facts are indeed indisputable. This should include a right to pre-

---

56 Elements of Crimes – Article 8*bis* – Crime of Aggression.

57 *See* OSCE Webpage online at <https://www.osce.org/odihr/elections/383577> (last accessed 7 November 2023).

58 Televised speech by President Putin, Televised speech of 24 February 2022, available online at <http://www.en.kremlin.ru/events/president/transcripts/67843> (last accessed 22 October 2023) (emphasis added).

sent evidence on how these facts are understood inside the Russian Federation or other parts of the world. Second, judicial notice should only presumptively establish the facts. Finally, the defense should have a meaningful opportunity to raise a reasonable doubt by calling evidence in relation to judicially noticed facts. This means that their defense team should be given the time and the funds to conduct a meaningful investigation and a reasonable opportunity to present rebuttal evidence. In other words, even though many may deem the alleged crime of aggression as a fact of common knowledge, this should not automatically lead a future tribunal to consider it conclusively established on the basis of judicial notice.

7 Conclusion

Regardless of whether one views the goal of international criminal prosecutions as limited to establishing the individual criminal responsibility of the accused or rather ascribes wider didactic or historiographic purposes, it is probably safe to assume that international criminal justice's objectives cannot be attained through show trials.[59] This means that the accused should genuinely be presumed innocent, that they are entitled to meaningfully confront all incriminating evidence, and that the prosecution's burden of proof should be rigorously enforced. At the same time, there is little to be gained from formalistically going through the motions of an adversarial trial if the adjudicator views some of the facts in the case as being beyond reasonable dispute at the start of the trial. Insisting on evidence being presented in relation to such facts would, quite literally, only be for show. Indeed, one may wonder whether the adjudicator's disposition to consider certain factual propositions as beyond reasonable dispute really dissipates simply by demanding that the prosecution presents evidence in relation to them.

Facts of common knowledge can thus give rise to something of a paradox. If the adjudicator takes judicial notice of them, they may be accused of not giving the accused a full and fair hearing. But if the adjudicator does not judicially notice them, the hearing may be not much more than a formality to legitimize a foregone conclusion. Yet, if used judiciously, judicial notice can help adjudicators to avoid both pitfalls.

---

59 The term show trial is defined in the Oxford English Dictionary as "[a] *judicial trial held in public with the intention of influencing or satisfying public opinion, and typically having a predetermined verdict.*"

As this chapter has argued, judicial notice of facts of common knowledge can help not only to streamline judicial proceedings, but also to stimulate a more open and meaningful dialogue about specific *notorious* historical events. For it to do so, the notion that judicially noticed facts are conclusively established should be abandoned. It is too inflexible and gives rise to due process concerns that make it difficult to take judicial notice of any factual proposition of consequence. Instead, the presumptive concept of judicial notice should be embraced and accompanied by robust procedural safeguards.[60] The latter must guarantee that the accused can meaningfully challenge the indisputable nature of the factual propositions. They must also allow for the possibility of submitting evidence to show that a given factual proposition, even though it may be believed by millions, can reasonably be doubted. It is true that this approach makes it more difficult for the accused to adopt a purely passive or subversive litigation strategy. But since the purpose of international prosecutions for aggression is to hold high-profile individuals accountable for their role in recent historical events, which, *ex hypothesi*, have been witnessed by and have affected the lives of millions, it is not by definition unfair to present them with the choice of either to adhere to the cognitive consensus of millions of people or to demonstrate why these millions of people were misinformed or got it wrong.

It is also more intellectually honest and fairer to the accused for the adjudicator to put their cards on the table and to give the accused a genuine opportunity to contest the incontestable nature of the relevant propositions. This may be especially valuable in the context of a specifically created tribunal for the crime of aggression, where it may be difficult to find adjudicators who are accepted by all sides as being truly neutral and having no preconceived ideas about what happened in Ukraine. Indeed, it is difficult to see why the interested States would want to set up a special tribunal specifically for the purpose of prosecuting aggression charges if they did not believe that there is a real possibility that aggression has taken place. If the adjudicators they appoint agree with this premise and consider it to be a fact of common knowledge, they should not be expected to affect a pretense of obliviousness. Instead, by taking presumptive judicial notice and by demonstrating a genuine openness to be proven wrong, they can only enhance the legitimacy of the proceedings.

60 *See*, for a similar proposal for the Israeli courts, Menashe, Doron, 'A New Paradigm for Understanding Judicial Notice and Its Implications in the Modern Digital Era' (2017) 9 *Elon Law Review* 267. Menashe calls this approach the 'participative model' – as opposed to the 'irrefutable model'.

After all, justice is not served by show trials, no matter how long they last or how much evidence is presented.

Notes and Acknowledgments

The author of this chapter is Legal Officer at the International Criminal Court. The views expressed are those of the author alone and do not reflect the views of the International Criminal Court. This chapter was edited at the insistence of the Office of the Registrar of the International Criminal Court as a condition for publication. The author is indebted to Ms. Hannah Bowcock for her invaluable research assistance during the preparation of this paper.

CHAPTER 8

Proceedings *in Absentia* in International Criminal Law and the Mechanism for Accountability for the Crime of Aggression Committed against Ukraine

Milan Lipovský

1 Introduction

Holding trials *in absentia* (or rather any proceedings *in absentia* as will be demonstrated below) has been one of the controversial issues in international criminal law since its modern beginnings. There are arguments both strongly in favor as well as strongly against holding them. Particularly in case of international tribunals that face the resistance of state(s) to cooperate with them, the real risk exists that not allowing any kind of proceedings *in absentia* might block the entire functioning of concerned judicial mechanisms. Along with possible waste of resources and energy, secondary harm to victims of crimes under international law threatens in such situations.

Consequently, the purpose of this chapter is to assess both legal and theoretical arguments in favor and against holding such proceedings under international criminal law, briefly analyze the practice of various international criminal tribunals existing so far (the goal is not to provide a full commentary but to briefly assess the regulation) and consider the issue with relation to the debates about a mechanism to assess international individual legal responsibility for the crime of aggression committed against Ukraine.

Thus, the following text is divided into several Parts: those deal with terminology (often neglected topic), theoretical reasons for and against holding proceedings *in absentia*, human rights requirements to hold fair proceedings *in absentia*, development of regulation in front of chosen international criminal tribunals, and a brief conclusion with regard to the crime of aggression in context of the situation in Ukraine.

2 Terminology

The debates focusing on the absence of the accused during criminal proceedings usually use the term trial *in absentia*. It should be noted however that

 | DOI:10.1163/9789004740945_010

such term is an oversimplification of various situations with significantly different legal consequences. Combining various understandings of the term is unfortunately not unusual.

Term *trial* indicates the stage (session or series of them sharing the same characteristics) of criminal proceedings during which guilt and eventually sentence are assessed by judge(s) and/or jury, and are finished with a judgment (in case of conviction).[1] The debates over so-called trials *in absentia* in international criminal law however revolve not only around trial stage itself, but also around pre-trial stages of criminal proceedings. Henceforth, the most general term that this chapter uses for criminal proceedings of *any* stage that takes place in the absence of the accused (or suspect, convict, etc. depending on the stage of the proceedings) is rather *proceedings in absentia*.[2]

Particularly in early stages of criminal proceedings, such as during an investigation, the suspect is usually not present, and this stage might be conducted in their absence without many controversies. It is logical because the identity of the perpetrator is often not yet known, or it would be detrimental to the exercise of justice to warn suspects about the investigative actions. Consequently, trials and pre-trial proceedings (as sub-categories of proceedings) *in absentia* are treated very differently and should be properly distinguished even in terminology. Thus, this chapter uses the phrase *pre-trial proceedings in absentia* for the early stages of criminal proceeding that precede trial itself, and *trial in absentia* for the trial stage as such.

Not uncommon is also a distinction being drawn between terms of a full/total and partial trial *in absentia*.[3] As the totality may refer to both pre-trial stage and trial stage, this Part avoids using this terminology because it may confuse the readers.

Sometimes, term *judgment in absentia* or a *conviction in absentia*[4] is also used to discuss "*any judgment rendered by a court after criminal proceedings at*

---

1 Appeals stage may follow of course and if an appeal proceedings share described characteristics of trial, the conditions for legitimate trial *in absentia* must apply therein as well.

2 Logically, it should be called criminal proceedings *in absentia* because criminal proceedings is at the center of this chapter. In order to simplify the text however, term *criminal* is to be automatically presumed.

3 *E.g.*, Zakerhossein, Mohammad H., De Brouwer, Anne-Marie, 'Diverse Approaches to Total and Partial *in Absentia* Trials by International Criminal Tribunals' (2015) 26 *Criminal Law Forum* 181, 183.

4 ECtHR, *Sejdovic v Italy*, app. no. 56581/00, Grand Chamber's Judgment of 1 March 2006, para. 99.

the hearing of which the sentenced person was not personally present."[5] Such terminology indicates that trial *in absentia* may also be distinguished based on whether the accused was at least initially present at the beginning of the trial stage or not at all. Despite the different treatment of these eventualities, they are a matter of exception to the rule of presence of the accused (during entire trial) and so the chapter uses term trial *in absentia* for both eventualities.

3 Reasons for the Proceedings *in Absentia*

This Part identifies both positive as well as negative arguments regarding holding proceedings *in absentia*. The goal is to find out whether a positive or negative attitude prevails at least on theoretical level.

At the beginning, it should be noted however that while multiple reasons have already been voiced both in favor as well as against the effectiveness and legitimacy of proceedings *in absentia*, they often ignore the differences associated with the absence of the accused during various stages of criminal proceedings. For example, the benefits/risks of a court being able to proceed to judgment in the absence of the accused will be significantly different from a situation when such a court will only be able to confirm charges or indictment in the absence of the accused. Thus, these different stages of criminal proceedings should be carried in mind when criticizing or praising proceedings *in absentia*.

One of the strongest arguments in favor of proceedings *in absentia* rests in the effectiveness of the criminal procedure. Should the accused be able to prevent the procedure by failing to attend, the impossibility is in fact serving justice badly.[6] This argument however has its other side as well. It may be stated that if the apparatus is ready to proceed but at the same time incapable of having the accused arrested, it is already lacking effectiveness and should be first improved. Additionally, it is questioned whether not being able to exercise any sentence does not render the proceedings useless.[7]

---

5 Tiribelli, Carlo, 'Judgment in Absentia in International Criminal Law: its Admissibility before the ad hoc Tribunals, the International Criminal Court and the European Arrest Warrant' (2006) 18 *Sri Lanka Journal of International Law* 369, 369.

6 The argument was mentioned as reasons behind amendment of Ukrainian legislation to allow trials *in absentia* following 2014. Marchuk, Iryna, 'Domestic Accountability Efforts in Response to the Russia-Ukraine War. An Appraisal of the First War Crimes Trials in Ukraine' (2022) 20 *Journal of International Criminal Justice* 787, 793.

7 Zakerhossein and De Brouwer, *supra* note 3, 199.

Building upon enhancing the effectivity of criminal structures, the character of criminal activity of the accused might play a role as well. Given the severity of crimes under international law (in comparison with "ordinary crimes"), the accused should not be able to prevent the proceedings by their absence especially in front of international criminal tribunals endowed with jurisdiction over crimes under international law. On the other hand, it might also be claimed that it is exactly the severity of crimes under international law why proceedings *in absentia* are too risky and might delegitimize the entire process and international criminal justice.

Another argument is based on judicial economy. If the criminal apparatus is fully prepared, not holding proceedings *in absentia* is a waste of finances already spent. On the other hand, it can be also stated that human rights requirements (see next Part) require right of re-trial. Thus, trial *in absentia* (this time trial rather than any proceedings) is in fact a waste of money because it would have to be fully repeated in most cases.

Alleged non-compliance of holding proceedings without the accused with due process is also often raised. This claim is very often presented as a difference of attitudes between common law countries (arguing against) and continental European countries (arguing in favor).[8] The truth is however that even the (allegedly) strictest domestic regulations, including the common law based ones, often contain certain exceptions to the presence of the accused[9] and the dividing line between common law countries and continental European countries is also not absolute.[10] In any case, the next Part proves

---

8 Ibid, 205–207. It is worth mentioning here that e.g., the legal system of the author of this chapter, i.e. Czech legal system, counts with proceedings *in absentia* (including trials *in absentia*). *See* the Czech Code of Criminal Procedure, Law no. 141/1961 Coll., §§ 302–306a. One of the interesting points, as will be seen below, is that in case of a re-trial, under the Czech law, new sentence must not be detrimental (in comparison to the judgment rendered *in absentia*) to the accused (§ 306a(4)). In relation to aggression, it is worth mentioning that e.g., Lithuania even allows for proceedings *in absentia* for this offense based on universal jurisdiction – *see* (as well as for comment on comparison of the Lithuanian definition with the international definition of the crime of aggression) Grigaite-Daugirde, Gabija, 'Crime of Aggression against Ukraine: Legality and Legitimacy of Domestic Prosecutions in Third States' (2023) 43 *Polish Yearbook of International Law* 299, 301.

9 *E.g.*, the US legislation and case law allow even for trial *in absentia* if the accused absconds. *See* USA, Supreme Court, *Crosby v United States*, 506 U.S. 255 (1993).

10 Schabas and Caruana claim that the usually presented common law versus continental European system disagreement regarding the matter is not really an issue of fundamental values but rather a matter of different practice and tradition. Schabas, Wiliam A. and Caruana, Veronique, 'Art. 63' in Ambos, Kai (ed), *Rome Statute of the International Criminal Court* (4th ed., Munich/Oxford/Baden-Baden: Beck/Hart/Nomos, 2022), 1849, mn. 2.

that the treaty-based international human rights regulation is not completely against the proceedings *in absentia.*[11]

An extremely important aspect of the possibility to hold at least certain part of proceedings in absence of the accused, is guaranteeing the availability of evidence for future. It is well known that the longer period there is between the criminal offense taking place and gathering of evidence, the less reliable the evidence is. People forget, documents may be lost or destroyed, and physical evidence may disintegrate. Thus, holding at least a part of proceedings *in absentia* may be very useful for securing verified and admissible evidence. On the other hand, this job may be to certain degree guaranteed by the police and prosecutorial service or truth-seeking commissions as well.

So far, the arguments have been focusing mainly on the accused and the effectiveness of the criminal procedure system. Since 1990s, victims' role as active participators of the international criminal proceedings is gaining its strength as well though. Being able to tell their story, or simply be heard is undoubtedly a very important part of victims' healing process.[12] It should also be carried in mind though that the effects of this process might be to some extent limited if despite all the effort, the accused was in fact not the perpetrator or satisfactory evidence was not found. Should that happen, the entire proceedings, including the efforts of the victims, might go in vain and lead to secondary harm. Thus, the positive effects of healing process for the victims depends very much on the correctness of the entire criminal proceedings and while proceedings *in absentia* may serve the healing process positively, they may also carry a certain risk from this perspective.

Last but not least, the historical memory role of criminal proceedings (particularly in case of prosecution of crimes under international law or in case of serious domestic criminal offenses) should not be ignored. To large extent,

11 And so is certainly not customary regulation because practice and opinio iuris are not satisfactorily uniform and widespread to create a binding rule prohibiting proceedings *in absentia.*

12 The Prosecutor of the International Criminal Court (ICC), Karim Khan, in fact highlighted the possible restorative role of proceedings *in absentia* in the case of Joseph Kony, the last remaining suspect in the situation in Uganda, who remains at large. The Prosecutor stated that his "*Office sought to take an initial step towards justice for the countless victims of* [*Kony's*] *alleged crimes, through our request to Pre-Trial Chamber II to authorise a hearing to confirm the charges against him in his absence.*" ICC, Office of the Prosecutor, Statement of the Prosecutor of the International Criminal Court, Karim A.A. Khan KC, Announcing his Decision to Conclude the Investigation Phase in the Situation in Uganda, 1 January 2023, available online at <https://www.icc-cpi.int/news/statement-prosecutor-international-criminal-court-karim-aa-khan-kc-announcing-his-decision> (last accessed 8 October 2024).

this role may be fulfilled even if the accused is not present.[13] The post-WW2 Nuremberg and Tokyo trials helped to solidify the customary nature of crimes under international law and brought a significant memory to the entire world. Should this be avoided due to the unavailability of proceedings *in absentia*, the international community would lose an important part of its development. On the other hand, the question remains whether the heritage would be the same if a majority of the trials were held in absence of the accused.

As it is clear from this Part, there are neither prevailing theoretical reasons in favor, nor against holding proceedings *in absentia*. There is in fact a situation of balance. The creators of any tribunal thus need to decide this matter based upon individual circumstances combined with the human rights considerations.

4 Human Rights Requirements

Any international criminal procedure (established by law) must satisfy the human rights protection standards.[14] And the tendency to strengthen human rights protection in written sources of international criminal law has so far culminated in Article 21(3) RS[15] that indicates a very strong position of human rights protection in international criminal law. Similar regulation should be present in any other modern statute as well.

Consequently, it is clear that in order to reach as high legitimacy as possible, modern international criminal procedure must satisfy the highest standards of human rights protection. For that reason, it is necessary to identify how human rights protection regulates proceedings *in absentia*. The following text of this Part deals with the universal and European protection of due process in that regard.

13 As a benefit of proceedings *in absentia*, *"reconstruction of historical individual and collective memory"* is mentioned by Irene Victoria Massimino alongside with an opportunity to voice their story by the victims and evidence examination. Massimino, Irene Victoria, 'The ICC and in-absentia Proceedings: Finding a Response to the Difficulties of Executing Arrest Warrants' (21 May 2024) *ESIL-Reflections*, vol. 13, issue 9.

14 ICTY, *Prosecutor v Tadić* (Decision on the Defence Motion for Interlocutory Appeal on Jurisdiction) IT-94-1-AR72, ACh, (2 October 1995), para. 45.

15 *"The application and interpretation of law pursuant to this article must be consistent with internationally recognized human rights, and be without any adverse distinction founded on grounds such as gender as defined in article 7, paragraph 3, age, race, colour, language, religion or belief, political or other opinion, national, ethnic or social origin, wealth, birth or other status."*

The International Covenant on Civil and Political Rights (ICCPR)[16] deals with right to fair trial in Article 14. Its paragraph 3 states among others that:

> In the determination of any criminal charge against him, everyone shall be entitled to the following minimum guarantees, in full equality:
> (a) To be informed promptly and in detail in a language which he understands of the nature and cause of the charge against him;
> (b) To have adequate time and facilities for the preparation of his defence and to communicate with counsel of his own choosing;
> [...]
> (d) To be tried in his presence, and to defend himself in person or through legal assistance of his own choosing; to be informed, if he does not have legal assistance, of this right; and to have legal assistance assigned to him, in any case where the interests of justice so require, and without payment by him in any such case if he does not have sufficient means to pay for it [...]

Of a particular significance is letter d) that explicitly demands the presence of the individual during process of determination of any criminal charge against them. The provision does not contain any exception, nonetheless the Human Rights Committee (HRC), a body created by the ICCPR and endowed with competence to determine complaints of individuals against States Parties, has qualified the right and confirmed possibility of exceptions to the rule. The quoted text contains other subparagraphs and, as it will be seen below, their content has crystalized in the requirements of compliance of the proceedings *in absentia* with the ICCPR as well.[17]

While Article 14(3)(d) ICCPR states that the accused has the right to be present at the proceedings during which determination of the charge takes place, it must be noted that it is a right, not a duty of the individual to be present.[18] For this reason, the HRC has for example allowed for absence of the accused when they "*decline to exercise their right to be present having*

16 International Covenant on Civil and Political Rights (adopted 16 December 1966, entered into force 23 March 1976) 999 UNTS 171.

17 Similar point was made by the ECtHR with reference to Art. 6 of the European Convention (see below) in ECtHR, *Demebukov v Bulgaria*, app. no. 68020/01, Chamber's Judgment of 28 February 2008, para. 44.

18 Which is why the HRC stated that "[t]*his provision and other requirements of due process enshrined in article 14 cannot be construed as invariably rendering proceedings in absentia inadmissible irrespective of the reasons for the accused person's absence.* [underlining omitted]" HRC, *Mbenge v Zaire*, comm. no. 16/1977, Views of 25 March 1983, para. 14.1.

been informed of the proceedings sufficiently in advance [footnote omitted]."[19] Nonetheless, the HRC also noted that any exception to the right of the accused to be present is only "*permissible if it is in the interest of the proper administration of justice.*"[20] In any case, due to the other requirement present in Article 14(3) ICCPR, even with trial *in absentia*, the accused must be duly notified. Thus, the accused must be notified of the date, place, and they must be requested to attend.[21] All in timely manner and the State Party must prove that it took measures to inform the accused of the charges and proceedings.[22]

Obviously, the requirement of notification of the accused may be problematic because it could be an opportunity for the suspects to effectively block judicial system. Consequently, an indication of what are reasonable methods of notification of the accused would be helpful for the States Parties. Unfortunately, there is no clear indication of those measures and they will depend on individual circumstances of each case.

The European Convention on Human Rights and Fundamental Freedoms (ECHR)[23] guarantees the right to fair trial in Article 6(3) which states among others:

> Everyone charged with a criminal offence has the following minimum rights:
> (a) to be informed promptly, in a language which he understands and in detail, of the nature and cause of the accusation against him;
> (b) to have adequate time and facilities for the preparation of his defence;
> (c) to defend himself in person or through legal assistance of his own choosing or, if he has not sufficient means to pay for legal assistance, to be given it free when the interests of justice so require; [...]

Unlike the ICCPR, the ECHR does not explicitly require presence of the accused during the proceedings. Nonetheless, the European Court of Human Rights (ECtHR) has stated that the presence of the accused is within the object

19 HRC, *Igor Kostin v Russian Federation*, comm. no. 2496/2014, Views of 4 May 2017, para. 7.2; similarly HRC, *Mbenge v Zaire*, comm. no. 16/1977, Views of 25 March 1983, para. 14.1.

20 HRC, *Igor Kostin v Russian Federation*, comm. no. 2496/2014, Views of 4 May 2017, para. 7.2.

21 HRC, *Mbenge v Zaire*, comm. no. 16/1977, Views of 25 March 1983, para. 14.1.

22 HRC, *Maleki v Italy*, comm. no. 699/1996, Views of 15 July 1999, paras. 9.3.–9.4.

23 (European) Convention for the Protection of Human Rights and Fundamental Freedoms (adopted 4 November 1950, entered into force 3 September 1953) ETS No. 5.

and purpose of the regulation.[24] Similarly, like the ICCPR, the ECHR however contains other guarantees that are reflected in the requirements of legitimacy and fairness of proceedings *in absentia*.

While the ECtHR accepted that an accused has the right to (explicitly or it may be implied) waive their right to be present at the trial, in case of implying the waiver, it must be "*shown that he could reasonably have foreseen what the consequences of his conduct* [leading to implying a waiver] *would be* [footnote omitted]."[25]

In order to be able to waive the right to be present, the accused must logically be aware of the proceedings. Like the HRC, the ECtHR demands that the waiver must be done in an unequivocal manner,[26] and it also demands the notification of the accused about the charges against them.[27] That may of course prove to be extremely difficult in cases where the address of the accused in unknown to the prosecution/court. The ECtHR indicated that an official evidence of delivering the notification may be replaced with sufficient evidence of the accused being "*aware of the existence of the criminal proceedings against him and of the nature and the cause of the accusation and* [not intending to] *to take part in the trial or wish*[ing] *to escape prosecution*."[28] Thus, while vague and informal knowledge (or even more, pure absence of the accused at the place of regular residence) will not suffice, evidence about the accused being aware of the proceedings and the charges might. The question is however whether by requiring the accused not to intend to take part, the ECtHR indicated that if the accused is prevented from attending despite their will to attend, the requirement would not be satisfied (this will prove problematic later, see Part on Special Tribunal for Lebanon). In any way, the theoretical conclusion of the ECtHR was that the notification delivery must either be official or implied and the ECtHR provided three examples of the latter:

24 ECtHR, *Sejdovic v Italy*, app. no. 56581/00, Grand Chamber's Judgment of 1 March 2006, para. 81; ECtHR, *Demebukov v Bulgaria*, app. no. 68020/01, Chamber's Judgment of 28 February 2008, para. 44.

25 ECtHR, *Sejdovic v Italy*, app. no. 56581/00, Grand Chamber's Judgment of 1 March 2006, para. 87.

26 ECtHR, *Demebukov v Bulgaria*, app. no. 68020/01, Chamber's Judgment of 28 February 2008, para. 47.

27 Art. 6(3)(a) ECHR.

28 ECtHR, *Sejdovic v Italy*, app. no. 56581/00, Grand Chamber's Judgment of 1 March 2006, para. 99.

> the accused states publicly or in writing that he does not intend to respond to summonses of which he has become aware through sources other than the authorities, or succeeds in evading an attempted arrest [...] or when materials are brought to the attention of the authorities which unequivocally show that he is aware of the proceedings pending against him and of the charges he faces.[29]

Of particular importance in situations where the accused is absent during the trial, is the right to appoint a defense counsel.[30]

A requirement that has not been voiced yet, is that in case of a judgment *in absentia* that has been issued in other circumstances than waiver of appearance and defending themselves by the accused, or where they intended to escape, there must be right to a full re-trial.[31]

As it is clear from the human rights regulation, the treaty law and case law of human rights protection bodies is primarily focusing on presence/absence of the accused during trial, rather than during pre-trial stages of criminal proceedings, thus confirming the view that absence of the accused is more legitimate during pre-trial stages. Regarding the trial stage, while treaty law regulation is not unform in explicitly demanding the presence of the accused, the possibility of exceptions from the presence of the accused have been accepted. Exercising any of those exceptions, however, must entail strict requirements guaranteeing fairness. Primarily, the accused must be properly notified of the charges, date, and place of the upcoming proceedings. There are nonetheless alternative possibilities of such notifications. Those must however be treated very carefully and the required unequivocal conclusion about the awareness of the accused of the notification may only be reached after all reasonable measures have been taken to inform the accused. And in case of the trial itself, the accused must be allowed to be defended by legal counsel. Should a judgment *in absentia* occur, there is a right to re-trial in other cases then in those where it is established that the sentenced waived their right to appear (and defend) themselves or where they intended to escape.

---

29 Ibid, para. 99.

30 Art. 6(3)(c) ECHR.

31 ECtHR, *Sejdovic v Italy*, app. no. 56581/00, Grand Chamber's Judgment of 1 March 2006, paras. 82 and 84; ECtHR, *Demebukov v Bulgaria*, app. no. 68020/01, Chamber's Judgment of 28 February 2008, para. 45. Gaeta also argues that in case of waiver to be present, subsequently fairly conducted proceedings are legitimate and the re-trial is not necessary. Gaeta, Paola, 'The Be (Present) or Not to Be (Present). Trial in Absentia before the Special Tribunal for Lebanon' (2007) 5 *Journal of International Criminal Justice* 1165, 1170.

5 Development

This Part is dedicated to the excurse of international criminal law development to depict its experience with proceedings *in absentia*.[32] International criminal law development commenced in real with the Nuremberg and Tokyo trials – those that resulted in the adoption of the Nuremberg principles,[33] a document containing codification of customary international law. For several subsequent decades, no international judicial mechanism endowed with jurisdiction over crimes under international law existed, nonetheless the International Law Commission continued in its work on articles concerning crimes under international law as well as on a draft code of a permanent mechanism. The following text deals with proposals contained therein as well. In the 1990s, the UN Security Council adopted statutes of two *ad hoc* international criminal tribunals and others followed. The development culminated (or so it seemed) in adoption of the Rome Statute of the International Criminal Court.[34] The text is divided accordingly.

It turned out however that adoption of the Rome Statute was not a final word in creating procedural mechanisms for investigation and prosecution of crimes under international law. Its jurisdictional gap[35] regarding crime of aggression in connection with the Russian invasion of Ukraine lead to renewed debates about a new mechanism. That will however be dealt with specifically in the next Part.

32 Scope of the chapter only allows for a brief overview. For a comprehensive study, *see e.g.*, Mertins, Lena, *Proceedings in Absentia in Comparative and International Criminal Law*. Studies in International and European Criminal Law and Procedure, vol. 50 (Berlin: Duncker & Humblot GmbH, 2022), part B.

33 International Law Commission (ILC), Principles of International Law Recognized in the Charter of the Nürnberg Tribunal and in the Judgment of the Tribunal (1950), YILC, 1950, vol. II, available online at <https://legal.un.org/ilc/texts/7_1.shtml> (last accessed 8 October 2024). The principles recognized by the Statute of the International Military Tribunal and in its Judgment were confirmed by the UN General Assembly already in 1946 in UNGA Res 95(I), Affirmation of the Principles of International Law recognized by the Charter of the Nürnberg Tribunal (11 December 1946).

34 Rome Statute of the International Criminal Court (adopted 17 July 1998, entered into force 1 July 2002) 2187 UNTS 3 (Rome Statute or RS). The Special Tribunal for Lebanon was created even later but unlike the ICC, it was another *ad hoc* tribunal.

35 It is basically the difference between the jurisdictional regimes of the ICC over genocide, crimes against humanity, and war crimes on one hand and the crime of aggression on the other. It results in the impossibility for the ICC to exercise jurisdiction over the crime of aggression committed against Ukraine due to the combination of lack of activity from the UN Security Council under Art. 15*ter* RS and effects of Art. 15*bis* (5) RS.

5.1 *International Military Tribunal*

Statute of the International Military Tribunal in Nuremberg (IMT)[36] explicitly allowed for trials *in absentia*. Its Article 12 stated that

> The Tribunal shall have the right to take proceedings against a person charged with crimes set out in Article 6 of this Charter in his absence, if he has not been found or if the Tribunal, for any reason, finds it necessary, in the interests of justice, to conduct the hearing in his absence.

During the major trial, this broadly designed provision was used in case against Martin Bormann, who was Hitler's secretary. Bormann could not even be successfully notified because it turned out that the accused was in fact already deceased. The IMT was informed by counsel that Bormann might be dead yet still it continued in the proceedings.[37]

It must be noted that formulation of conditions for trial *in absentia* in Article 12 was a very broad provision. While one exception was based on the accused not being found, the other allowed the tribunal to hold the trial *in absentia* if it found it necessary in the interests of justice.

The exception of "not being found" can be identified in some modern tribunals' statutes as well, but it is not universally accepted as legitimate. And the latter exception gave the tribunal such a wide discretion that would certainly not be legitimate in the 21st century.

5.2 *ICTY*

Statute of the International Criminal Tribunal for the former Yugoslavia (ICTY)[38] contained an explicit guarantee of the presence of the accused during their trials in Article 21(4)(d):

---

36 Annex to the Agreement by the Government of the United Kingdom of Great Britain and Northern Ireland, the Government of the United States of America, the Provisional Government of the French Republic and the Government of the Union of Soviet Socialist Republics for the Prosecution and Punishment of the Major War Criminals of the European Axis (adopted and entered into force 8 August 1945) 82 UNTS 279.

37 IMT, *USA, France, UK, and USSR v Hermann Wilhelm Goring, et al.*, Judgment, Trial of the Major War Criminals (1 October 1946), available online at <https://www.legal-tools.org/doc/f41e8b/> (last accessed 8 October 2024), 340.

38 Statute of the Tribunal for the Prosecution of Persons Responsible for Serious Violations of International Humanitarian Law Committed in the Territory of the former Yugoslavia since 1991, established by UNSC Res 827 (1993) (25 May 1993), as amended.

> In the determination of any charge against the accused pursuant to the present Statute, the accused shall be entitled to the following minimum guarantees, in full equality:
>
> [...]
>
> (d) to be tried in his presence, and to defend himself in person or through legal assistance of his own choosing; [...]

The provision very clearly runs counter to any trial in absence of the accused. As such, and in combination with the inability of certain states to obtain certain suspects and hand them over to the tribunal, the prohibition caused tension. Subsequent frustration was probably the root for adoption of Rule 61 of the Rules of Procedure and Evidence (RPE) of the tribunal that allowed for special pre-trial stage proceedings.

Rule 61 basically allowed for a Trial Chamber to confirm that there were reasonable grounds to confirm the Prosecutor's indictment and have it publicly read.[39] It was only possible if there was a failure to execute an arrest warrant and reasonable time has passed since its adoption.[40] Under those circumstances and if the Prosecutor had proved that all reasonable steps to secure the arrest were taken and to ascertain the whereabout of the accused, yet still the whereabouts of the accused were unknown,[41] the judge could have ordered the Prosecutor to send the indictment to Trial Chamber. Subsequently, the Trial Chamber was allowed to call for further witnesses[42] and if it was satisfied (with the evidentiary standard set to *reasonable grounds for believing* that the accused has committed the crimes in the indictment against them), it could determine so and have the relevant parts of the indictment read out.[43] Additionally, the Trial Chamber could have ordered freezing of the accused's assets.[44]

Clearly, such pre-trial proceedings are not the same as a trial or judgment *in absentia*. Neither is the evidentiary standard as high as the one necessary to convict anyone (i.e., beyond all reasonable doubt). Nonetheless, the proceedings could have served as a useful tool to press states to a more effective search

39 To large extent, it later became an equivalent with confirmation of charges proceedings in front of the ICC. Schabas, William A., Chaitidou, Eleni and El Zeidy, Mohamed, 'Art. 61' in Ambos, Kai (ed.), *Rome Statute of the International Criminal Court* (4th ed., Munich/Oxford/Baden-Baden: Beck/Hart/Nomos, 2022), mn 1.

40 ICTY RPE, Rule 61(A).

41 ICTY RPE, Rule 61(A)(i, ii).

42 ICTY RPE, Rule 61(B).

43 ICTY RPE, Rule 61(C).

44 ICTY RPE, Rule 61(D).

for the accused (after the Rule 61 proceedings had successfully finished and the accused was thus denoted, to a certain degree, to be responsible for the crimes described in indictment) because the lack of effective action in such a situation is logically even less defendable. It could even serve the victims as a moral sanction of a sort, should the accused never be found or handed over. On the other hand, the presumption of innocence must be kept in mind. The effects of any determination in pre-trial proceedings of this kind must be understood as preliminary.

While the Rule 61 procedure was only used briefly,[45] the reason was not any claim of lack of legitimacy of proceedings *in absentia*. It rather rested in the fact that the tribunal became too busy with the accused that were already present. And in any case, there was no obligation to hold the hearings under Rule 61.[46] When it comes to the trial *in absentia* as such, the ICTY Appeals Chamber briefly commented negatively upon it and claimed that they might only be exceptionally legitimate in case of contempt of court.[47]

5.3 *ICTR*

Statute of the International Criminal Tribunal for Rwanda also contained a guarantee of the accused's presence during trial. Article 20(4)(d) of the Statute of the ICTR is in relevant part word-by-word the same as the above-quoted Article 21(4)(d) of the Statute of the ICTY.

The ICTR judges have however (in addition to Rule 61) adopted a special Rule 71*bis*. This rule, although sharing certain similarities in the reasons for allowing the procedure with proceedings *in absentia* in front of other courts, was in fact serving a different purpose. The reasons for the procedure under Rule 71*bis* was the preservation of evidence for a future trial, not to confirm charges. It may have been requested either when an arrest warrant was not executed in reasonable time or when it has been executed but the accused has not been transferred to the tribunal.[48]

The ICTR RPE however also contained Rule 82*bis*:

> If an accused refuses to appear before the Trial Chamber for trial, the Chamber may order that the trial proceed in the absence of the accused

---

45 During 1995 and 1996 for example in cases of Karadžić, Mladić and others.

46 Schabas, Chaitidou, El Zeidy, *supra* note 39, mn 1.

47 ICTY, *Prosecutor v Blaškić* (Judgment on the Request of the Republic of Croatia for Review of the Decision of Trial Chamber II of 18 July 1997) ICTY-95-14-AR, ACh (29 October 1997), para. 59.

48 ICTR RPE, Rule 71*bis* (A and B).

for so long as his refusal persists, provided that the Trial Chamber is satisfied that:
(i) the accused has made his initial appearance under Rule 62;
(ii) the Registrar has duly notified the accused that he is required to be present for trial;
(iii) the interests of the accused are represented by counsel.

Due to those requirements, it was an example of a waiver of a right to be present during the trial, i.e., a trial *in absentia* with initial appearance. The obligatory initial appearance turned it into less controversial regulation. Also, due to the obligatory representation, the non-appearance of the accused may have been a rather formalistic issue. It may be however also concluded that wording of this Rule, combined with case law, shifted the right to be present during trial to a sanctionable obligation.[49]

5.4 *International Residual Mechanism for Criminal Tribunals* (MICT)

The Statute of the MICT[50] also counted on the right of the accused to be present during trial.[51] Nonetheless, the RPE allowed for removal of the accused from the courtroom if despite warnings, they persisted in disruptive conduct,[52] and also to hold a trial in the absence of the accused if 5 conditions were met: i) initial appearance of the accused, ii) notification about the need of the accused to be present at trial, iii) the accused being physically and mentally fit to stand trial, iv) voluntary and unequivocal waiver or forfeiture of the right by the accused, and v) representation by a defense counsel.[53]

As such, the exceptions are rather straightforward, particularly due to the requirement of a waiver.

5.5 *Draft Code of Crimes against Peace and Security of Mankind and Draft Code of ICC*

The cold war period was a time without any international judicial mechanism existing to investigate and prosecute crimes under international law. Nonetheless, it was not a period of complete inactivity. The ILC worked on the Draft

49 Mertins, *supra* note 32, 46–47.
50 Statute of the International Residual Mechanism for Criminal Tribunals, annex 1 to UNSC Res 1966 (2010) (22 December 2010).
51 Art. 19(4)(d) Statute of the MICT.
52 MICT RPE, Rule 94(B).
53 MICT RPE, Rule 98.

Code of Crimes against the Peace and Security of Mankind[54] and the Draft Statute for an International Criminal Court.[55] The latter was adopted in 1994 and contained Draft Article 37. With regard to the general rule and its exceptions, it stated the following:

> 1. As a general rule, the accused should be present during the trial.
> 2. The Trial Chamber may order that the trial proceed in the absence of the accused if:
> (a) The accused is in custody, or has been released pending trial, and for reasons of security or the ill-health of the accused it is undesirable for the accused to be present;
> (b) the accused is continuing to disrupt the trial; or
> (c) the accused has escaped from lawful custody under this Statute or has broken bail.[56]

As such, the ILC Draft Code contained a general rule[57] together with broadly defined exceptions to it. They entailed the security/health exception (letter a), disrupting the trial exception (letter b), and the so-called absconding exception (letter c). While the third exception is often not considered very problematic (provided guarantees of fairness are upheld, see below)[58] and similarly, the second one is often considered acceptable (it is even present in the Rome Statute as will be seen below), the first one turned out controversial. The first exception presupposed that the accused would be initially present (in custody) and would either remain in custody or would be released pending trial. In that regard (initial presence), it is similar to the third exception. However, instead of absconding (under the third exception), here the problematic reasons for the absence of the accused were supposed to be their ill-health or security. Regarding the security grounds, it can be stated that if the tribunal

---

54 ILC, Draft Code of Offences against the Peace and Security of Mankind (1954), YILC, 1954, vol. II; and Draft Code of Crimes against the Peace and Security of Mankind (1996), YILC, 1996, vol. II, Part II.

55 ILC, Draft Statute for an International Criminal Court with commentaries (1994), YILC, 1994, vol. II, Part Two.

56 Ibid, Art. 37(1 and 2).

57 In commentaries, the ILC confirmed its importance and stated that exceptions are legitimate in very limited situations. Ibid, 54, para. 4.

58 As stated above, even US system, based on common law and thus opposing trial *in absentia* in general, accepts such exception. *See* Brown, Daniel J., 'The International Criminal Court and Trial in Absentia' (1999) 24 *Brooklyn Journal of International Law* 763, 780.

would be unable to secure a safe trial, it could hardly be imagined that the process would be fair no matter whether in presence or absence of the accused.[59] And regarding the ill-health exception, if an accused suffered from sickness so serious to prevent their presence during trial, it can hardly be accepted that the accused would be aware of what the trial even meant.

It should be kept in mind however that the 1994 Draft Statute did not count on an exception that would allow for trial *in absentia* where the accused was not initially present at the early stages of trial.[60] All three exceptions count on the accused being present at least at the beginning. From that point of view, the draft was conservative. Which is why it is surprising how liberal it was in case of the exception contained in letter a). Should the court however decide to hold a trial in absence of the accused under the proposed article, there were guarantees in it to be maintained. In line with human rights requirements, the court would have to ensure itself that "*all reasonable steps have been taken to inform the accused of the charge; and* [... that] *the accused* [was] *legally represented, if necessary by a lawyer appointed by the Court.*"[61] The first requirement is simple because since the court would be obligated to have the accused in custody at the beginning, it would not have been a problem to hand over the charges. What is striking however (especially in relation to the first exception where it may be that the accused would not have waived the right to be present), is that the Draft Article omitted the inclusion of the right of re-trial, despite actually mentioning it in commentaries as one of the human rights requirements.[62]

As will be seen further, almost all these exceptions to the presence of the accused were rejected during the negotiations of the Rome Statute.[63] Nonetheless, an inspiration may be seen in pre-trial stages in front of the ICC.

Regarding the pre-trial stage, the Draft also allowed for an Indictment Chamber similar to the one governed by Rule 71*bis* of the ICTR RPE. The court was supposed to be allowed to establish an Indictment Chamber to

---

59 "[I]*t is difficult to conceive of a situation in which the Court is able to marshal the resources necessary to initiate an investigation, apprehend and indict a suspect and yet somehow not be able to guarantee that suspect's security at trial.* [... A]*bsent extraordinary circumstances, like a global war, the chances of security problems are likely to be remote.*" Brown, *supra* note 58, 782.

60 Unlike Art. 44(1)(h) of the 1993 version of the Draft Code. That allowed for trial *in absentia* in case of deliberate absence of the accused. YILC, 1993, vol. II, Part. 2.

61 ILC, Draft Statute for an International Criminal Court, *supra* note 55, Art. 37(3).

62 Ibid, 53, para. 3.

63 It is not surprising considering the divided positions of States during the ILC work already as is seen e.g., in Tiribelli, *supra* note 5, 374–381.

record evidence, consider whether the crime(s) was(were) *prima facie* committed, and issue an arrest warrant.[64] Unlike with trial, this stage was counted on in situations of deliberate absence of the accused.

The debates surrounding the ILC's work clearly show the divided nature of the opinions of States and scholars regarding the proceedings *in absentia*. The ILC attempted to counter those criticisms by narrowing down the exceptions to trials *in absentia* (although including a controversial one as well) and by adding a Pre-Trial Indictment Chamber. The latter option has proven to be more successful considering the fact that the ICC is obliged to hold a confirmation of charges hearing and the fact that under certain circumstances, those can also be held in absence of the accused.

5.6 *Special Tribunal for Lebanon*

The Special Tribunal for Lebanon (STL) was a body that allowed for trials *in absentia* in a wide manner (especially in comparison to other international and internationalized criminal tribunals with the exception of the IMT). The reasons for this divergence probably sprang from the influence of Lebanese law, that allowed for trials *in absentia*, and the fact that the accused were already at the beginning expected to be absent from the proceedings.[65]

The Statute of the Tribunal (STL Statute)[66] contained a provision called Trials *in Absentia* which stated:

> 1. The Special Tribunal shall conduct trial proceedings in the absence of the accused, if he or she:
> (a) Has expressly and in writing waived his or her right to be present;
> (b) Has not been handed over to the Tribunal by the State authorities concerned;
> (c) Has absconded or otherwise cannot be found and all reasonable steps have been taken to secure his or her appearance before the Tribunal and to inform him or her of the charges confirmed by the Pre-Trial Judge.

64 ILC, Draft Statute for an International Criminal Court, *supra* note 55, Art. 37(4).

65 Gardner, Maggie, 'Reconsidering Trials in Absentia at the Special Tribunal for Lebanon: An Application of the Tribunal's Early Jurisprudence' (2011) 43 *George Washington University Law Review* 91, 107.

66 Attachment to the Agreement between the United Nations and the Lebanese Republic on the Establishment of a Special Tribunal for Lebanon annexed to the UNSC Res 1757 (2007) (30 May 2007).

> 2. When hearings are conducted in the absence of the accused, the Special Tribunal shall ensure that:
> (a) The accused has been notified, or served with the indictment, or notice has otherwise been given of the indictment through publication in the media or communication to the State of residence or nationality;
> (b) The accused has designated a defence counsel of his or her own choosing, to be remunerated either by the accused or, if the accused is proved to be indigent, by the Tribunal;
> (c) Whenever the accused refuses or fails to appoint a defence counsel, such counsel has been assigned by the Defence Office of the Tribunal with a view to ensuring full representation of the interests and rights of the accused.
>
> 3. In case of conviction in absentia, the accused, if he or she had not designated a defence counsel of his or her choosing, shall have the right to be retried in his or her presence before the Special Tribunal, unless he or she accepts the judgement.[67]

The STL Statute included a general provision that guaranteed right of the accused to be present during trial,[68] however subject to Article 22. First paragraph of Article 22 then allowed for three exceptions to the general rule: waiver (a), not being handed over (b), and absconding or otherwise not being found (c).

The first exception might be considered as common ground because as it has been discussed above, the right of the accused to be present during trial is not the same as an obligation to be present.[69] The exception was even made stronger by the requirement of the waiver being in writing and express. It is also worth mentioning that, to a certain degree, a similar exception (initially appearing and subsequently refusing to appear) was also contained in the RPE of the Special Court for Sierra Leone.[70]

67 Art. 22 STL Statute.

68 Art. 16(4)(d) STL Statute.

69 Though there may be a special regulation in any tribunal's law. For an example of obligatory appearance, *see* Part on the Rome Statute.

70 RPE of the Special Court for Sierra Leone, available online at <https://s3.eu-west-1.amazonaws.com/rscsl.org/wp-content/uploads/2022/09/24162759/RSCSL-Rules.pdf> (last accessed 8 October 2024), Rule 60(A)(i).

There are various possible interpretations of the second exception.[71] Based on the text and taken systematically together with the third exception (that builds upon the accused's willful non-appearance), the second exception could either be understood as a situation where the reason for the accused's non-appearance is not their free will but lack of it from the concerned State. Thus, it would count with situations of the concerned State having the accused in custody or otherwise prohibiting them from voluntary appearance before the Tribunal. Or the second possible interpretation could be understood as claiming that letter b) *"refers to the scenario in which the defendant does not flee from justice or go into hiding, but instead continues as normal and relies on the governing authority's unwillingness to cooperate with the Tribunal by arresting him."*[72] As such, the disagreement between the two interpretations lies in the matter of whose will (or lack thereof) is the root for absence of the accused.[73] It must be noted that the plain text of the STL Statute is not of much help in the identification of the correct interpretation. Nonetheless, those two interpretations overlook a common ground between them. Regardless of the attitude of the concerned State (whether willing or not), if it was not in control of a part of its territory where the accused was known by the Tribunal to reside/hide, the concerned State would not hand the accused over rather due to its inability than its own lack of will. Should at the same time the accused not be present at the Tribunal at the initiation of the proceedings, they could not be considered as having absconded. And because their whereabouts would be known, the letter c) exception would be excluded from use. The letter a) exception would also be excluded had the accused not expressly waived the right. Thus, letter b) would apply to such *common ground* between those two interpretations regardless of whether the lack of will to hand over was upon the concerned State or not. While outside the scope of this "common ground", the intended interpretation of the letter b) exception is somehow foggy, the second paragraph of Article 22 is helpful in identifying the correct path (see below).

71 Discussed for example by Shaw, Garry J., 'Convicting Inhumanity in Absentia: Holding Trials in Absentia at the International Criminal Court' (2012) 44 *George Washington International Law Review* 107, 122.

72 Gardner, *supra* note 65, 117–118.

73 In that regard, it should be pointed out that many authors (including author of this chapter) refuse legitimacy of trial *in absentia* when the reason for non-appearance of the accused is not *their* free will, while they in fact wish to participate. *See e.g.*, Mertins, *supra* note 32, 69.

The third exception counts on absconding[74] and a situation where the accused cannot be "otherwise found". Those two eventualities are different from each other however. Absconding exception means that the accused initially appeared but managed to escape.[75] "Not being otherwise found" is a situation where the accused did not even initially appear, and the Tribunal did not know where they were. The latter is thus one of the centerpieces of controversies regarding the trial *in absentia* among its supporters and opponents.[76] In both cases, however there is a second stage of consideration present in the provision of letter c). The provision requires that "*all reasonable steps have been taken to secure both the appearance of the accused before the Tribunal and inform him of the charges.*"[77] Some of the reasonable steps are then dealt with in the subsequent paragraph together with guarantees required even in other exceptions to the presence of the accused during trial.

As such, while the waiver (in limited meaning of letter a) exception) and absconding exceptions are relatively acceptable, not being handed over and the "otherwise not being found" exceptions are problematic. The reason is particularly in the fact that in situation of absconding and/or waiver, the accused was handed the charges and either explicitly (in case of waiver) or implicitly (in case of absconding) waived their right to be present during trial. The same is not as straightforward for the remaining two exceptions. Which is why the requirement of notification is extremely important.

The notification guarantee is then dealt with in the subsequent paragraph 2 together with legal representation. Regarding notice, it might however be questionable whether it would truly have been guaranteed that the accused was notified of the charges and trial if the reason for trial *in absentia* was the concerned State's non-cooperation (paragraph 1, letter b) and the notification was attempted by media publication and/or by communication to the State of residence or nationality (paragraph 2, letter a)). One can easily imagine a situation where the concerned State held the accused in custody (or prevented

74 Similarly (initial appearance and later at large refusing to participate) was also present in the RPE of the Special Court for Sierra Leone, *supra* note 70, Rule 60(A)(ii).

75 Implicitly also contained in the following quote: It "[r]*equires knowledge of the charges by the accused, and therefore a conscious decision on his part to evade service, arrest and prosecution, whereas the* [otherwise not being found] *does not.*" STL, *Prosecutor v Ayyash* (Decision to Hold Trial *in Absentia*) STL-18-10/I/TC, TChII (5 February 2020), para. 45.

76 But because it demands that the accused's whereabouts are unknown, it does not include a situation where the accused is "*openly at home, relying on the state's unwillingness to cooperate with the Tribunal.*" Gardner, *supra* note 65, 115.

77 STL, *Prosecutor v Ayyash* (Decision to Hold Trial *in Absentia*) STL-18-10/I/TC, TChII (5 February 2020), para. 46.

them from appearing in front of the Tribunal in any other way) and did not notify them of the trial. This scenario leads us back to the discussion on various interpretations of exception under letter b) and the source of lack of will to appear before the Tribunal.

This concern was implicitly addressed by the Appeals Chamber of the STL. It established a three-pronged test for the notification. Thus, three following steps must have been satisfied:

> i) reasonable efforts have be taken to notify the accused personally; ii) the evidence as to notification satisfies the Trial Chamber that the accused actually knew of the proceedings against them; and that iii) it does so with such degree of specificity that the accused's absence means they must have elected not to attend the hearing and therefore have waived their right to be present.[78]

By adding those requirements based on the STL Statute, RPE, and human rights demands, the Appeals Chamber filled in certain holes in the written law of the Tribunal and solved the above-mentioned problem regarding the source of lack of will to cooperate (under exception contained in letter b)) because had the accused not been informed and the concerned State prevented them from knowing about the charges, the quoted notification requirement could hardly be ever satisfied.[79] And also, by requiring the accused to elect not to attend, the Appeals Chamber ruled out the lack of will of the State concerned as a ground for letter b) exception. Thus, this exception should be read as only counting with i) the lack of will on the part of the accused (despite the unfortunate wording of Article 22(1)(b) STL Statute) combined with that State's non-cooperation, or ii) the inability of the concerned State to arrest and hand over the accused (e.g., due to lack of control over piece of territory as described above) combined with the accused's willful non-appearance.

As the Appeals Chamber hinted, the notification delivery may also be implied but material supporting an implied inference must be of unequivocal

78 STL, *Prosecutor v Ayyash, Badreddine, Oneissi and Sabra* (Decision on Defence Appeals against Trial Chamber's Decision on Reconsideration of the Trial *in Absentia* Decision) STL-11-01/PT/AC/AR126.1, ACh (1 November 2012), para. 31.

79 Since in situation of absconding, the accused actually was initially present at the Tribunal (and thus probably was informed about the charges and upcoming trial), it would be logical to conclude that the test is more relevant in case of "otherwise not being found". Which is why, it is striking that the Trial Chamber stated exactly the opposite in STL, *Prosecutor v Ayyash* (Decision to Hold Trial *in Absentia*) STL-18-10/I/TC, TChII (5 February 2020), para. 51.

manner leading to a conclusion that the accused was aware (phrase coming from the human rights demands, see above) of the charges.

In any case, it should be kept in mind that Article 22(3) of the STL Statute counts on the right of re-trial. Possibly (from certain point) in a wider manner than is necessary under human rights regulation. As it was discussed above, should the accused waive their right to be present (or intend to escape) and the subsequent proceedings were conducted in a fair manner, there should be no need for a re-trial. Still the STL Statute allowed for it even when e.g., the accused waived the right to be present (and did not appoint a counsel).[80] Even in case of a necessary re-trial though, there is a problem. The STL Statute counts on the re-trial to be conducted by the STL itself. But the STL has already concluded its functions and ceased to exist. Thus, such right would be illusory without any special regulation.[81]

In conclusion, while the legacy of the STL may succumb to criticism both for existence of exceptions as well as for the way the law was interpreted, it has proven that there are situations where a tribunal may not work without the ability to hold a trial *in absentia*. And the STL helped, certainly on theoretical level, to secure certain human rights standards of holding such trials. It is also noteworthy that the exceptions to the trial *in absentia* cover those without need of initial appearance of the accused. That might prove crucial in relation to the mechanism for prosecuting the crime of aggression committed against Ukraine.

The significant points of the STL were thus briefly summarized e.g., as follows:

> The Statute permits trials to commence and to end also without an accused ever having showed up in court, and even where they have failed to appoint a defence lawyer, on the mere conditions that, where the indictment could not be served or notified to the accused, it was duly publicized through the media or communicated to the state of residence or nationality of the accused, and where the accused failed to appoint a

80 Should letter b) exception be understood as based on lack of will of the concerned State, it could lead to an absurd situation where if the accused appointed their own counsel but would not be allowed to appear, they would not be entitled to a re-trial.

81 Especially considering possible consequences of Art. 5(1) of the STL Statute confirming that "[n]*o person shall be tried before a national court of Lebanon for acts for which he or she has already been tried by the Special Tribunal.*" A partial possible solution would be in interpreting this provision to only apply in case of final conviction, i.e., one not susceptible to re-trial. Mertins, *supra* note 32, 76.

defence counsel, the Defence Office assigned counsel to represent the accused in his absence.[82]

5.7 *International Criminal Court*

In 1998, the Rome Statute was concluded after long debates during which there were many controversial issues that various delegations considered as an obstacle to compromise, including the matter of trials *in absentia*.[83] It is visible on provisions dealing with proceedings *in absentia* that the previously outlined experience of the *ad hoc* tribunals materialized in the debates and text of the Rome Statute and was probably a basis to reach a common ground and circumvent the disagreements in that regard.

The trial *in absentia* as such, is however not allowed under the sole text of the Rome Statute.[84] Article 63(1) RS states that "[t]*he accused shall be present during the trial.*"[85] And in paragraph 2 it adds that:

> If the accused, being present before the Court, continues to disrupt the trial, the Trial Chamber may remove the accused and shall make provision for him or her to observe the trial and instruct counsel from outside the courtroom, through the use of communications technology, if required. Such measures shall be taken only in exceptional circumstances after other reasonable alternatives have proved inadequate, and only for such duration as is strictly required.

The very narrow exception is not really a trial *in absentia*. Even if removed from the hearing due to disrupting the trial, the accused is in fact still present before the ICC. The removal is conditioned by exhaustion of all other reasonable alternatives and still guaranteeing the accused the right to participate via

---

82 Gaeta, *supra* note 31, 1168–1169.

83 For an overview of the debates, *see e.g.*, Schabas and Caruana, *supra* note 10, 1852–1853, mns. 7–11.

84 Wording of Art. 76(4) RS ("*The sentence shall be pronounced in public and, wherever possible, in the presence of the accused.*"), seemingly allowing for judgment *in absentia*, is considered as forgotten remainder of discussions regarding trial *in absentia*. Mertins, *supra* note 32, 96.

85 The phrase is a deviation from the human rights regime where being present is a right, not a duty. *See* ICC, *Prosecutor v Ruto and Sang* (Decision on Mr. Ruto's Request for Excusal from Continuous Presence at Trial) ICC-01/09-01/11-777, TChV(a) (18 June 2013), para. 104: "*the presence of the accused during the trial is not only a right* [...] *but also a duty.*" Thus, it is both a right and a duty under the RS. Nonetheless, presence may be excused by the ICC.

their counsel.[86] As such, the accused is not absent completely even if the strictest measures allowed are adopted. Thus, a typical trial *in absentia* is not truly allowed under the text of the RS itself despite numerous attempts to reinterpret this position.[87] These attempts, though motivated by effective exercise of justice, are hardly consistent with the RS given the fact that Article 63 imposes a duty to be present,[88] allows for very limited exceptions, and Article 67(1)(d) RS explicitly conditions the right to be present only by Article 63(2) RS. One should also not forget that the wording of the RS is a result of a clear rejection of trial *in absentia* as such during negotiations of the Rome Statute. Interpreting the RS, as it is now, contrarily to the rejection of trial *in absentia* could run counter to Articles 31 and 32 of the Vienna Convention on the Law of Treaties.[89]

The further exceptions developed by in the ICC RPE must be read in light of the above-stated limitations. Thus, they are quite special and very limited. Under Rule 134*bis*, the accused may be physically absent during trial but they are connected via telecommunications technologies. And under Rules 134*ter* and 134*quarter*, they are voluntarily absent and excused but still represented by a counsel. Although wording of the Rules ("*accused subject to a summons to appear*") clearly indicates that those Rules do not apply to trial where the accused was not initially present, these new exceptions stretch interpretation of the text of the RS provisions towards its limits in the latter two cases.

The experience of the *ad hoc* tribunals materialized predominantly in the pre-trial stage. Article 61 RS allows for pre-trial proceedings *in absentia*, i.e., for confirmation of charges hearing. It contains certain similarities to Rule 61 of

86 "[A] *defendant who is virtually present by participating via video link is often deemed to be present.*" Mertins, *supra* note 32, 35.

87 Described e.g., in Schabas and Caruana, *supra* note 10, 1881–1883, mns. 93–95.

88 Grounds presented by various ICC Chambers for the presence of the accused during trial (and basically defending it being both a right and a duty) have been summarized as including the following: "*that it reflects 'the gravitas of the proceedings* [footnote omitted ...] *that it provides the victims with the opportunity to face the accused in Court and is important for the morale of the victims and witnesses;* [footnote omitted] *that it helps to create a 'comprehensive record of the relevant events';* [footnote omitted] *that it protects the rights of the accused and ensures that the accused is in a position to identify any incongruities between personal memories and those presented in the testimonial evidence brought by the prosecution* [footnote omitted ...] *that it provides judges with 'the opportunity to observe all the parties, including the accused, as the evidence is presented'*[footnote omitted]." Ibid, 1861.

89 Vienna Convention on the Law of Treaties (adopted 22 May 1969, entered into force 27 January 1980) 1155 UNTS 331.

the ICTY RPE. Like in front of the ICTY, the ICC confirms charges. On the other hand, while the evidentiary standard under the ICTY RPE was reasonable grounds to believe, the RS requires substantial grounds to believe. Further, unlike with ICTY, the process is obligatory in front of the ICC in every case and as a general rule, the accused is supposed to be present during the proceedings in front of the ICC. In front of ICTY, the proceedings were counted on in situation of absence of the accused only.

Thus, generally under Article 61(1) RS, the charged person, their counsel and Prosecutor shall be present during a hearing to confirm charges before the Pre-Trial Chamber. Paragraph two counts on two alternative exceptions to presence of the charged person however if:

i. the charged person has waived the right to be present, or
ii. the charged person has *"fled or cannot be found and all reasonable steps have been taken to secure his or her appearance before the Court and to inform the person of the charges and that a hearing to confirm those charges will be held."*

Where the Pre-Trial Chamber decides that it is in the interest of justice, the charged person will also be obligatorily represented by a counsel during the confirmation of charges hearing conducted in their absence. Paragraph 3 adds that the charged person will be provided with the charges and informed of the evidence within a reasonable time before the hearing.

From the perspective of proceedings *in absentia*, the confirmation of charges hearing in the RS is a peculiar regulation. On one hand, it is not a trial *in absentia*, it is pre-trial procedure. As such, the human rights requirements guaranteeing fairness of criminal proceedings *in absentia* are arguably not so strictly applicable. The authors of the RS nonetheless decided to apply some of those human rights requirements to it (legal representation to a certain degree, notification of the charges). The right of re-trial is not dealt with in this hearing though in the RS because there is logically no judgment issued as a result of the confirmation of charges hearing. The purpose of the proceedings to confirm charges under the RS is to sort out the cases submitted by the Prosecutor, and only allow to go forward those that are supported by evidence satisfying the *substantial grounds to believe* standard; and to inform the charged person in detail about the charges and evidence collected to be used during trial.[90]

---

90 *"Confirmation hearings serve to protect 'the suspect from wrongful and unfounded accusations, by ensuring that only those persons against whom sufficiently compelling charges going beyond mere theory or suspicion have been brought are committed for trial'* [footnote omitted]" ICC, *Prosecutor v Joseph Kony* (Decision on the Prosecution's Request to Hold a

The exception to the general rule of the charged person's presence during the hearing consists of a waiver (in narrow meaning of letter i)) and absconding/not being found. The first one is based upon availability (and logically even initial appearance) of the charged person, while the latter expects that the charged person is not available to the ICC. Subsequently, while absconding logically also requires initial appearance (and subsequent absconding), "not being found" does not. Thus, an initial appearance is not necessary in the second exception when the charged person "cannot be found".[91]

The exceptions are similarly constructed like those to trial *in absentia* in front of the STL. Nonetheless, the second STL exception is missing in the RS (not being handed over by the concerned State). The consequence is that under the RS, if the charged person did not initially appear (thus the waiver and absconding do not apply) and the ICC is generally aware of their location or residence, the confirmation hearing *in absentia* may not take place. In front of the STL (and in case of a trial), that was possible due to the second exception. The RS does not contain such exception even in relation to pre-trial proceedings though.[92]

Under the first exception, the waiver request must be made in writing and will only be granted if the Pre-Trial Chamber is satisfied that the charged person understands the right and the consequences of a decision not to be present.[93]

The second provision containing exceptions (Article 61(2)(b) RS), based on absconding and not being found, has another similarity to the STL Statute. There is also explicitly stated a second stage to be considered by the Pre-Trial Chamber. After deciding that the charged person absconded, or cannot be found, it has to make sure that all reasonable (although not necessarily suc-

---

Confirmation of Charges Hearing in the Kony case in the Suspect's Absence) ICC-02/04-01/05-466, PTChII (23 November 2023), para. 25.

91 The Pre-Trial Chamber had to clarify that fact due to the (rejected) submissions claiming (based on Art. 60(1) RS) that even second exception required initial appearance of the charged person. ICC, *Prosecutor v Joseph Kony* (Decision on the Prosecution's Request to Hold a Confirmation of Charges Hearing in the Kony case in the Suspect's Absence) ICC-02/04-01/05-466, PTChII (23 November 2023), paras. 24–30.

92 In relation to the "cannot be found" exception, the ICC confirmed that "[t]*he concept* [...] *does not cover a situation in which the approximate whereabouts of the person are known but the Court is unable to have an arrest warrant executed due to reasons unrelated to the identification of the suspect's location, for instance due to lack of cooperation from relevant States.*" ICC, *Prosecutor v Joseph Kony* (Decision on the Prosecution's Request to Hold a Confirmation of Charges Hearing in the Kony case in the Suspect's Absence) ICC-02/04-01/05-466, PTChII (23 November 2023), para. 32.

93 ICC RPE, Rule 124(1 and 2).

cessful)[94] steps to have been taken with the purpose of securing the appearance of the charged person before the ICC, to inform them of the charges, and additionally (in comparison to the text of the STL Statute) about the hearing. In any case, the second stage must be preceded with all reasonable measures to locate and arrest the person.[95]

The decision by the Pre-Trial Chamber to hold the confirmation hearing *in absentia* is purely discretionary though. The sources of law regulate the requirements to be fulfilled but the arguments whether to hold the hearings or not, are left upon the judges. The Pre-Trial Chamber thus discussed issues similar (and going beyond)[96] to those contained in the Part above dealing with arguments in favor and against holding any proceedings *in absentia* (not just pre-trial proceedings). And after doing so, the Pre-Trial Chamber observed that "[e]*ven if the charges were to be confirmed following a hearing in absentia, the Court's ability to fully realise the objectives of the Statute and address the victims' interests in justice and accountability would remain limited*,"[97] because the RS does not allow for trial *in absentia*. Thus, the judges made a powerful statement that resonates even with regard to the situation in Ukraine and any future proceedings in front of the ICC. The quote deserves a full repetition:

> The Chamber recalls that the [Rome] Statute does not allow proceedings *in absentia* to be held beyond the confirmation of charges hearing. In the view of the Chamber, to fully materialise the objectives outlined above, the statutory framework should have foreseen the possibility to conduct a trial *in absentia*, when charges are confirmed pursuant to article 61(2)(b) of the Statute and the interests of justice so demand. This, without prejudice to the rights of the defendant to have a re-trial

94 When stating so, the Pre-Trial Chamber even referred to STL case law. ICC, *Prosecutor v Joseph Kony* (Decision on the Prosecution's Request to Hold a Confirmation of Charges Hearing in the Kony case in the Suspect's Absence) ICC-02/04-01/05-466, PTChII (23 November 2023), para. 33.

95 ICC RPE, Rule 123(3). Although the Rule says so in case where "*the warrant of arrest has not been executed*" (i.e., to "not being found" exception, not to absconding) and in fact, in case of absconding, it may have already been executed (but the charged person later absconded), the requirement to locate and arrest the person should equally apply (again) to absconding situation because the charged person's presence has to be secured again.

96 ICC, *Prosecutor v Joseph Kony* (Decision on the Prosecution's Request to Hold a Confirmation of Charges Hearing in the Kony case in the Suspect's Absence) ICC-02/04-01/05-466, PTChII (23 November 2023), paras. 59–68.

97 Ibid, para. 66.

> if he or she later appears before the Court. Although this cannot relate to the present case, it would be valuable for States Parties to reconsider the discipline of *in absentia* trial proceedings before the Court, in this regard for any future instances.[98]

In conclusion, while the authors of the Rome Statute declined to adopt a provision on trials *in absentia*, they were still likely inspired by the experience of previous tribunals when formulating the requirements of the pre-trial hearings *in absentia*. Even so far limited experience of the ICC practice regarding this provision however already shows the limited effectiveness of such proceedings.

The 1990s decade, when the Rome Statute was concluded, was a period of more optimistic view regarding co-operation between members of the international community than it is today. It may have been that the idea of trial in absence of the accused seemed unnecessary because States were more willing to cooperate in general and possibly even in surrendering the accused to the ICC. Unfortunately, that optimism has to certain degree disappeared and it may be the right time to reconsider the approach to trials *in absentia* not just under the Rome Statute but also in case of the mechanism to assess the crime of aggression committed against Ukraine.

6 Mechanism for the Crime of Aggression Committed against Ukraine

A lot has already been written upon the reasons for need of a new mechanism[99] and this Part will not repeat them. It builds upon the fact that States and other stakeholders have already begun investing into the new mechanism.

98 Ibid, para. 70.

99 *See. e.g.*, contributions to section *crime of aggression* of the Justsecurity.org blog, available online at <https://www.justsecurity.org/82513/just-securitys-russia-ukraine-war-archive/> (last accessed 8 October 2024); or Lipovský, Milan, 'What is 'a Certain International Criminal Court' and Does the Choice of a Fully International or Internationalized (Hybrid) Court/Chambers Matter for the Crime of Aggression Committed against Ukraine?' (2023) 43 *Polish Yearbook of International Law* 213; or in Czech language: Lipovský, Milan, 'Nový (zvláštní) mezinárodní trestní tribunál pro zločin agrese vůči Ukrajině anebo "staré" cesty? [New (special) international criminal tribunal for the crime of aggression against Ukraine or "old" paths?]' (2023) 2 *Jurisprudence* 12.

The negotiations between the so-called Core Group of States regarding creation of a tribunal have considered several forms.[100] No matter the specific eventually chosen type, the topic of proceedings *in absentia* must surely be raised due to the fact that the suspects themselves as well as their State(s) of nationality/residence will likely not want to cooperate with the mechanism.[101]

In addition to the arguments in favor of proceedings *in absentia* discussed above, it might be added that due to its large-scale character, the crime of aggression turns entire nations into victims.[102] In such a situation, justice should be served even with potential risks (such as justice served *in absentia*). While truth commissions could bring certain positive outcomes as well, their role is different from judicial criminal proceedings. They do not determine individual criminal responsibility, an aspect certainly important for victims.

As the previous Parts have proven, pre-trial proceedings *in absentia* (e.g., an indictment confirmation chamber or confirmation of charges hearing) may be more acceptable for the wider forum of States. Such proceedings might be helpful in collecting and safeguarding evidence and providing basic grounds for historical memory. How strong it would be, depends on the chosen evidentiary standard. The choice would most likely be between reasonable grounds to believe and substantial grounds to believe. But that is still not the same as finding an individual criminally responsible and pointing a judicial finger beyond all reasonable doubt.

When the mechanism (for the assessment of international individual criminal responsibility for the crime of aggression committed against Ukraine) starts functioning, there is a risk that its performance will only be possible in absence of the accused. With all previously written in mind, the trial (in best case) *in absentia*, and/or pre-trial proceedings *in absentia* should be counted on in its formation. Obviously with all relevant human rights guarantees applicable.

---

100 *See e.g.*, chapters in this book by Jennifer Trahan, Pavel Šturma, and Emil Ruffer.

101 It would neither be a first trial *in absentia* for offense of crime of aggression conducted in relation to the situation in Ukraine. For a description of the case against the former Ukrainian president Viktor Yanukovych (and criticism regarding certain aspects of it), *see* Marchuk, *supra* note 6, 791–792.

102 Korynevych, Anton, Senatorova, Oksana, Shepitko, Mykhaylo, 'Prosecution of the Crime of Aggression in International and Ukrainian Jurisdiction: Challenges and Prospects' (2023) *Polish Yearbook of International Law* 367, 373.

7 Conclusions

The chapter discussed various argument in favor as well as against the proceedings *in absentia* in international criminal law. It found that both the legal as well as theoretical arguments in that regard are deeply divided. Eventually, it is thus upon the authors of statutes of individual tribunals to consider whether the circumstances are so special that they warrant for the choice of a solution that big part of international community considers controversial.

Nonetheless, it must be clearly stated that there are no total legal obstacles even to full trials *in absentia* from the human rights perspective. With guarantees, such as notification, representation, and re-trial, even trial *in absentia* as such may be conducted in compliance with human rights standards.

Pre-trial proceedings *in absentia* are more often adopted in the practice of international criminal tribunals (as opposed to trials *in absentia*). However, despite best efforts, the outcomes that such proceeding can deliver, are largely limited. Especially in case of first proceedings for a crime of aggression at the international level since Nuremberg and Tokyo, the pre-trial proceedings *in absentia* may not be sufficient solution.

Controversies surrounding holding proceedings *in absentia* grow in strength along with later stages of criminal proceedings. It is paradoxical however, that so do risks of passivity of criminal justice, especially in cases of serious crimes, including crimes under international law.

In conclusion and in relation to the situation in Ukraine with regard to the crime of aggression (and not only), it should be stated that as long as there will be lack of cooperation between relevant actors to bring the suspects to court, proceedings *in absentia* should counted on.

Bibliography

International Treaties

General Treaty for Renunciation of War as an Instrument of National Policy (adopted 27 August 1928, entered into force 25 July 1929) 94 LNTS 57

(London) Charter of the International Military Tribunal, Annexed to the Agreement by the Government of the United Kingdom of Great Britain and Northern Ireland, the Government of the United States of America, the Provisional Government of the French Republic and the Government of the Union of Soviet Socialist Republics for the Prosecution and Punishment of the Major War Criminals of the European Axis (adopted and entered into force 8 August 1945) 82 UNTS 279

Charter of the United Nations (adopted 26 June 1945, entered into force 24 October 1945) 892 UNTS 119

(UN) Convention on the Prevention and Punishment of the Crime of Genocide (adopted 9 December 1948, entered into force 12 January 1951) 78 UNTS 277

Statute of the Council of Europe (adopted 5 May 1949, entered into force 3 August 1949) ETS No. 1

(European) Convention for the Protection of Human Rights and Fundamental Freedoms (adopted 4 November 1950, entered into force 3 September 1953) ETS No. 5

International Covenant on Civil and Political Rights (adopted 16 December 1966, entered into force 23 March 1976) 999 UNTS 171

Vienna Convention on the Law of Treaties (adopted 22 May 1969, entered into force 27 January 1980) 1155 UNTS 331

(UN) Convention against Torture and other Cruel, Inhuman or Degrading Treatment or Punishment (adopted 10 December 1984, entered into force 26 June 1987) 1465 UNTS 85

Rome Statute of the International Criminal Court (adopted 17 July 1998, entered into force 1 July 2002) 2187 UNTS 3

Agreement between the United Nations and the Government of Sierra Leone on the Establishment of a Special Court for Sierra Leone (adopted 16 January 2002, entered into force 12 April 2002) 2178 UNTS 137

Case Law

Nuremberg Trials

IMT, U.S.A, France, UK, and USSR v Hermann Wilhelm Goring, et al., Judgment, Trial of the Major War Criminals (1 October 1946)

International Court of Justice

ICJ, *Reparation for Injuries Suffered in the Service of the United Nations*, Advisory Opinion, ICJ Reports 1949

ICJ, *Effect of Award of Compensation by the United Nations Administrative Tribunal*, Advisory Opinion, ICJ Reports 1954

ICJ, *Certain Expenses of the United Nations (Article 17, paragraph 2, of the Charter)* Advisory Opinion, ICJ Reports 1962

ICJ, *Legality of the Use by a State of Nuclear Weapons in Armed Conflict*, Advisory Opinion, ICJ Reports 1996

ICJ, *Arrest Warrant of 11 April 2000* (Democratic Republic of the Congo v. Belgium) Judgment of 4 February 2002, ICJ Reports 2002

ICJ, *Questions Relating to the Obligation to Prosecute or Extradite* (Belgium v Senegal) Judgment of 20 July 2012, ICJ Reports 2012

International Criminal Court

ICC, *Prosecutor v Omar Hassan Ahmad Al Bashir* (Decision Pursuant to Article 87(7) of the Rome Statute on the Failure by the Republic of Malawi to Comply with the Cooperation Requests Issued by the Court with Respect to the Arrest and Surrender of Omar Hassan Ahmad Al Bashir) ICC-02/05-01/09-139, PTChI (12 December 2011)

ICC, *Prosecutor v Omar Hassan Ahmad Al Bashir* (Decision pursuant to Article 87(7) of the Rome Statute on the refusal of the Republic of Chad to comply with the cooperation requests issued by the Court with respect to the arrest and surrender of Omar Hassan Ahmad Al Bashir) ICC-02/05-01/09-140, PTChI (13 December 2011)

ICC, *Prosecutor v Omar Hassan Ahmad Al Bashir* (Decision on the Cooperation of the Democratic Republic of the Congo Regarding Omar Al Bashir's Arrest and Surrender to the Court) ICC-02/05-01/09-195, PTChII (9 April 2014)

ICC, *Prosecutor v Omar Hassan Ahmad Al Bashir* (Decision under Article 87(7) of the Rome Statute on the non-compliance by South Africa with the request by the Court for the arrest and surrender of Omar Al-Bashir) ICC-02/05-01/09-302, PTChII (6 July 2017)

ICC, *Prosecutor v Omar Hassan Ahmad Al Bashir* (Decision under Article 87(7) of the Rome Statute on the non-compliance by Jordan with the request by the Court for the arrest and surrender of Omar Al-Bashir) ICC-02/05-01/09-309, PTChII (11 December 2017)

ICC, Request by Professor Roger O'Keefe for Leave to Submit Observations on the Merits of the Legal Questions Presented in 'The Hashemite Kingdom of Jordan's appeal against the "Decision under Article 87(7) of the Rome Statute on the non -compliance by Jordan with the request by the Court for the arrest and surrender [of] Omar Al-Bashir" of 12 March 2018 (ICC-02/05-01/09-326), ICC-02/05-01/09-334 (19 April 2018)

ICC, Observations by Professor Roger O'Keefe, pursuant to Rule 103 of the Rules of Procedure and Evidence, ICC-02/05-01/09-360 (18 June 2018)

ICC, *Prosecutor v Omar Hassan Ahmad Al-Bashir* (Judgment in the Jordan Referral Re Al-Bashir Appeal) ICC-02/05-01/09-397-Corr, ACh (6 May 2019)

ICC, Joint Concurring Opinion of Judges Eboe-Osuji, Morrison, Hofmański and Bossa to Judgment in the Jordan Referral Re Al-Bashir Appeal, ICC-02/05-01/09-397-Anx1 (6 May 2019)

ICC, *Prosecutor v Joseph Kony* (Decision on the Prosecution's Request to Hold a Confirmation of Charges Hearing in the Kony case in the Suspect's Absence) ICC-02/04-01/05-466, PTChII (23 November 2023)

ICC, *Prosecutor v Ruto and Sang* (Decision on Mr. Ruto's Request for Excusal from Continuous Presence at Trial) ICC-01/09-01/11-777, TChV(a) (18 June 2013)

International Criminal Tribunal for the Former Yugoslavia

ICTY, *Prosecutor v Blaškić* (Judgment on the Request of the Republic of Croatia for Review of the Decision of Trial Chamber II of 18 July 1997) ICTY-95-14-AR, ACh (29 October 1997)

ICTY, *Prosecutor v Milošević* (Decision on Review of Indictment and Application for Consequential Orders) IT-99-37-I (24 May 1999)

ICTY, *Prosecutor v Tadić* (Decision on the Defence Motion for Interlocutory Appeal on Jurisdiction) IT-94-1-AR72, ACh (2 October 1995)

International Criminal Tribunal for Rwanda

ICTR, *Prosecutor v Karemera et al.* (Decision on Prosecutor's Interlocutory Appeal of Decision on Judicial Notice) ICTR-98-44-AR73(c), ACh (16 June 2006)

ICTR, *Prosecutor v Laurent Semanza* (Decision on the Prosecutor's Motion for Judicial Notice and Presumptions of Facts Pursuant to Rules 94 and 54) ICTR-97-20-I, TChIII (3 November 2000)

Special Court for Sierra Leone

SCSL, *Prosecutor v Norman et al., Fofana* (Decision on Appeal against 'Decision on Prosecution's Motion for Judicial Notice and Admission of Evidence) SCSL-2004-14-AR73, ACh (16 May 2005)

SCSL, Submissions of the Amicus Curiae on Head of State Immunity by Professor Philippe Sands and Alison Macdonald to Decision on Immunity from Jurisdiction, SCSL-01-I-1669 (23 October 2003)

SCSL, *Prosecutor v Taylor* (Decision on Immunity from Jurisdiction) SCSL-2003-01-I, ACh (31 May 2004)

Special Tribunal for Lebanon

STL, *Prosecutor v Ayyash, Badreddine, Oneissi and Sabra* (Decision on Defence Appeals against Trial Chamber's Decision on Reconsideration of the Trial *in Absentia* Decision) STL-11-01/PT/AC/AR126.1, ACh (1 November 2012)

STL, *Prosecutor v Ayyash* (Decision to Hold Trial *in Absentia*) STL-18-10/I/TC, TChII (5 February 2020)

Human Rights Committee

HRC, *Maleki v Italy*, comm. no. 699/1996, Views of 15 July 1999

HRC, *Mbenge v Zaire*, comm. no. 16/1977, Views of 25 March 1983

HRC, *Igor Kostin v Russian Federation*, comm. no. 2496/2014, Views of 4 May 2017

European Court of Human Rights

ECtHR, *Demebukov v Bulgaria*, app. no. 68020/01, Chamber's Judgment of 28 February 2008

ECtHR, *Sejdovic v Italy*, app. no. 56581/00, Grand Chamber's Judgment of 1 March 2006

ECtHR, *Ukraine and the Netherlands v Russia*, app. nos. 8019/16, 43800/14 and 28525/20, Grand Chamber's Decision of 25 January 2023

Domestic Case Law

Canada, *R. v. Zundel*, [1992] 2 S.C.R. 731

Canada, *R. v. Zundel*, 1987 CanLII 121

Canada, *R. v. Zundel*, Ontario Court of Appeal, 1990 CarswellOnt 1075

U.S.A, *City Bank Farmers Trust Co. v. United States*, 74 F.2d 692 (2d Cir. 1935)

U.S.A, Supreme Court, *Crosby v. United States*, 506 U.S. 255 (1993)

UN Sources

UN General Assembly

UNGA Res 95(I), Affirmation of the Principles of International Law Recognized by the Charter of the Nürnberg Tribunal (11 December 1946)

UNGA Res 351 A(IV), Establishment of a United Nations Administrative Tribunal (24 November 1949)

UNGA Res 377, Uniting for Peace (3 November 1950)

UNGA Res 3314 (XXIX), Definition of Aggression (14 December 1974)

UNGA Res 57/228, Khmer Rouge Trials (22 May 2003)

UNGA Res 57/228 B, Khmer Rouge Trials (22 May 2003)

UNGA Res ES-11/1, Aggression against Ukraine (2 March 2022)

UNGA Res ES-11/3, Suspension of the Rights of Membership of the Russian Federation in the Human Rights Council (7 April 2022)
UNGA Res 76/262, Standing Mandate for a General Assembly Debate When a Veto is Cast in the Security Council (26 April 2022)
UNGA Res ES-11/5, Furtherance of Remedy and Reparation for Aggression against Ukraine (14 November 2022)
UNGA Res ES-11/6, Principles of the Charter of the United Nations Underlying a Comprehensive, Just and Lasting Peace in Ukraine (23 February 2023)
UNGA Res ES-11/7, Advancing a Comprehensive, Just and Lasting Peace in Ukraine (24 February 2025)
UNGA Res ES-11/8, The Path to Peace (25 February 2025)

UN Security Council

UNSC Res 687 (1991) (3 April 1991)
UNSC Res 808 (1993) (19 February 1993)
UNSC Res 827 (1993) (25 May)
UNSC Res 955 (1994) (8 November 1994)
UNSC Res 1264 (1999) (15 September 1999)
UNSC Res 1272 (1999) (25 October 1999)
UNSC Res 1315 (2000) (14 August 2000)
UNSC Res 1503 (2003) (28 August 2003)
UNSC Res 1593 (2005) (31 March 2005)
UNSC Res 1757 (2007) (30 May 2007)
UNSC Res 1966 (2010) (22 December 2010)
UNSC Res 2774 (2025) (24 February 2025)

International Law Commission

ILC, Principles of International Law Recognized in the Charter of the Nürnberg Tribunal and in the Judgment of the Tribunal (1950), YILC, 1950, vol. II
ILC, Draft Code of Offences against the Peace and Security of Mankind (1954), YILC, 1954, vol. II
ILC, Draft Statute for an International Criminal Court with commentaries (1994), YILC, 1994, vol. II, Part Two
ILC, Draft Code of Crimes against the Peace and Security of Mankind (1996), YILC, 1996, vol. II, Part II
ILC, Articles on Responsibility of States for Internationally Wrongful Acts with commentaries (2001), YILC, 2001, vol. II, Part Two
ILC, Identification of Customary International Law, Third Report by Sir Michael Wood, Special Rapporteur, A/CN.4/682, 27 March 2015

ILC, Draft Conclusions on Subsequent Agreements and Subsequent Practice in Relation to the Interpretation of Treaties (2018), YILC, vol. II, Part Two

ILC, Report of the ILC, Seventy-seventh Session, Supplement No. 10, UN Doc. A/77/10

Other UN Documents

UN Office of Legal Affairs Webpage, United Nations Diplomatic Conference of Plenipotentiaries on the Establishment of an International Criminal Court. Rome, 15 June – 17 July 1998, available online at <https://legal.un.org/icc/rome/proceedings/contents.htm>

Report of the Group of Experts for Cambodia, UN Doc. A/53/850 – S/1999/231

UNTAET/REG/2000/15 (6 June 2000)

Report of the International Commission of Inquiry on East Timor to the Secretary General, UN Doc. A/54/726, S/2000/59 (2000)

UNMIK/REG/2000/64 (15 December 2000), on assignment of international judges / prosecutors and/or change of venue, as amended by UNMIK/REG/2001/34 (15 December 2001)

UNGA, A/CN.4/L.969, International Law Commission, Seventy-Third Session, 'Draft Articles on Immunity of State Officials from Foreign Criminal Jurisdiction', Draft Art. 7 (31 May 2022)

UN, Preparatory Commission for the International Criminal Court, PCNICC/2002/WGCA/L 1.Add.1

UN Office of Legal Affairs Webpage, Preparatory Commission for the International Criminal Court, available online at <https://legal.un.org/icc/prepcomm/prepfra.htm>

Security Council Report, Article 27(3) and Parties to a Dispute: An Abridged History, available online at <https://www.securitycouncilreport.org/atf/cf/%7B65BFCF9B-6D27-4E9C-8CD3-CF6E4FF96FF9%7D/article_27_3_and_parties_to_a_dispute.pdf>

Other International Organizations

African Union

African Union (Assembly) 'Decision on the Meeting of African States Parties to the Rome Statute of the International Criminal Court (ICC) Doc. Assembly/AU/13(XIII)' (3 July 2009), Assembly/AU/Dec.245(XIII) Rev. 1

African Union (Assembly) 'Decision on the Progress Report of the Commission on the Implementation of Decision Assembly/AU/Dec.270(XIV) on the Second Ministerial Meeting on the Rome Statute of the International Criminal Court (ICC) Doc. Assembly/AU/10(XV)' (27 July 2010), Assembly/AU/Dec.296(XV)

African Union (Assembly) 'Decision on the Implementation of the Decisions on the International Criminal Court (ICC) Doc. EX.CL/639(XVIII)' (30–31 January 2011), Assembly/AU/Dec.334(XVI)

African Union (Assembly) 'Decision on the Implementation of the Assembly Decisions on the International Criminal Court. Doc. EX.CL/670(XIX)' (30 June 1 July 2011), Assembly/AU/Dec.366(XVII)

Statute of the Extraordinary African Chambers (2012), *International Legal Materials*, vol. 52, 2013

Council of Europe

Council of Europe (Parliamentary Assembly) 'The Russian Federation's Aggression against Ukraine: Ensuring Accountability for Serious Violations of International Humanitarian Law and Other International Crimes' (28 April 2022), resolution 2436 (2022)

Council of Europe (Committee of Minister's Deputies) 'Consequences of the Aggression of the Russian Federation against Ukraine – Accountability for International Crimes' (15 September 2022), decision CM/Del/Dec(2022)1442/2.3

Council of Europe (Parliamentary Assembly), 'Legal and Human Rights Aspects of the Russian Federation's Aggression against Ukraine' (26 January 2023), resolution 2482 (2023)

Council of Europe, 'United Around Our Values, Declaration of 4th Summit of Heads of State and Government of the Council of Europe', Reykjavík (16-17 May 2023)

Council of Europe (Committee of Minister's Deputies), 4th Summit of Heads of State and Government of the Council of Europe (Reykjavík, Iceland, 16-17 May 2023) – Follow-up (5 July 2023), CM/Del/Dec(2023)1471/1.6

Council of Europe (Committee of Minister's Deputies) '*Core Group* on the Establishment of a Special Tribunal for the Crime of Aggression of the Russian Federation against Ukraine' (30 April 2024) CMD CM/Del/Dec(2024)1497/10.2

Council of Europe (Parliamentary Assembly) 'Legal and Human Rights Aspects of the Russian Federation's Aggression against Ukraine' (26 June 2024), resolution 2556 (2024)

Council of Europe (Parliamentary Assembly) 'European Commitment to a Just and Lasting Peace in Ukraine' (30 January 2025), resolution 2588 (2025)

Council of Europe (Parliamentary Assembly) 'Russian War of Aggression against Ukraine: the Need to Ensure Accountability and Avoid Impunity' (9 April 2025), resolution 2598 (2025)

European Union

European Union (European Parliament), Resolution 2022/3017(RSP) on the Establishment of a Tribunal on the Crime of Aggression against Ukraine (19 January 2023), Official Journal of the EU 2023/C 214/10

International Criminal Court

ICC, Assembly of States Parties, Continuity of Work in Respect of the Crime of Aggression, ICC-ASP/1/Res.1 (9 September 2002), available online at <https://asp.icc-cpi.int/sites/asp/files/asp_docs/Resolutions/icc-asp-asp1-Res-01-ENG.pdf>

ICC, Assembly of States Parties, Review Conference, The Crime of Aggression, Annex I, ICC Doc. RC/Res.6 (11 June 2010), available online at <https://treaties.un.org/doc/source/docs/RC-Res.6-ENG.pdf>

ICC, Assembly of States Parties, ICC-ASP/3/SWGCA/INF.1

ICC, Assembly of States Parties, ICC-ASP/5/SWGCA/INF.1

ICC, Assembly of States Parties, ICC-ASP/6/SWGCA/INF.1

Report of the Special Working Group on the Crime of Aggression, ICC-ASP/6/20/Add.1, Annex II (June 2008)

ICC, Assembly of States Parties, ICC-ASP/7/20/Add/1

ICC, Assembly of States Parties, Activation of the Jurisdiction of the Court over the Crime of Aggression, ICC-ASP/16/Res.5 (14 December 2017)

ICC, Office of the Prosecutor, Statement of the Prosecutor of the International Criminal Court, Karim A.A. Khan K.C, Announcing his Decision to Conclude the Investigation Phase in the Situation in Uganda, 1 January 2023, available online at <https://www.icc-cpi.int/news/statement-prosecutor-international-criminal-court-karim-aa-khan-kc-announcing-his-decision>

ICC, Assembly of States Parties, Strengthening the International Criminal Court and the Assembly of States Parties, ICC-ASP/22/Res.3 (13 December 2023), available online at <https://asp.icc-cpi.int/sites/default/files/asp_docs/ICC-ASP-22-Res3-ENG.pdf>

Document ICC-ASP/23/10, available online at <https://asp.icc-cpi.int/sites/default/files/asp_docs/ICC-ASP-23-10-ENG.pdf>

ICC, Assembly of States Parties, Strengthening the International Criminal Court and the Assembly of States Parties, ICC-ASP/23/Res.1 (6 December 2024), available online at <https://asp.icc-cpi.int/sites/default/files/asp_docs/ICC-ASP-23-Res.1-ENG.pdf>

Other Intergovernmental Organizations

Official Records of the United Nations Conference on the Law of Treaties between States and International Organizations or between International Organizations, vol. II

Report of the Conference of the Heads of Governments of Great Britain, the United States and USSR (Potsdam, 2 August 1945), *American Journal of International Law*, vol. 39 (1945), Suppl.

Domestic Legislation

Belarus, Criminal Code of 1999

Cambodia, Law on the Establishment of the Extraordinary Chambers, with inclusion of amendments as promulgated on 27 October 2004, ns/rkm/1004/006

Czech Republic, Code of Criminal Procedure, Law no. 141/1961 Coll.

Kosovo, Assembly, Law No. 04/L-274, On Ratification of the International Agreement Between the Republic of Kosovo and the European Union on the European Union Rule of Law Mission in Kosovo

Kosovo, Assembly, Amendment of the Constitution of the Republic of Kosovo, Amendment no. 24, No.05-D-139, 3 August 2015

Kosovo, Assembly, Law On Specialist Chambers and Specialist Prosecutor's Office, Law No. 05/L-053

Poland, Criminal Code of 1932

Poland, Criminal Code of 1997

Romania, Criminal Code of 1936

Russia, Criminal Code of 1996

Ukraine, Constitution of Ukraine, adopted at the Fifth Session of the Verkhovna Rada of Ukraine on 28 June 1996, as amended

Ukraine, Criminal Code of 2001

State Representatives' Speeches, Acts, Press Releases, Papers

Charter of the International Military Tribunal for the Far East in Tokyo, proclaimed at Tokyo, *T.I.A.S.* No. 1589

Control Council Law no. 10, available online at <https://www.legal-tools.org/doc/ffda62/pdf/>

Final Report to the Secretary of the Army on the Nuernberg War Crimes Trials Under Control Council Law No. 10 by Telford Taylor, Brigadier General, U.S.A. Chief of Counsel for War Crimes, Washington, D.C. (15 August 1949)

Address by President of the Russian Federation (18 March 2014), available online at <http://en.kremlin.ru/events/president/news/20603>

UK House of Commons Library, Briefing Paper, *Chilcot Inquiry*, No. CBP 6215, 1 July 2016, available online at <https://researchbriefings.files.parliament.uk/documents/SN06215/SN06215.pdf>

Speech by Foreign Minister Annalena Baerbock at the Commemoration of the 25th Anniversary of the Adoption of the Rome Statute of the International Criminal Court, 17 July 2021, available online at <https://www.auswaertiges-amt.de/en/newsroom/news/-/2609126>

Address by the President of the Russian Federation (24 February 2022), available online at <http://en.kremlin.ru/events/president/news/67843>

Letter dated 24 February 2022 from the Permanent Representative of the Russian Federation to the United Nations addressed to the Secretary-General, S/2022/154 (5 March 2022)

Ukraine: New Laws Criminalize Collaboration with an Aggressor State, available online at <https://www.loc.gov/item/global-legal-monitor/2022-04-04/ukraine-new-laws-criminalize-collaboration-with-an-aggressor-state/>

Letter dated 12 August 2022 from the Representatives of Latvia, Liechtenstein and Ukraine to the United Nations Addressed to the Secretary-General, UN Doc. A/ES-11/7-S/2022/616 (17 August 2022), available online at <https://www.justsecurity.org/wp-content/uploads/2022/09/UNSC-Letter-12-August-2022.pdf>

International Nuremberg Principles Academy, Nuremberg Declaration on the Crime of Aggression (8 May 2023), available online at <https://crimeofaggression.info/wp-content/uploads/Nuremberg_Declaration_on_the_Crime_of_Aggression.pdf>

Speech by the Federal Foreign Minister of Germany, Annalena Baerbock in The Hague entitled "Strengthening International Law in Times of Crisis" (16 January 2023), available online at <https://www.auswaertiges-amt.de/en/newsroom/news/strengthening-international-law-in-times-of-crisis/2573492>

UK Government Press Release, UK Joins Core Group Dedicated to Achieving Accountability for Russia's Aggression against Ukraine, 20 January 2023, available online at <https://www.gov.uk/government/news/ukraine-uk-joins-core-group-dedicated-to-achieving-accountability-for-russias-aggression-against-ukraine>

Joint Statement by Albania, Belgium, Costa Rica, Czech Republic, Estonia, Guatemala, Latvia, Liechtenstein, Lithuania, Luxembourg, Marshall Islands, North-Macedonia, and Poland on the Accountability for the Crime of Aggression Committed on the Territory of Ukraine (17 April 2023), available online at <https://un.mfa.ee/joint-statement-on-the-accountability-for-the-crime-of-aggression-committed-on-the-territory-of-ukraine/>

G7 Japan 2023 Foreign Ministers' Communiqué (18 April 2023) Karuizawa, Nagano, available online at <https://www.gov.uk/government/publications/g7-japan-2023-foreign-ministers-communique/g7-japan-2023-foreign-ministers-communique-18-april-2023-karuizawa-nagano>

Ambassador Van Schaack's Remarks on the U.S. Proposal to Prosecute Russian Crimes of Aggression (27 March 2023), available online at <https://www.state.gov/ambassador-van-schaacks-remarks/>

President of Ukraine, Volodymyr Zelenskyy, Official website, President: Ukraine Stands against Hybrid Formats of Tribunal for Russian Crime of Aggression, 4 May 2023, available online at <https://www.president.gov.ua/en/news/ukrayina-vistupaye-proti-gibridnih-formativ-tribunalu-shodo-82669>

Core Group, Joint Statement on Efforts to Establish a Tribunal on the Crime of Aggression against Ukraine (9 May 2023) available online at <https://www.president.gov.ua/en/news/spilna-zayava-stoso vno-zusil-zi-stvorennya-tribunalu-shodo-z-82785>

'"Hybrid Tribunal"': Does Not Give an Answer on How to Punish the Leaders of the Russian Federation', *Kuleba*, 9 September 2023, available online at <https://www.eurointegration.com.ua/news/2023/09/9/7169055/>

Letter to the Permanent Representatives of States Parties to the Rome Statute from the Permanent Missions of Costa Rica, Sierra Leone, Vanuatu, Germany and Slovenia to the United Nations, Mandated Review of the Kampala Amendments on the Crime of Aggression, dated 8 November 2024, available online at <https://crimeofaggression.info/wp-content/uploads/Letter-to-all-ICC-SPs_distribution-of-discussion-paper-on-review-of-Kampala-Amendments-on-the-Crime-of-Aggression_Nov-2024.pdf>

President of Ukraine, Official Website: On January 1, 2025, Ukraine Will Become the 125th Member State of the International Criminal Court, 25 October 2024, available online at <https://www.president.gov.ua/en/news/z-1-sichnya-2025-roku-ukrayina-stane-125-yu-derzhavoyu-uchas-94061>

Books

Anderson, Terence, Schum, David and Twining, William, *Analysis of Evidence* (Cambridge University Press, 2005)

Arendt, Hannah, *Eichmann in Jerusalem: A Report on the Banality of Evil* (Penguin Classics, 1963)

Ascensio, Hervé, Lambert Abdelgawad, Elisabeth., Sorel, Jean-Marc, *Les juridictions pénales internationalisées*, CERDIN (Université de Paris 1/SLC, Paris, 2006)

Blanc, Alexis A. et al.,*'The Russian General Staff. Understanding the Military's Decisionmaking Role in a "Besieged Fortress"* (Rand Corporation, 2023)

Blum, Y.Z., *Eroding the United Nations Charter* (Brill Nijhoff, 1993)

Brownlie, Ian, *International Law and the Use of Force by States* (Oxford: Oxford University Press, 1968)

Cohen, L. Jonathan, *The Probable and the Provable* (Oxford University Press, 1977)

Combacau, Jean, Sur, Serge, *Droit international public* (8e éd., Paris: LGDJ, 2008)

Combs, Nancy, *Fact-Finding Without Facts* (Cambridge University Press, 2011)

Corten, Olivier, *The Law against War* (2nd edn., Oxford: Hart Publ., 2021)

Corten, Olivier, Koutroulis, Vaios, *Tribunal for Crime of Aggression against Ukraine – a Legal Assessment*. In-depth Analysis (Brussels: EU, December 2022)

Dinstein, Yoram, *War, Aggression and Self-Defence* (4 edn., Cambridge: Cambridge University Press, 2005)

Epstein, Catherine, *Model Nazi: Arthur Greiser and the Occupation of Western Poland* (Oxford: Oxford University Press, 2010)

Faix, Martin, *The Law of International Organizations* (Olomouc: Palacký University, 2012)

Finder, Gabriel and Prusin, Alexander, *Justice Behind the Iron Curtain: Nazis on Trial in Communist Poland* (Toronto: University of Toronto Press, 2018)

Fletcher, George P., *Romantics at War. Glory and Guilt in the age of terrorism* (Princeton-Oxford: Princeton University Press, 2002)

Fox, Hazel, *The Law of State Immunity* (Oxford University Press, 2004)

Franck, Thomas M., *Recourse to Force: State Action Against Threats and Armed Attacks* (Cambridge University Press, 2001)

Glaser, Stefan, *Droit international pénal conventionnel* (Bruxelles: Bruylant, 1970)

Glover, Richard, *Murphy on Evidence* (15th edn, Oxford University Press, 2017)

Grant, Thomas D., *Aggression Against Ukraine. Territory, Responsibility, and International Law* (New York: Palgrave, 2015)

Grzebyk, Patrycja, *Criminal Responsibility for the Crime of Aggression* (London-New York, Routledge, 2013)

Hajdin, Nikola, *Individual Responsibility for the Crime of Aggression* (Stockhom: Stockhom University, 2021)

Harris, Whitney R., *Tyranny on Trial. The Evidence at Nuremberg* (Dallas: Southern Methodist University Press, 1954)

Heller, Kevin, *The Nuremberg Military Tribunals and the Origins of International Criminal Law* (Oxford: Oxford University Press, 2011)

Hobza, Antonín, *Přehled mezinárodního práva válečného. Dodatek: Trestání válečných zločinů* [Survey of International Law of War. Punishment of War Crimes] (Praha: Všehrd, 1946)

Kahn, Robert A., *Holocaust Denial and the Law* (Palgrave, 2004)

Keane, Adrian and McKeown, Paul, *The Modern Law of Evidence* (14th edn, Oxford University Press, 2022)

Kearney, Michael, *Prohibition of Propaganda for War in International Law* (Oxford: Oxford University Press, 2007)

Kittichaisaree, Kriangsak, *International Criminal Law* (Oxford: Oxford University Press, 2001)

Kolb, Robert, *International Law on the Maintenance of Peace* (Edward Elgar, 2018)

Maugham, Viscount, *U.N.O. and War Crimes* (London: Johny Murray Albebarle Stree, 1951)

Mälksoo, Lauri, *Russian Approaches to International Law* (Oxford: Oxford University Press, 2015)

Martineau, Anne-Charlotte, *Les juridictions pénales internationalisées: un nouveau modèle de justice hybride?* (Paris: Pedone, 2007)

May, Larry, *Aggression and Crimes against Peace* (Cambridge: Cambridge University Press, 2008)

McDermott, Yvonne, *Proving International Crimes*, (forthcoming)

McDougall, Carrie, *The Crime of Aggression under the Rome Statute of the International Criminal Court* (2nd edn, Cambridge University Press, 2021)

Mertins, Lena, *Proceedings in Absentia in Comparative and International Criminal Law*. Studies in International and European Criminal Law and Procedure, vol. 50 (Berlin: Duncker & Humblot GmbH, 2022)

Munday, Roderick, *Cross and Tapper on Evidence* (13th edn, Oxford University Press, 2018)

Pompe, C. A., *Aggressive War. An International Crime* (The Hague: Martinus Nijhoff, 1953)

Pritchard, John and Zaide, Sonia M. (eds.), *The Tokyo War Crimes Trial*, vol. 22

Röling, Bernard V. A. and Rüter, Christiaan F., *The Tokyo Judgment, The International Military Tribunal for the Far East (I.M.T.F.E.) 29 April 1946 – 12 November 1948* (Amsterdam, University Press Amsterdam, 1977), vol. 2

Schabas, William, *The International Criminal Court, A Commentary on the Rome Statute* (Oxford University Press, 2010)

Šturma, Pavel, Čepelka, Čestmír and Balaš, Vladimír, *Právo mezinárodních smluv* [Law of International Treaties] (Plzeň: Aleš Čeněk, 2011)

Šturma, Pavel, Chovancová, Katarína, Šmigová, Katarína, Větrovský, Jaroslav, *Immunities of States and Their Officials in Contemporary International Law* (Passau-Berlin -Prague: RW&W Science & New Media, 2017)

Tan, Yudan, *The Rome Statute as Evidence of Customary International Law* (Leiden: Brill, 2021)

Taylor, Telford, *The Anatomy of the Nuremberg Trials* (Back Bay, 1992)

Thayer, James B., *A Preliminary Treatise on Evidence at the Common Law* (1898)

Uhlířová, Kateřina, *Head of State Immunity in International Law – The Charles Taylor Case before the Special Court for Sierra Leone* (Acta Universitatis Brunensis Iuridica, 2013)

Van Alebeek, Rosanne, *The Immunity of States and Their Officials in International Criminal Law and International Human Rights Law* (Oxford University Press, 2008)

Vergès, Jacques M., *De la stratégie judiciaire* (Les Editions de Minuit, 1968)

Villiger, Mark E., *Commentary on the 1969 Vienna Convention on the Law of Treaties* (Leiden: Nijhoff, 2009)

Wigmore, John H., *9 Evidence § 2567* (3rd ed. 1940)

Werle, Gerhard, Vormbaum, Moritz, *The African Criminal Court. A Commentary on the Malabo Protocol* (Springer, 2017)

Wilson, Richard A., *Writing History in International Criminal Trials* (Cambridge University Press, 2011)

The Case Against the Nazi War Criminals, Opening Statement for the United States of America by Robert H. Jackson and Other Documents, with Preface by Gordon Dean of Counsel for United States (New York: Alfred A. Knopf, 1946)

Trials of War Criminals before the Nuernberg Military Tribunals under Control Council Law No. 10, Nuernberg October 1946-April 1949 (Washington: United States Government Printing Office), vol. XIV

United Nations War Crimes Commission, *Law Reports of Trials of War Criminals* (London: His Majesty's Stationery Office, 1947–1949)

Articles and Chapters in Books

Akande, Dapo, 'The Competence of International Organizations and the Advisory Jurisdiction of the International Court of Justice' (1998) 9 *European Journal of International Law*

Akande, Dapo, 'International Law Immunities and the International Criminal Court' (2004) 98 *American Journal of International Law* 3

Akande, Dapo and Shah, Sangeeta, 'Immunities of State Officials, International Crimes and Foreign Domestic Courts: A Rejoinder to Alexander Orakhelashvili' (2011) 22 *European Journal of International Law* 3

Barriga, Stefan, 'Negotiating the Amendments on the Crime of Aggression' in Barriga, Stefan and Kreβ, Claus (ed.), *The Travaux Préparatoires of the Crime of Aggression* (Cambridge: Cambridge University Press, 2011)

Bassiouni, M. Cherif, 'Introduction to the History of Establishing an International Criminal Court' in Bassiouni, M. Cherif (ed.), *International Criminal Law, vol. III, Enforcement* (Transnational Publ. Inc., Dobbs Ferry, N.Y., 1986)

Bellin, Jeffrey and Ferguson, Andrew G., 'Trial by Google: Judicial Notice in the Information Age' (2014) 108 *Northwestern University Law Review* 1137

Bílková, Veronika, 'The Use of Force by the Russian Federation in Crimea' (2015) 75 *Heidelberg Journal of International Law* 27

Bogush, Gleb,''Committed by Men': Individual Criminal Responsibility for Aggression against Ukraine' (2023) 2 *Polish Review of International and European Law* (forthcoming)

Borda, Aldo Z., 'History in International Criminal Trials – The "Crime-Driven Lens" and Its Blind Spots' (2020) 18 *Journal of International Criminal Justice* 543

Bridgeman, Tess, 'When Does the Legal Basis for U.S. Forces in Syria Expire?' (blog *Justsecurity.org*, 14 March 2018) <https://www.justsecurity.org/53810/legal-basis-u-s-forces-syria-expire/>

Bridgeman, Tess, Rosen, Brianna, 'Still at War: The United States in Syria' (blog *Justsecurity.org*, 29 April 2022) <https://www.justsecurity.org/81313/still-at-war-the-united-states-in-syria/>

Brown, Daniel J., 'The International Criminal Court and Trial in Absentia' (1999) 24 *Brooklyn Journal of International Law* 763

Butchard, Patrick, 'Conflict in Ukraine: A Special Tribunal on the Crime of Aggression' (*House of Commons Library Research Briefing*, 27 August 2024) <https://commonslibrary.parliament.uk/research-briefings/cbp-9968/#:~:text=Two%20years%20after%20Russia's%20full-scale%20invasion&#x003E

Chappell, John Ramming and Svoboda, Emma, 'Must Russia Abstain on Security Council Votes Regarding the Ukraine Crisis?' (blog Lawfare, 11 February 2022) <https://www.lawfaremedia.org/article/must-russia-abstain-security-council-votes-regarding-ukraine-crisis>

Cassese, Antonio, 'The Role of Internationalized Courts and Tribunals in the Fight Against International Criminality' in Romano, Cesare P. R., Nollkaemper, André, Kleffner, Jaan K. (eds.), *Internationalized Criminal Courts: Sierra Leone, East Timor, Kosovo and Cambodia* (Oxford University Press, 2004)

Chawryło, Katarzyna, 'Weapons of Mass Deception. Russian Television Propaganda in Wartime' (*OSW Commentary*, 6 May 2022) <https://www.osw.waw.pl/en/publikacje/osw-commentary/2022-05-06/weapons-mass-deception-russian-television-propaganda-wartime>

Clark, Roger S., 'Negotiating Provisions Defining the Crime of Aggression, its Elements and the Conditions for ICC Exercise of Jurisdiction over it' (2010) 20 *European Journal of International Law* 1103

Combs, Nancy, 'Deconstructing the Epistemic Challenges to Mass Atrocity Prosecutions' (2018) 75 *Washington and Lee Law Review* 223

Corell, Hans, 'A Special Tribunal for Ukraine on the Crime of Aggression – The Role of the U.N. General Assembly' (blog *Justsecurity.org*, 14 February 2023) <https://www.justsecurity.org/85116/a-special-tribunal-for-ukraine-on-the-crime-of-aggression-the-role-of-the-u-n-general-assembly/>

Dannenbaum, Tom, 'Mechanisms for Criminal Prosecution of Russia's Aggression Against Ukraine' (blog *Justsecurity.org*, 10 March 2022) <https://www.justsecurity.org/80626/mechanisms-for-criminal-prosecution-of-russias-aggression-against-ukraine/>

Davis, Kenneth C., 'Judicial Notice' (1955) 55 *Columbia Law Review* 945

Deen-Racsmány, Zsuzsanna, '*Prosecutor v. Taylor*: The Status of the Special Court for Sierra Leone and its Implications for Immunity' (2005) 18 *Leiden Journal of International Law*

de Souza Dias, Talita, 'The Activation of the Crime of Aggression before the International Criminal Court: Some Overlooked Implications Arising for States Parties and Non-States Parties to the Rome Statute' (2019) 24(3) *Journal of Conflict and Security Law* 567

Douglas, Lawrence, 'The Memory of Judgment: The Law, the Holocaust, and Denial' (1995) 7 *History and Memory* 100

Douzinas, Costas, 'History Trials: Can Law Decide History?' (2012) 8 *Annual Review of Law and Social Science* 273

Drumbl, Mark, 'Germans are the Lords and Poles are the Servants': The Trial of Arthur Greiser in Poland, 1946, in Heller, Kevin and Simpson, Gerry (eds.), *The Hidden Histories of War Crimes Trials* (Oxford: Oxford University Press, 2013)

Fitzmaurice, Malgosia, 'Third Parties and the Law of Treaties (2002) 6 *Max Planck Yearbook of United Nations Law*

Fitzpatrick, Daniel, 'Developing a Legal System in East Timor: Some Issues of UN Mandate and Capacity' (2000) 5 *Austrian Review of International and European Law*

Friedlander, Robert A., 'Problems of Enforcing International Criminal Law' in Bassiouni, M. Cherif (ed.), *International Criminal Law, vol. III, Enforcement* (Transnational Publ. Inc., Dobbs Ferry, N.Y., 1986)

Gaeta, Paola, 'The Be (Present) or Not to Be (Present). Trial in Absentia before the Special Tribunal for Lebanon' (2007) 5 *Journal of International Criminal Justice* 1165

Galand, Alexandre S., 'A Hidden Reading of the ICC Appeals Chamber's Judgment in the Jordan Referral Re Al-Bashir' (blog *Ejiltalk.org*, 6 June 2019) <https://www.ejiltalk.org/a-hidden-reading-of-the-icc-appeals-chambers-judgment-in-the-jordan-referral-re-al-bashir/>

Gardner, Maggie, 'Reconsidering Trials in Absentia at the Special Tribunal for Lebanon: An Application of the Tribunal's Early Jurisprudence' (2011) 43 *George Washington University Law Review* 91

Green, James, Henderson, Christian, Ruys, Tom, 'Russia's Attack on Ukraine and the *Jus ad Bellum*' (2022) 9(4) *Journal on the Use of Force and International Law* 4

Grigaite-Daugirde, Gabija, 'Crime of Aggression against Ukraine: Legality and Legitimacy of Domestic Prosecutions in Third States' (2023) 43 *Polish Yearbook of International Law* 299

Grover, Leena, 'Interpreting the Crime of Aggression' in Kreβ, Claus, Barriga, Stefan (eds.), *The Crime of Aggression: A Commentary* (Cambridge University Press, 2016)

Grzebyk, Patrycja, 'The Role of the Polish Supreme National Tribunal in the Development of Principles of International Criminal Law' in Bergsmo, Morten, Ling, Cheah Wui and Ping, Yi (eds.), *Historical Origins of International Criminal Law*, vol. 2 (Torkel Opsahl Academic EPublisher, 2014)

Grzebyk, Patrycja, 'Classification of the Conflict between Ukraine and Russia in International Law (Ius ad Bellum and Ius in Bello)' (2014) 34 *Polish Yearbook of International Law* 39

Grzebyk, Patrycja, 'Crime of Aggression against Ukraine: The Role of Regional Customary Law' (2023) 21(3) *Journal of International Criminal* Justice 435

Haas, Peter, 'Introduction: Epistemic Communities and International Policy Coordination' (1992) 46 *International Organization* 1

Hathaway, Oona A., 'The Case for Creating an International Tribunal to Prosecute the Crime of Aggression Against Ukraine (Part I)' (blog *JustSecurity.org*, 20 September 2022) <https://www.justsecurity.org/83117/the-case-for-creating-an-international-tribunal-to-prosecute-the-crime-of-aggression-against-ukraine/>

Hathaway, Oona A., Mills, Maggie, Zimmerman, Heather, 'The Legal Authority to Create a Special Tribunal to Try the Crime of Aggression Upon the Request of the UN General Assembly' (blog *Justsecurity.org*, 5 May 2023) <https://www.justsecurity.org/86450/the-legal-authority-to-create-a-special-tribunal-to-try-the-crime-of-aggression-upon-the-request-of-the-un-general-assembly/>

Hathaway, Oona A., Mills, Maggie M., Poston, Thomas M., 'War Reparations: The Case for Countermeasures' (2024) Stanford Law Review, vol. 76, no. 5, <https://ssrn.com/abstract=4548945>

Heinsch, Robert, 'The Crime of Aggression After Kampala: Success or Burden for the Future?' (2010) 2 *Goetingen Journal of International Law* 713

Heller, Kevin, 'Retreat from Nuremberg: The Leadership Requirement in the Crime of Aggression' (2007) 18(3) *European Journal of International Law* 477

Heller, Kevin J., 'Prosecutor v. Karemera, Ngirumpatse, & Nzirorera' (2007) 101 *American Journal of International Law* 157

Heller, Kevin J., 'Options for Prosecuting Russian Aggression Against Ukraine: A Critical Analysis' (2022) *Journal of Genocide Research* 26

Heller, Kevin J., 'The AU's Position on Personal Immunity: A Response to Coracini & Trahan' (blog *OpinioJuris.org*, 9 November 2022) <https://opiniojuris.org/2022/11/09/the-aus-position-on-personal-immunity-a-response-to-trahan/>

Jílek, Dalibor, 'Přemítání o založení Mezinárodního tribunálu pro stíhání osob odpovědných za závažná porušení mezinárodního práva humanitárního spáchaná na území bývalé Jugoslávie od roku 1991 [Reflections on the Establishment of an International Tribunal for the Prosecution of Persons Responsible for Serious Violations of International Humanitarian Law Committed on the Territory of the Former Yugoslavia Since 1991]' (1996) *Časopis pro právní vědu a praxi* 1

Johnson, Larry D., '"Uniting for Peace": Does it still serve any useful purpose?' (2014) 108 *AJIL Unbound* 106

Komarov, Alexander, Hathaway, Oona A., 'Ukraine's Constitutional Constraints: How to Achieve Accountability for the Crime of Aggression' (blog *Justsecurity.org*, 5 April 2022) <https://www.justsecurity.org/80958/ukraines-constitutional-constraints-how-to-achieve-accountability-for-the-crime-of-aggression/>

Korynevych, Anton, Sanatorova Oksana, Shepitko, Mykhaylo, 'Prosecution of the Crime of Aggression in International and Ukrainian Jurisdiction: Challenges and Prospects', (2023) 43 *Polish Yearbook of International Law* 367

Koskenniemi, Marti, 'Between Impunity and Show Trials' (2002) 6 *Max Planck Yearbook of United Nations Law* 1

Kosso, Peter, 'Historical Evidence and Epistemic Justification: Thucydides as a Case Study' (1993) 32 *History and Theory* 1

Kreß, Claus, 'Time for Decision: Some Thoughts on the Immediate Future of the Crime of Aggression: A Reply to Andreas Paulus' (2009) 20 *European Journal of International Law* 1129

Kreß, Claus, 'The International Criminal Court and Immunities under International Law for States Not Party to the Court's Statute' in Bergsmo, Morten, Ling, Yan (ed.), *State Sovereignty and International Criminal Law* (FICH Publication Series No. 15, 2012)

Kreß, Claus, 'On the Activation of ICC Jurisdiction over the Crime of Aggression' (2018) 16 *Journal of International Criminal Justice* 1

Kreß, Claus, 'Article 98' in Ambos, Kai (ed.), *Rome Statute of the International Criminal Court: Article-by-Article Commentary* (München-Oxford-Baden-Baden: Beck-Hart -Nomos, 2022)

Kulaga, Lukasz, 'Domestic and International Criminal Jurisdiction in the Context of the Initiative for a Special Tribunal for the Crime of Aggression' (2023) 43 *Polish Yearbook of International Law* 339

Labuda, Patryk, 'Making Counter-Hegemonic International Law: Should a Special Tribunal for Aggression Be International or Hybrid?' (blog *Justsecurity.org*, 19 September 2023) <https://www.justsecurity.org/88373/making-counter-hegemonic-international-law-should-a-special-tribunal-for-aggression-be-international-or-hybrid/>

Lipovský, Milan, 'Nový (zvláštní) mezinárodní trestní tribunál pro zločin agrese vůči Ukrajině anebo "staré" cesty? [New (special) international criminal tribunal for the crime of aggression against Ukraine or "old" paths?]' (2023) 2 *Jurisprudence* 12

Lipovský, Milan, 'What is 'a Certain International Criminal Court' and Does the Choice of a Fully International or Internationalized (Hybrid) Court/Chambers Matter for the Crime of Aggression Committed against Ukraine?' (2023) 43 *Polish Yearbook of International Law* 213

Lipovský, Milan, 'Assessing the Legal Boundaries of Military Support to Ukraine from the Perspective of Use of Force' (2025) 50 (1-2) *Review of Central and East European Law* 87

Lippman, Matthew, 'Nuremberg: Forty Five Years Later' (1991) 7 *Connecticut Journal of International Law* 1

Lumb, R. D., 'Individual Responsibility for Aggressive War: The Crime Against Peace', (1956-59) 3(4) *University of Queensland Law Journal* 333

Malloy, Katy, 'Ukraine v. Russia: A Case for Change in International Enforcement' (2024) 65(5) *William & Mary Law Review* 1231

Mamiya, Ralph, 'Taking Judicial Notice of Genocide – The Problematic Law and Policy of the Karemera Decision' (2007) 25 *Wisconsin International Law Journal* 1

Marchuk, Iryna, 'Domestic Accountability Efforts in Response to the Russia-Ukraine War. An Appraisal of the First War Crimes Trials in Ukraine' (2022) 20 *Journal of International Criminal Justice* 787

Massimino, Irene V., 'The ICC and in-absentia Proceedings: Finding a Response to the Difficulties of Executing Arrest Warrants' (21 May 2024) *ESIL-Reflections*, vol. 13, issue 9

Matuszak, Sławomir and Żochowski, Piotr, 'Ukraine: New Wartime Legislation' (*OSW Analyses*, 17 March 2022) <https://www.osw.waw.pl/en/publikacje/analyses/2022-03-17/ukraine-new-wartime-legislation>

May, Larry, 'Act and Circumstance in the Crime of Aggression, Symposium: War & Responsibility' (2007) 15 *Journal of Political Philosophy* 169

McDougall, Carrie, 'Why Creating a Special Tribunal for Aggression Against Ukraine is the Best Available Option: A Reply to Kevin Jon Heller and Other Critics' (blog *OpinioIuris.org*, 15 March 2022) <http://opiniojuris.org/2022/03/15/why-creating-a-special-tribunal-for-aggression-against-ukraine-is-the-best-available-option-a-reply-to-kevin-jon-heller-and-other-critics/>

McDougall, Carrie, 'Why Ukraine Needs an International – not Internationalised – Tribunal to Prosecute the Crimes of Aggression Committed Against It', (2023) 12:2 *Polish Review of International and European Law* 65

McCormick, Charles, 'Judicial Notice' (1952) 5 *Vanderbilt Law Review* 296

McNaughton, John, 'Judicial Notice–Excerpts Relating to the Morgan-Wigmore Controversy' (1961) 14 *Vanderbilt Law Review* 779

Menashe, Doron, 'A New Paradigm for Understanding Judicial Notice and Its Implications in the Modern Digital Era' (2017) 9 *Elon Law Review* 267

Milano, Enrico, 'Russia's Veto in the Security Council: Whither the Duty to Abstain under Art. 27(3) of the UN Charter?' *Max-Planck-Institute* (2015) <https://www.zaoerv.de/75_2015/75_2015_1_a_215_232.pdf>

Milanovic, Marko, 'North Korea's Troop Deployment in the Russian War of Aggression against Ukraine: The DPRK as a Principal or as an Accomplice?' (blog *Ejiltalk.org*, 4 November 2024) <https://www.ejiltalk.org/north-koreas-troop-deployment-in-the-russian-war-of-aggression-against-ukraine-the-dprk-as-a-principal-or-as-an-accomplice/>

Morgan, Edmund, 'Judicial Notice' (1944) 57 *Harvard Law Review* 269

Nouwen, Sarah, 'The Special Court for Sierra Leone and the Immunity of Taylor: The Arrest Warrant Case Continued' (2005) 18 *Leiden Journal of International Law*

Nouwen, Sarah, 'Return to Sender: Let the International Court of Justice Justify or Qualify International-Criminal-Court Exceptionalism Regarding Personal Immunities' (2019) 78(3) *Cambridge Law Journal*

Politi, Mauro, 'The Debate within the Preparatory Commission for the International Criminal Court' in Politi, Mauro, Nesi, Giuseppe (eds.), *The International Criminal Court and the Crime of Aggression* (Aldershot: Ashgate, 2004)

Prusin, Alexander, 'Poland's Nuremberg: The Seven Court Cases of the Supreme National Tribunal, 1946–1948' (2010) 24 *Holocaust and Genocide Studies* 1

Ratner, Steven R. 'The United Nations Group of Experts for Cambodia' (1999) 93 *American Journal of International Law* 948

Reisinger Coracini, Astrid, Trahan, Jennifer, 'The Case for Creating a Special Tribunal to Prosecute the Crime of Aggression Committed Against Ukraine (Part VI): On the Non-applicability of Personal Immunities' (blog *Justsecurity.org*, 8 November 2022) <https://www.justsecurity.org/84017/the-case-for-creating-a-special-tribunal-to-prosecute-the-crime-of-aggression-committed-against-ukraine-part-vi-on-the-non-applicability-of-personal-immunities/>

Reisinger Coracini, Astrid, 'Is Amending the Rome Statute the Panacea Against Perceived Selectivity and Impunity for the Crime of Aggression Committed Against Ukraine?' (blog *Justsecurity.org*, 21 March 2023) <https://www.justsecurity.org/85593/is-amending-the-rome-statute-the-panacea-against-perceived-selectivity-and-impunity-for-the-crime-of-aggression-committed-against-ukraine/>

Sander, Barrie, 'Unveiling the Historical Function of International Criminal Courts: Between Adjudicative and Sociopolitical Justice' (2018) 12 *International Journal of Transitional Justice* 334

Schabas, William A., Chaitidou, Eleni and El Zeidy, Mohamed, 'Art. 61' in Ambos, Kai (ed.), *Rome Statute of the International Criminal Court* (4th ed., Munich/Oxford/Baden-Baden: Beck/Hart/Nomos, 2022)

Schabas, Wiliam, Caruana, Veronique, 'Art. 63' in Ambos, Kai (ed), *Rome Statute of the International Criminal Court* (4th ed., Munich/Oxford/Baden-Baden: Beck/Hart/Nomos, 2022)

Scheffer, David J., 'Forging a Cooperative Relationship Between International Criminal Court and a Special Tribunal for Aggression Against Ukraine' (blog *Justsecurity.org*, 25 October 2022) <https://www.justsecurity.org/83757/forging-a-cooperative-relationship-between-intl-crim-court-and-a-special-tribunal-for-russian-aggression-against-ukraine/>

Shaw, Garry J., 'Convicting Inhumanity in Absentia: Holding Trials in Absentia at the International Criminal Court' (2012) 44 *George Washington International Law Review* 107

Sloan, F. Blaine, 'The Binding Force of a 'Recommendation' of the General Assembly of the United Nations' (1948) 25 *British Book of International Law* 1

Šturma, Pavel, 'Povinnost aut dedere aut judicare a nový smíšený trestní tribunál pro stíhání zločinů podle mezinárodního práva [Obligation Aut Dedere Aut Judicare and a New Mixed Criminal Tribunal for Prosecution of Crimes under International Law]' (2014) 4 *Jurisprudence*

Šturma, Pavel, 'Back to the ILC's Legislative History: Code of Crimes against the Peace and Security of Mankind' (2015) 6 *Czech Yearbook of Public & Private International Law* 37

Tiribelli, Carlo, 'Judgment in Absentia in International Criminal Law: its Admissibility before the ad hoc Tribunals, the International Criminal Court and the European Arrest Warrant' (2006) 18 *Sri Lanka Journal of International Law* 369

Trahan, Jennifer, 'Negotiating the Amendment on the Crime of Aggression: Proceedings at the Kampala Review Conference on the International Criminal Court' (2011) 11 *International Criminal Law Review* 49

Trahan, Jennifer, 'From Kampala to New York—The Final Negotiations to Activate the Jurisdiction of the International Criminal Court over the Crime of Aggression' (2018) 18 *International Criminal Law Review* 197

Trahan, Jennifer, 'Why a 'Hybrid' Ukrainian Tribunal on the Crime of Aggression is not the Answer (blog *Justsecurity.org*, 6 February 2023) <https://www.justsecurity.org/85019/why-hybrid-ukrainian-tribunal-on-crime-of-aggression-is-not-the-answer/>

Trahan, Jennifer, 'Amending the Kampala Amendments: Proposal to Harmonize the ICC's Jurisdiction over the Crime of Aggression with its Jurisdiction over its Other Core Crimes' (blog *Opinionjuris.org*, 2 November 2023) <https://opiniojuris.org/2023/10/02/amending-the-kampala-amendments-a-proposal-to-harmonize-the-iccs-jurisdiction/>

Trahan, Jennifer, 'Proposals for the Formation of a Crime of Aggression Tribunal for the Situation of Ukraine' in Dutton, Yvonne, Scharf, Michael, Sterio, Milena, William, Paul (eds.) *Ukraine, Accountability, and the New Global Order* (Routledge, forthcoming 2024)

van Alebeek Rosanne, van den Herik, Larissa and Ryngaert, Cedric, 'Prosecuting Russian Officials for the Crime of Aggression: What About Immunities?' (2023) *European Convention on Human Rights Law Review* 4

Wilson, Richard A., 'Humanity's Histories Evaluating the Historical Accounts of International Tribunals and Truth Commissions' (2007) 4 *Politix* 31

Zakerhossein, Mohammad H., De Brouwer, Anne-Marie, 'Diverse Approaches to Total and Partial *in Absentia* Trials by International Criminal Tribunals' (2015) 26 *Criminal Law Forum* 181

International Court's and Tribunal's Webpages

Webpage of the International Court of Justice, available online at <https://icj-cij.org/how-the-court-works>

Webpage of the International Criminal Court, Ukraine, Situation in Ukraine, available online at <https://www.icc-cpi.int/situations/ukraine>

Webpage of the International Criminal Court, The States Parties to the Rome Statute, available online at <https://asp.icc-cpi.int/states-parties>

Webpage of the International Criminal Court, Press Release, Situation in Ukraine: ICC Judges Issue Arrest Warrants against Vladimir Vladimirovich Putin and Maria Alekseyevna Lvova-Belova (17 March 2023), available online at <https://www.icc-cpi.int/news/situation-ukraine-icc-judges-issue-arrest-warrants-against-vladimir-vladimirovich-putin-and>

ICC ASP Webpage <https://asp.icc-cpi.int/crime-of-aggression/History-CoA>

ICC ASP Webpage, Newsletter, December 2010, available online at <https://asp.icc-cpi.int/sites/asp/files/asp_docs/Publications/Newsletter-ASP-5-Web-ENG.pdf>

Webpage of the Kosovo Specialist Chambers, Background, available online at <https://www.scp-ks.org/en/background>

Webpage of the Kosovo Specialist Chambers, Chambers, available online at <https://www.scp-ks.org/en/specialist-chambers/chambers>

Webpage of the Kosovo Specialist Chambers, available online at <https://www.scp-ks.org/en>

News Reports

Brunsden, Jim, 'EU Deal Struck on Trials in Absentia' *Politico* (6 June 2008) <https://www.politico.eu/article/eu-deal-struck-on-trials-in-absentia/>

Gadzo, Mersiha, 'Record High Deaths in the Russia-Ukraine War: What You Should Know', *AL JAZEERA* (16 October 2024) <https://www.aljazeera.com/news/2024/10/16/russia-ukraine-wartime-deaths>

Grynszpan, Emmanuel, 'Russian Oligarchs Get Richer from the War in Ukraine' *Le Monde* (3 August 2023) <https://www.lemonde.fr/en/international/article/2023/08/03/russian-oligarchs-get-richer-from-the-war-in-ukraine_6077914_4.html>

Hansler, Jennifer, 'U.S. Announces It Supports Creation of Special Tribunal to Prosecute Russia for 'Crime of Aggression' in Ukraine' *CNN* (28 March 2023) <https://edition.cnn.com/2023/03/28/politics/us-support-special-tribunal-crime-of-aggression/index.html>

McKenzie, David, 'Putin Will Not Attend BRICS Summit in South Africa, as ICC Arrest Warrant Overshadows Key Talks' *CNN* (20 July 2023) <https://edition.cnn.com/2023/07/19/world/putin-brics-summit-south-africa-intl/index.html>

Sands, Philippe, 'Putin's Use of Military Force is a Crime of Aggression' *Financial Times* (28 February 2022) <https://www.ft.com/content/cbbdd146-4e36-42fb95e1-50128506652c&#x003E>

Tass, 'Putin Orders Creation of Special Council for Military Operation Needs' *Tass* (19 October 2022) <https://tass.com/politics/1524957>

Walter, Jan D., 'Military Hardware for Ukraine: Who Plans to Supply What?' *DW* (3 June 2022) <https://www.dw.com/en/military-hardware-for-ukraine-who-plans-to-supply-what/a-62015239#:~:text=Military%20hardware%20for%20Ukraine%3A%20Who%20plans%20to%20supply,5%20Czech%20Republic%20...%206%20Other%20states%20>

Other Sources

Handbook, Ratification and Implementation of the Kampala Amendments to the Rome Statute of the ICC: Crime of Aggression, War Crimes (November 2012)

Justsecurity.org blog, available online at <https://www.justsecurity.org/82513/just-securitys-russia-ukraine-war-archive/>

RPE of the Special Court for Sierra Leone, available online at <https://s3.eu-west-1.amazonaws.com/rscsl.org/wp-content/uploads/2022/09/24162759/RSCSL-Rules.pdf>

OSCE Webpage online at <https://www.osce.org/odihr/elections/383577>

NASDAQ Webpage, available online at <https://www.nasdaq.com/market-activity/quotes/historical>

Frequently Asked Questions (FAQ), Endorsed by Albania, Belgium, Estonia, Guatemala, Latvia, Liechtenstein, Lithuania, Luxembourg, Marshall Islands, North Macedonia, Poland and Ukraine, available online at <https://www.justsecurity.org/wp-content/uploads/2023/01/FAQ_Special-Tribunal-for-the-Crime-of-Aggression.pdf>

Webpage of the Global Institute for the Prevention of Aggression, available online at <https://crimeofaggression.info/wp-content/uploads/GIPA-model-amendment-proposal.pdf>

Law Society of Scotland, Iraq: A Basis in Law?, available online at <https://www.lawscot.org.uk/members/journal/issues/vol-61-issue-08/iraq-a-basis-in-law/>

GIPA Webpage <https://crimeofaggression.info/wp-content/uploads/GIPA-Proposal-Short.pdf>

Blog Series: The Case for Creating an International Tribunal to Prosecute the Crime of Aggression against Ukraine (Parts I, II, III, IV), blog series *Justsecurity.org*, available online at <https://www.justsecurity.org/tag/prosecuting-the-crime-of-aggression-against-ukraine/>

Statement by President von der Leyen on the Establishment of the International Centre for the Prosecution of Crimes of Aggression against Ukraine (4 March 2023), available online at <https://ec.europa.eu/commission/presscorner/detail/es/statement_23_1363>

Nuremberg Declaration on the Crime of Aggression (8 May 2023), available online at <https://crimeofaggression.info/wp-content/uploads/Nuremberg_Declaration_on_the_Crime_of_Aggression.pdf>

Index

www.ingramcontent.com/pod-product-compliance
Lightning Source LLC
Chambersburg PA
CBHW071246230926
51849CB00001B/246
9789004740938